ProActive
Hospitality & Catering

City & Guilds

Hospitality Supervision & Leadership

Level 3

For Level 3 Diploma in Hospitality, Supervision & Leadership (NVQ)
and Level 3 Award in Hospitality, Supervision & Leadership Principles

Series Editor: **Pam Rabone**

Holly Bamunuge • Peter Brindley • Marjory Clark
Ann Dennis • Trevor Eeles • Darren Garwood • Fiona Mills

AND B... working together

City&
Guilds

Heinemann
Part of Pearson

Heinemann is an imprint of Pearson Education Limited, a company incorporated in England and Wales, having its registered office at Edinburgh Gate, Harlow, Essex, CM20 2JE. Registered company number: 872828

www.heinemann.co.uk

Heinemann is a registered trademark of Pearson Education Limited

Text © Pearson Education Limited 2009

First published 2009

12 11 10 09
10 9 8 7 6 5 4 3 2 1

British Library Cataloguing in Publication Data

A catalogue record for this book is available from the British Library

ISBN 978 0 435467 97 5 ⊢

Designed and typeset by Kamae Design, Oxford
Original illustrations © Pearson Education Ltd.
Illustrated by Kamae Design and Alistair Bright
Cover design by Pearson Education Ltd.
Cover photo/illustration © Pearson Education Ltd./Ben Nicholson
Printed in Italy by Rotolito

Acknowledgements

The author and publisher would like to thank the following organisations for permission to reproduce material:

Sodexo (logo, p2); Charlton House Catering Services Limited (logo, p2); Vacherin Limited (logo, p2); Compass Group PLC (logo, p2); Procter&Gamble (Bounce safety data sheet, p134); APACS - The UK Payments Association (Chip & PIN symbol, p147); EFQM (EFQM Excellence Model, p175); Institute of Customer Service (evidence requirements, Unit 24, p3).

The author and publisher would like to thank the following individuals and organisations for permission to reproduce photographs:

© Pearson Education Ltd. Oliver Beamish, p22; © Asia Images Group/Alamy, p24; © Chuck Place/Alamy, p28; © Photodisc. Photolink, p33; © LondonPhotos - Homer Sykes/Alamy, p41; © Oliver Knight/Alamy, p44; © Oliver Knight/Alamy, p50; © Camilla Sjodin/Etsa/Corbis, p66; © Oliver Knight/Alamy, p72; © Mark Bassett, p89; © Leah-Anne Thompson. Shutterstock, p113; © Cultura/Alamy, p161; © David Gilder. Shutterstock, p164; © JUPITERIMAGES/ Comstock Images/Alamy, p169; © Olly. Shutterstock, p174; © David Gilder. Shutterstock, p180.

Every effort has been made to contact copyright holders of material reproduced in this book. Any omissions will be rectified in subsequent printings if notice is given to the publishers.

Websites
The websites used in this book were correct and up-to-date at the time of publication. It is essential for tutors to preview each website before using it in class so as to ensure that the URL is still accurate, relevant and appropriate. We suggest that tutors bookmark useful websites and consider enabling students to access them through the school/college intranet.

Contents

Introduction to the Hospitality Supervision and Leadership Qualification

The Hospitality Supervision and Leadership qualification has been written by People 1st, the sector skills council responsible for the development of qualifications for the hospitality and catering sector, and awarding bodies such as City & Guilds. The qualification is based upon research carried out within the industry to identify the skills and knowledge required to be a supervisor within the hospitality sector. You may have some of the skills and parts of the knowledge already but this textbook and accompanying CD-ROM have been designed to help you work towards the qualification, helping you to identify the evidence you require and supporting your knowledge development.

This qualification consists of five mandatory units (Group A) and a range of optional units (Groups B and C). See table on pages ix-x for the full list. These units are all on the Qualifications and Credit Framework (QCF) and each unit is worth a certain number of credits. In order to achieve the full Diploma in Hospitality Supervision and Leadership (NVQ) you will need to achieve a minimum of 45 credits. All units in Group A are mandatory. One unit in Group B is mandatory. Two further units can be taken from either Group B or Group C. The choice of optional units will vary depending upon the job role that you undertake and the choice of units should be selected by reviewing the units with your assessor.

Mandatory units – textbook

HS1 Provide leadership for your team – MSC
HS2 Develop productive working relationships with colleagues – MSC
HS3 Contribute to the control of resources
HS4 Maintain the health, hygiene, safety and security of the working environment
HS5 Lead a team to improve customer service – ICS

Optional units section B – on CD-ROM

HSL6 Contribute to promoting hospitality services and products
HSL7 Supervise food production operations
HSL8 Supervise functions
HSL9 Contribute to the development of recipes and menus
HSL10 Supervise food services
HSL11 Supervise drink services
HSL17 Supervise housekeeping services/
HSL18 Supervise linen services
HSL21 Supervise reception services/HSL22 Supervise reservation and booking services
HSL24 Providing learning opportunities for colleagues
HSL25 Supervise the use of technological equipment in hospitality services
HSL26 Supervise practices for handling payments
HSL30 Ensure food safety practices are followed in the preparation and serving of food and drink

The mandatory units have been written as a textbook and underpin the other units' supervisory knowledge. The CD-Rom contains workbooks covering 14 of the most popular option units that previous candidates have selected. These can be used to support your knowledge and help to suggest the types of evidence that can be collected.

Some of the units have been imported from other qualifications and this is stated at the beginning of the units. When you look at the specification, these units will be slightly different in content and unit layout so will be easily recognisable. However, the approach to evidence collection and assessment will be the same as the other units.

How you will be assessed

You should naturally be able to demonstrate the inference of competence – this simply means that you need to collect enough evidence to show you competently repeated the task required by the qualification in your everyday job.

The exact method of assessment will vary for every candidate but the processes should be the same. Your assessor should conduct an initial assessment (sometimes called a skill scan) – this will determine a number of things that will help you and your assessor decide which units you should do and the approach to assessment. The initial assessment should identify what you can already do and may be ready for summative assessment on, and what you need some tutoring to achieve. The process of initial assessment is critical as it supports the identification of the sources of evidence and helps to identify the best methods for your assessor to use to support you while you are working towards your qualification.

The process of collecting evidence varies but you must cover everything in the qualification. What you will notice as you work towards one unit is that you will use the same evidence in other units – so one piece of evidence is not used in isolation. This is known as holistic assessment, and will only be noticeable as you move on through your qualification. The book and the work pack have been designed to help support you and your assessor to identify evidence. The evidence grids in each option unit will be useful in helping you not only to identify evidence for that unit but also to see where the evidence can be used in other units. This will clearly impact on the way in which you build your evidence. When organising your evidence, it is much simpler to number each piece of evidence and keep them in one section of your portfolio until you need to reference them later in another unit. In fact, you do not need to put evidence in your portfolio – you can leave it where it is normally kept and 'signpost' where this is so that anyone who needs to know how you have achieved the qualification can find the evidence.

Collecting evidence: where to start

The amount of evidence you need and the way in which you collect it will depend upon your job role and experience. It is therefore important that you produce a portfolio to reflect your experience and likely competence. It is called a portfolio of evidence because it should demonstrate what you could show someone to convince them that you are able to do this task.

Getting started

After the skill scan or initial assessment there are some basic pieces of evidence you should include, even if you choose to signpost most of the other evidence. These include:

o a detailed, up-to-date curriculum vitae

o job description – if this is not detailed, you may want to provide a description of a 'typical' day. Some very detailed job descriptions can be cross-referenced to the units to provide a useful point of reference as well

o information on your place of work, such as brochures or menus

o an organisational chart highlighted to indicate where you are, whom you report to and who reports to you

o any forms of appraisals (these may be confidential so you may not want to include them in your portfolio) or statements completed by colleagues, customers or your line manager.

All of these help to build a picture of you and your likely competence, and they contextualise the remaining evidence. Sometimes it is useful to include any jargon you may use in the portfolio, to help anyone looking at it to understand to what you are referring.

To identify to you what is 'enough or sufficient evidence' is impossible as each individual learner will have different experience, assessment needs and sources of evidence. The way in which you are assessed will be decided upon between you and your assessor after the initial assessment, and on subsequent meetings.

The criteria used for assessing evidence

No matter what method of assessment is used, all evidence must be valid, authentic, current and sufficient.

Valid – is this the most valid way to show that I can do the task and the best method for assessment?

Authentic – can the evidence be attributed to me?

Current – does the evidence show that I can still do the job? Is the evidence recent enough?

Sufficient – is there enough evidence to 'infer competence'?

Methods of assessment
Observation

This is one of the most common methods of evidence collection and is now often supported by DVDs and photographs – in some cases these may be used in place of observation. At level 3 the use of observation is required less because as a supervisor you will naturally generate most of the evidence you require to infer competence and show you are doing the job. Your assessor will discuss the need for an observation with you and together you will decide when and what are good opportunities to collect evidence. Observation may only take place when you have collected some other sorts of evidence. It can underpin knowledge and the behaviours that underpin your performance which are required in some units. This simply means it is a good way of showing you know what you are doing and that this is evident when you carry out your job. The observation will be recorded either within the individual unit or on a generic observation report that may be used later for other units too.

Work products

These are pieces of evidence that occur naturally from you carrying out your normal job. They are a good source of evidence and reduce or remove the need for direct observation to take place. The types of work product you can collect or signpost will vary depending upon your job role but may include menus, stock-taking documents, delivery notes, minutes of meetings you have conducted, rotas and so on. The work must clearly indicate that you have carried out the task and you may be asked to highlight sections and write a brief description of the work product.

Professional discussion

This is sometime called a 'job chat' as you will be talking about what you do, how you do it, when you do it and why you do it. It may refer to other people who are involved while you do your job. You will be told when you are going to have a professional discussion so you can prepare for it. You should think about the areas it will cover, and refer to your portfolio or evidence in the workplace as you talk about the tasks you undertake. It can be daunting at first, as it needs to be recorded. Professional discussions can be used at the beginning of the assessment process as they can help your assessor to better understand your role. Equally, they can be conducted throughout or used right at the end to finish off units, particularly where there are difficult or impossible things to cover as they do not form part of your normal job. They are easier than writing long narratives and can be authenticated because of the uniqueness of your voice.

Simulation

This is not a permitted assessment method unless it is used for assessment of 'contingencies' such as accidents or emergencies, equipment failure, or overspends.

Witness testimony

The use of witness testimony is a really helpful form of assessment, especially when the assessor is not present, and is therefore a good source of evidence. There are two definitions used to describe witness testimony:

○ The first is that generated by an expert witness (for example, a line manager). This expert witness testimony may be sufficient for the assessor to consider that competence has been proved. The expert witness must be able to demonstrate experience and knowledge of the unit(s) for which they are providing evidence.
○ The other is simply termed a witness testimony and may be provided by a colleague, customer or supplier. This type of witness testimony contributes to the assessment process and will be used with other forms of evidence to support the inference of competence.

Candidate report/reflective account

The use of candidate reports can be useful where an assessor may not be present. The report should be clearly written and explain what took place. It could be supported by a witness testimony. Once written, the report will need to be cross-referenced to the units it covers and, as with all forms of evidence, it must be signed and dated. It is possible that the tasks undertaken were done in the past but the evidence must 'infer' that the candidate is still able to do the task.

Assessment of knowledge and understanding

Knowledge and understanding can be assessed in a variety of different ways, and describes what the candidate understands; for example, 'understands how to supervise food production operations'.

All of these methods of assessment listed on pages vi-vii can be used to assess knowledge and understanding. The methods below can be used in addition to these.

Questioning

Questioning can be in the form of written or oral questions. All of the answers need to be clearly matched to the knowledge and understanding. Some answers may provide evidence across a number of units.

Projects and assignments

Projects and assignments are used to cover gaps in the evidence and can cover parts of different learning outcomes. It is not necessarily the best method of assessment and will depend upon how comfortable you are at writing the project or assignment. This is something that you and your assessor will discuss and agree upon.

Inferring knowledge from performance

When the assessor is observing you it may be possible for them to identify that you are applying knowledge in a practical situation. The good thing about implicit knowledge is that it helps to prevent over-assessment and since the assessor has observed the application of the knowledge, they will not need to use other methods of assessment. The assessor may also, as part of the observation, be able to examine work-related products that contribute to your knowledge of how to do a task.

The Technical Certificate

This consists of one Technical Certificate called the Level 3 Award in Hospitality, Supervision and Leadership Principles, which has two units that underpin the knowledge requirements of the five mandatory units.

The titles of the two units are:
o Principles of leading a team in the hospitality industry
o Supervision of operations in the hospitality industry.

This Technical Certificate is based upon taught units that are called Vocationally Related Qualifications (VRQs). They are assessed by multiple choice questions which are set by the awarding body.

The Technical Certificate forms part of the Advanced Modern Apprenticeship framework that you are working towards.

The Advanced Modern Apprenticeship consists of:
o employment rights and responsibilities
o one Technical Certificate – two units
o 45 credits achieved from the Level 3 Diploma units.
Key Skills* – Level 2 Application of Number and Level 2 Communication*

* Functional Skills will replace Key Skills from September 2010.

Level 3 Diploma in Hospitality Supervision and Leadership (NVQ)

To attain the qualification candidates would have to complete 8 units in total. This comprises of:

o   all of the mandatory units in Section A

o   at least one unit from Section B

o   the remaining two units can come from either Section B or C

SECTION A MANDATORY UNITS	
HSL1	Provide leadership for your team (MSC B5)
HSL2	Develop productive working relationships with colleagues (MSC D1)
HSL3	Contribute to the control of resources
HSL4	Maintain the health, hygiene, safety and security of the working environment
HSL5	Lead a team to improve customer service (ICS 42)

SECTION B OPTIONAL UNITS	
HSL7	Supervise food production operations
HSL8	Supervise functions
HSL10	Supervise food services
HSL11	Supervise drink services
HSL17	Supervise housekeeping services
HSL20	Supervise portering and concierge services
HSL21	Supervise reception services
HSL22	Supervise reservation and booking services

Candidates that select any of the following units, HSL7, HSL10 or HSL11 from Section B are strongly recommended to take unit HSL30.

SECTION C OPTIONAL UNITS	
HSL6	Contribute to promoting hospitality services and products
HSL9	Contribute to the development of recipes and menus
HSL12	Supervise off-site food delivery services
HSL13	Supervise cellar and drink storage operations
HSL14	Manage the receipt, storage or dispatch of goods (SfL WS20)
HSL15	Supervise the wine store/cellar and dispense counter
HSL16	Supervise vending services
HSL18	Supervise linen services
HSL19	Monitor and solve customer service problems (ICS 32)
HSL23	Improve relationships with customers (ICS 26)
HSL24	Provide learning opportunities for colleagues (MSC D7)
HSL25	Supervise the use of technological equipment in hospitality services
HSL26	Supervise practices for handling payments
HSL27	Contribute to the development of a wine list
HSL28	Manage the environmental impact of your work (MSC E9)
HSL29	Contribute to the selection of staff for activities
HSL30	Ensure food safety practices are followed in the preparation and serving of food and drink (People1st 3GEN1)
HSL31	Lead meetings (MSC D11)

The art of supervision

In the busy world of hospitality there might seem to be layer upon layer of staff, all bustling about in order to make sure that the customer gets what they paid for, be it a service or a product or a combination of the two. Each department in a hotel or each section in a restaurant consists of a team of people, each with their own role, and all working together with the same end in sight. The General Manager has the ultimate position of control and therefore responsibility for the business, but they will only be as good as their team members who actually carry out the day-to-day tasks of the business, e.g. the operative staff guided by their supervisor and manager.

As the **supervisor,** you have a unique role to play in the general structure of the business. Supervisors tend to come into their job having spent some time, maybe even years, as a first line operative, e.g. a room attendant, a commis chef, a bartender, a barista, or a porter. 'First line' people are those who come into direct contact with the customer in their ordinary duties, like a waiter or a receptionist, or who provide very direct services for the customer, like cleaning their room, cooking their food or carrying their bags.

As a supervisor, you work both with the department manager and the staff in the department. Supervisors represent the staff to the manager, working alongside them on a day-to-day basis. Supervisors also represent the manager to the staff, working with the manager to run an effective department. As a supervisor, you really are in the middle of everything that goes on in the department.

The supervisor has, as we have said, a unique role, but why unique?

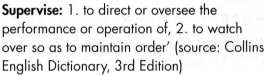

> **Definitions**
> **Supervise:** 1. to direct or oversee the performance or operation of, 2. to watch over so as to maintain order' (source: Collins English Dictionary, 3rd Edition)
> **Supervisor:** a person who manages or supervises

Although there is a difference between managing and **supervising** (see 'Supporting and Encouraging a Team', page 37), here we will be focusing on the supervisor who is there maintaining order and overseeing the performance of the departmental tasks to the benefit of the company, therefore providing direct benefit to the customer.

The role of the supervisor

An example taken from the National Occupational Standards (NOS) for housekeeping states that as a supervisor you should normally:

- supervise the housekeeping service
- supervise the linen service
- supervise the health, hygiene, safety and security of the working environment
- supervise the work of staff
- be in charge of the housekeeping department during the absence of the head housekeeper
- undertake daily inspections to monitor standards of occupied and vacated rooms, laundry and linen

- monitor the correct use of cleaning materials and produce an analysis of results
- assist in ensuring the department operates within budget.

But what does it mean to 'supervise the linen service' or, in the case of a catering supervisor, 'supervise the food service'? To break down your role in order to understand it better, we will go through the supervisor's role, guided by the NVQ standards, looking at how as a supervisor you:

- provide leadership for your team
- develop productive working relationships with colleagues
- manage resources
- ensure the health and safety of your colleagues and customers
- encourage excellent customer service.

The topics already mentioned can be applied to cooking, restaurant service, housekeeping, portering and reception – in fact, any other practical job that is part of a team effort and where you are present as the supervisor.

The manager establishes what the business needs to do in order to go forward, with the help of his or her managers and you as the supervisor. As supervisor, you then have to communicate these objectives to the staff and work with them on the actual day-to-day tasks, training the staff where necessary, monitoring the quality of the product or service, and then providing feedback to the manager when the tasks are complete or seeking help from the manager when there are situations beyond your authority or experience.

As you can see from the diagram, the supervisor's role is a cycle and each new objective is based on the experience of the previous one, thus improving the products and services all the time. The supervisor has the responsibility of carrying out the tasks which will ensure that the business objectives will be attained, while looking after the staff who carry out these tasks.

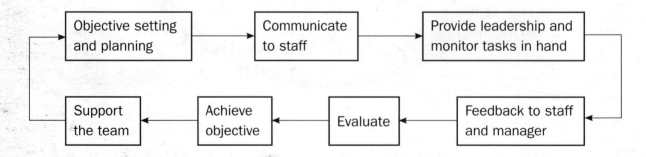

Overview of the hospitality industry

Introduction

The hospitality industry is Britain's largest and fastest-growing industry. In 2008, more than 2.5 million people were working in some role in the industry. But what is the hospitality industry?

According to the Collins English Dictionary (1991), 'Hospitality' means 'kindness in welcoming strangers or guests', so this is an industry where care of people is the core business. This in turn means that customer service is of the highest importance no matter what level of service is being offered; e.g. someone paying £450 for a hotel room for one night expects a high level of service but someone paying £45 a night still expects basic good service e.g. a clean room, even if it is not luxurious, and to be treated 'kindly'. Customer service is something that a business should always be trying to improve.

To understand the many aspects of hospitality, let us look at the different areas and services that make up the industry. The industry broadly divides into the public service sector and the private sector.

The public service sector (or cost sector) does not mean cheap or poor quality as it includes, for example, the Houses of Parliament at Westminster and conferences which are five-star catering events. It also includes hospitals, schools, residential homes and prisons which are funded by the state. Employee catering (staff restaurants and so on) is also included in this group; however, in some instances it is commercial catering provided by contract food service providers.

○ 'in-house services' or 'hospitality services' are owned and managed by the company itself. People 1st, the sector skills council for hospitality, leisure, travel and tourism, defines hospitality services as 'hospitality occupations within an organisation where the main purpose is not hospitality (for example, an in-house cook working in an on-site canteen within a manufacturing company)'.

○ contract food service providers (these used to be called contract caterers) are companies who are contracted to provide a service to the clients of the company which contracts them. For example, the Scottish Exhibition Centre in Glasgow contracts Leith's (part of the Compass Group) to provide their catering for them; all the catering staff are employed by Leith's and not directly by the Centre. Likewise, some school meals services are not owned and run by the school but the schools pay catering companies to provide the catering services. Currently around 20 per cent of UK school meal catering is outsourced in this way. The largest of these companies in Britain are the Compass Group and Sodexo, but there are many smaller companies like Charlton House and Vacherin.

Figure B Some well-known catering companies.

Commercial catering usually means a business which exists to make profit from its services. The private sector includes:

- those companies where a profit is necessary to survive, e.g. hotels, pubs, restaurants, theme parks, fast food outlets, clubs, caravan parks, etc.
- self-employed people providing services for private households/yachts as cooks, butlers, housekeepers, etc.
- restaurant staff, who make up about 27 per cent of the industry according to People 1st (the sector skills council for the industry) and hotel staff just 12 per cent.

The public service and private sectors then divide into the following.

- Catering: those establishments which offer food and drink only, e.g. restaurants, bars, events caterers, contract caterers, in-house catering and public sector catering such as the NHS, prisons, schools, day care centres, etc.
- Accommodation: those establishments which offer accommodation only, e.g. guest houses, lodges, self-catering chalets and caravans.
- Hospitality: those businesses which offer catering and accommodation services, e.g. hotels, cruise ships, residential care homes.
- Tourism, leisure and retail outlets: those businesses offering catering and/ or accommodation in the context of a tourism, leisure or retail environment.

All of the above can range in scale from an SME (small- to medium-sizes enterprise), like a privately-owned bed and breakfast, to national and global chains and franchises like Hilton Hotels, Café Rouge or even McDonald's.

The following tables can help you to gain a broad understanding of the services offered by these different areas of the industry.

Luxury hotels	Budget hotels	Hostels	Bed and breakfast
Provide food and accommodation	Provide food and accommodation	Provide food and accommodation	Provide food and accommodation
24-hour room service	Tea- and coffee-making facilities in rooms		Tea- and coffee-making facilities in rooms
Full staff including night housekeeping staff	Minimal staff	Minimal staff	Usually just the owner/s
In-house restaurants and bars	Have a franchise restaurant, or are next to a restaurant e.g. Premier Inns are always next to Brewers Fayre or Beefeater restaurants (all owned by Whitbread)	Usually a communal dining room and guests help to set and clear tables, and wash up	Only provide breakfast

Table A Services offered in different parts of the hospitality industry.

Luxury hotels	Budget hotels	Hostels	Bed and breakfast
Long-stay and business	Short-stay, high turnover	Short-stay, high turnover	One night or short holidays
Personal guest services, e.g. laundry		Do it yourself	May offer this
Lounge areas	Small seating area	Communal sitting area	Shared sitting room
Portering services	Basic		
Banqueting facilities			
Meeting rooms for hire	May have this facility		
High standard of furnishing and fabric	Basic comfort standards	Basic and could be a little run-down	Could be very well decorated or quite basic
Privately owned, e.g. the Goring Hotel, London, or part of a group, e.g. Hilton	Group or chain of hotels, e.g. Travelodge, Ibis	Youth hostel, charity-owned	Privately owned and run

Restaurants	Traditional cafés	Brasserie outlets	Fast food outlets
Provide food and drink	Provide food and drink	Provide food and drink	Provide food and drink
Simple one-hour meal to very expensive Michelin-star fine dining experience taking tow to three hours, e.g. (lower end) Ask and Nando's, or (high end) Gordon Ramsey at Claridges	Simple all-day-breakfast type food and comfort food, e.g. shepherd's pie, pasta, sausages and chips, etc.	More European than British, e.g. are licensed and the emphasis is on quick, good food, e.g. Cafe Rouge, Patisserie Valerie	Standard menu, food to eat in or take away. Little or no waiting
Can be conventional, e.g. varied style of food or themed, e.g. tapas, Thai or Chinese food	Low cost, very basic	Could be coffee and pastries, quick home-made snacks or a full meal	Limited and set menu
Open lunch and dinner but this depends on food style	Open usually only in daytime	Open all day and sometimes late into evening	Some can be 24-hour opening, e.g. McDonald's or just at meal times, e.g. fish and chip shops

Table A Services offered in different parts of the hospitality industry.

Price depends on food offer. Can be up to £150 a head, e.g. Sketch in London	Cheap and tending to disappear now with so much competition	Mid-range to slightly expensive pricing	Emphasis on budget meals
Type of food depends on locality and clientele, e.g. Giorgio Locatelli in the Churchill Hotel in London is 'fine dining' whereas Pizza Express is in most high streets	On travel routes and busy roads	High street relying on passing trade	Usually in busy shopping centres or high streets

Travel and leisure outlets:		Tourism and recreation outlets	Retail store outlets
Trains, airlines, coaches	Cruises		
Catering depends on class of travel, e.g. standard or first class	Provide accommodation and extensive catering	Examples of these are museums, historic buildings, theme parks and visitor attractions	Food courts with fast food outlets often, but sometimes with more expensive brands
Provided at terminals, service stations on motorways and on board, often by contract caterers		Often fast food outlets or quick service restaurants. Food not usually prepared freshly on the premises	Emphasis on turnover in fast food areas but on high spend in more expensive brands, e.g. Cafe Rouge
Trains: trolley service, buffet car and first class have good quality meals	Catering can be to a very high standard	Some places use well known brands, e.g. Sodexo, Costa Coffee	Some stores have specialised outlets, e.g. Harrods, Harvey Nichols

Table A Services offered in different parts of the hospitality industry.

Event catering is commercial and usually takes place in hotels or outside venues e.g. garden parties, wedding parties held in marquees, racing events. Events can be completely organised by one company to include food, drinks, tables, decoration, music, or provided by a combination of companies, each offering their speciality.

Characteristics of different types of hospitality businesses

The different businesses that come together to make up the hospitality industry are themselves made up of many different job roles. The industry is 'labour intensive', meaning there are many people working to provide the services in relation to the number of customers being served. In a five-star London hotel it may well be that there are 300 rooms and around 300 staff, i.e. a ratio of 1:1 staff to customer. This gives the industry a very large wages bill and is why good customer service is important, because this helps to increase the revenue, thus securing people's jobs.

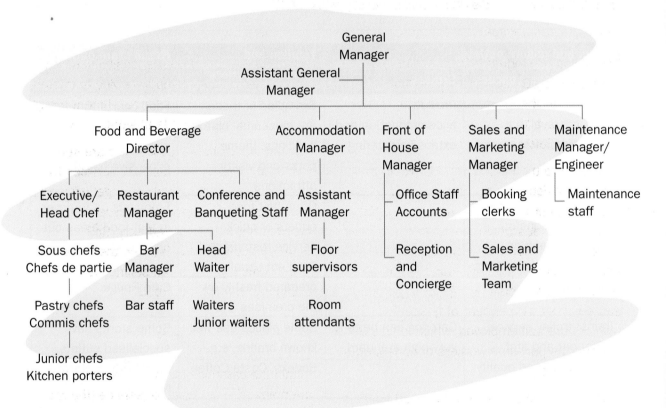

Figure C A typical hotel organisation chart.

All establishments are slightly different from one another but the organisation chart above gives some idea of the different roles within a hotel. The line of reporting, i.e. who is responsible for which area, differs depending on the size and quality of the establishment. For example, in a large five-star hotel, the Executive Chef is usually at the same level in the organisation as the Food and Beverage Director or Manager.

Employment types

Industry data: Employment in the UK hospitality industry

	2004*	2005*	2006	2007
Contract food service provider	179,600	178,300	182,600	181,600
Hotels	247,100	238,400	238,500	245,000
Pubs, bars and nightclubs	368,400	333,900	297,700	319,600
Restaurants	518,700	514,700	499,700	526,700
Hospitality services	402,100	379,900	390,300	417,400
Total Workforce	1,917,300	1,843,000	1,866,300	1,960,300

Table D Employment in the UK hospitality industry 2004–2007.

(Source: Labour Force Survey (30 April 2008))

The hospitality industry in the UK employed more than 1.96 million people in 2007, according to the latest Labour Force Survey by People 1st, the sector skills council for hospitality, leisure, travel and tourism.

According to the People 1st 'Key Facts and Figures' of February 2008 (www.people1st. co.uk), 51 per cent of the industry are 'full-time' employees which means they work more than 20 hours a week (usually 40–50 hours) and most jobs are found in the kitchen or as catering assistants. According to the same survey, 10 per cent of hospitality workers are self-employed, which leaves 39 per cent as part-time workers or consultants to the industry.

'Part-time' employees work up to 20 hours a week. For example, to cover the busy lunch period in a department store restaurant, some staff will be employed from 11 a.m. to 3 p.m. five days a week, i.e. 20 hours a week. The industry has many opportunities for part-time workers like students who work in bars and cafes while studying or for working mothers who cannot take up full-time work because of family responsibilities. The shift pattern where 24-hour service is offered also gives opportunities for part-time working to cover the busy periods at work.

Consultants or freelance workers are self-employed people who sell their services to the industry, e.g. financial and legal advisors, event organisers, those who deliver training programmes within the industry. Self-employed people can also own their own small company, e.g. a van selling ice creams or food at the side of a road.

Service types

Within the catering side of the industry there are many different types of service (the way food is served), including:

- **fast food**: take away or eat on the premises e.g. Burger King, Pizza Hut
- **self-service**: e.g. staff restaurants, store restaurants where the customers serve themselves their own food from a selection set out by the catering staff. Breakfast buffets in a hotel are also self-service

- **plated service:** food is served ready-plated, usually at a high level of presentation, e.g. in 'fine dining' and banqueting; however, in a cheap café the food is also served plated but this is not usually described as 'plated' service
- **silver service:** this is the opposite of plated service because here the food is served on to the plate by the waiter in front of the customer. The waiter in this case is a skilled person, as the craft of silver service takes time to learn
- **buffet service:** this is where hot and cold food is laid out for the customer to serve themselves or for it to be served to them by a member of staff, who may sometimes be a chef
- **function:** a function is not so much a style of catering but a place where different styles may be used. A function differs from a restaurant in that it is where a group of people sit down, as guests or customers, to the same menu at the same time, e.g. a meeting of 10 people or an awards ceremony of 750 people.

Within the accommodation side of the industry the service types are:

- **un-serviced:** e.g. self-catering operations and holiday homes
- **serviced:** e.g. places where the rooms are cleaned by staff, not the client, e.g. hotels, serviced flats.

Hotels and restaurants – star rating system

You will have often hear about three-star or five-star hotels, but what does this mean and who awards these stars? It is the AA (Automobile Association) in conjunction with the UK tourist authorities, i.e. VisitBritain, VisitScotland and VisitWales, that rate the accommodation. Opposite is a table of the standards used to assess the star rating of a hotel or guest accommodation.

Accommodation standards star ratings

Star ratings, from one to five, show the standard of quality for hotels and guest accommodation. The following brief summary gives the main standards within their ratings.

A similar system is in place for restaurants with the AA Rosette Awards.

Star rating
Hotel
Guest accommodation

Courteous staff provide an informal yet competent service. The majority of rooms are en suite, and a designated eating area serves breakfast daily and dinner most evenings.

Minimum quality requirements for cleanliness, maintenance, hospitality, facilities and services. A cooked or substantial continental breakfast is served in a dining room or eating area, or bedroom only.

All rooms are en suite or have private facilities. A restaurant or dining room serves breakfast daily and dinner most evenings.

Courteous service, well-maintained beds, and breakfast prepared with a good level of care.

Staff are smartly and professionally presented. All rooms are en suite, and the restaurant or dining room is open to residents and non-residents.

Friendly welcome, and good-quality, well-presented beds and furniture. A choice of good-quality, freshly-cooked food is available at breakfast.

Professional, uniformed staff respond to your needs or requests, and there are usually well-appointed public areas. The restaurant or dining room is open to residents and non-residents, and lunch is available in a designated eating area.

Attentive, more personalised service. At least half of the bedrooms are en suite or have private bathrooms (from 1 January 2008). Very good beds and high-quality furniture. Breakfast offers a greater choice, and fresh ingredients are cooked and presented with a high level of care.

Luxurious accommodation and public areas, with a range of extra facilities and a multilingual service available. Guests are greeted at the hotel entrance. High-quality menu and wine list.

Awareness of each guest's needs with nothing being too much trouble. All bedrooms are en suite or have a private bathroom (from 1 January 2008). Excellent-quality beds and furnishings. Breakfast includes specials/home-made items, high-quality ingredients and fresh local produce.

Figure D The AA star ratings. (Source: www.theaa.com)

Factors that affect hospitality businesses

Like all industries the hospitality industry does not work in isolation. It is subject to fluctuations in the market as much as retail, for example. While some areas of hospitality are a necessity, e.g. hospital meals, other areas are a luxury, e.g. five-star hotels, cruise catering.

Tourism

The dictionary definition of a 'tourist' is 'a person who travels for leisure purposes'. Tourism and hospitality go hand-in-hand as people who visit somewhere in Britain also need to sleep and eat somewhere. VisitBritain and travel companies are constantly marketing Britain as a tourist destination point, thus providing the hospitality industry with more and more customers.

The exchange rate

This is the rate at which one country can exchange its currency with that of another, e.g. one Euro was worth 90p in March 2009 whereas five years ago it was worth 75p. This means that visiting Britain is becoming cheaper for foreign visitors as they can buy more with their money now than a few years ago; therefore tourism numbers are increasing.

Media

Printed publicity is only a small way of promoting tourism and therefore hospitality. The Internet has provided very easy access to information about hotels, travel, restaurant booking services and package holiday deals. The tourist and hospitality industries have taken advantage of this means of promoting their services to the world, thus attracting more and more business. The Internet site for VisitBritain (www.visitbritain.co.uk) is a real source of information for people travelling to and around the UK with information on places to go, places to stay, places to eat and how to travel around the country. On a smaller scale, the restaurant booking services on the Internet bring information very close to the consumer and allow easy access to booking restaurant tables without a queue; this is so important in today's world where speed is of the essence.

Globalisation

Globalisation means 'the process by which a company expands to operate throughout the world'.

With the globalisation of companies, business travel has increased tremendously and the air and train companies have been providing a 'business class' service. This means they can charge more than the basic fare, including specific services for the business traveller, e.g. Internet access, faster booking-in times, special lounges with meeting rooms.

Business travellers are among the high-spend guests at hotels with their companies or clients paying the bill. The five-star hotels charge high prices for their rooms and can offer different luxury services to the business customer, e.g. spa, gym, swimming pool, on-site laundry and room service 24 hours a day (important when the customer has jet-lag and cannot yet fit into the meal pattern of the host country).

Finance

The hospitality industry contributes around £21 billion to the national economy as well as employing around 7 per cent of the total workforce in the UK. Due to the world recession in 2008–9 many businesses are struggling to compete and survive. However, economics goes in cycles and businesses are working towards an end to the recession. The Olympics in 2012 will provide thousands of extra jobs in the hospitality industry but at the moment there is a skills shortage and a shortage of staff generally. Only 13 per cent of the total workforce in hospitality has a qualification and more and more it is considered that particular skills are needed within the industry, not just at management levels but at operative levels where the greatest numbers of people work.

Social trends to consider:

- Disposable incomes:
  - The dictionary definition for disposable income is 'the money a person has available to spend after paying taxes, pension contributions etc'. This money is spent on consumer goods and services.
  - Unless there is a recession period there is a high amount of disposable income (spending money) especially from young people aged 14 to 24 and from the over-60 age groups. It is now normal for students to travel around the world before they go to university whereas ten years ago it was quite rare.

- Standards of living:
  - It is more common now for people to eat out than ten years ago, and this can be seen by the increase of all types of eating places on the high street. This is because the standard of living has risen. This means that people expect a certain quality of lifestyle which is higher than in previous generations, e.g. in the past it was a luxury to own a computer; now it is a basic part of nearly every household.
- Leisure activities:
  - People have a higher expectation of their leisure time which means they travel more, and use more facilities such as gyms, theatres, cinemas and eating places.
- Cultural influences:
  - The hospitality industry has been greatly affected by the high numbers of non-British people living in the country as well as by the effect of many British people travelling abroad. The culinary experience of most people is now quite broad and most high streets will have varied cuisine available, such as British, Caribbean, Eastern, Indian and Chinese.
- Population growth:
  - Population growth studies are important for forecasting future trends in catering, e.g. falling numbers of children have a negative effect on the school meals service and possibly the number of fast food outlets.
  - The growing number of older people in the population has an influence on the hospitality industry because this affects the types of food and accommodation

on offer, e.g. more accessible accommodation is needed, such as walk-in showers for those who find steps difficult to negotiate, lower light switches for those who cannot stretch so easily.

Legislation

Legislation has a direct effect on the industry as it acts as a regulatory body to promote and maintain standards and control abuses. For example, the Food Safety Act 1990 made managers improve, monitor and train staff in food handling, storage, etc. which is a cost to the business. Also a licence is needed before opening a hotel, restaurant or bar and in the case of a licensed premises, e.g. an outlet selling alcohol, a person needs to hold a specific qualification, e.g. the National Certificate for Personal Licence Holders (NCPLH) qualification. To obtain these qualifications one needs time and money, not always readily available.

There is a lot of regulation controlling the running of these businesses, such as:

- daily operational laws regarding food hygiene, the display of tariffs, weights and measures, etc.
- business laws covering contracts, workers rights, fire precautions, health and safety, disability discrimination, etc.
- the introduction of a minimum wage
- EU regulations.

See also Appendix 1: Legislation, page 199.

Education and training

Britain has a long history of education for the hospitality industry and was one of the first countries in Europe to provide Hospitality Management degrees at university level. The training and education in this country provides training from the basic level, such as a GCSE or a Diploma, up to the highest levels of Masters and PhD. From 2009 the new Diplomas for 14 to 19-year-olds will provide a new form of studies on the industry in order to encourage people to go into an industry that has so many opportunities for so many different types of jobs and yet which does not yet attract enough people. The new Diplomas should help students to have a better understanding of the industry and to dispel some of the myths while promoting the positive side of the industry, e.g. building friendships, wide choice of jobs, travel opportunities, good promotion prospects and some beautiful places to work. Training at work is carried out extensively in the hospitality industry and in-house training schemes are well developed in large organisations. In small businesses the training is informal with skills and techniques being passed from person to person.

Time management

The ability to manage time effectively and efficiently is important in all aspects of your life:

○ as a learner
○ privately
○ at work.

Some people manage time better than others because they have natural time management skills or because they have learnt how to manage time by working more effectively and efficiently.

You may be able to identify if you have poor time management by using the checklist below.

Checklist ✓

☐ Find meeting deadlines a problem

☐ Avoid tackling difficult tasks

☐ Do things that do not really need to be done

☐ Find it difficult to decide between conflicting priorities

☐ Feel out of control

☐ Leave things to the last minute

☐ Tend to take over other people's work

☐ Find it difficult to be on time for appointments

☐ Get stressed when interrupted

☐ Find yourself wondering 'Where did the day go?'

☐ Keep shuffling the same papers around

If you ticked one or more of the above you are likely to benefit from managing your time more effectively.

Managing your time more effectively

A good place to start is by listing all the tasks to be done and prioritising them into order of:

○ what is important
○ what is urgent.

Step 1

By prioritising the most important or urgent tasks first, once they are dealt with you can start to spend more time on important tasks that are less urgent.

Step 2

Avoiding tasks is something is that all people do when they do not like doing something or find a particular task difficult. So spend ten minutes a day working on those tasks until you find them less daunting. This will help you to maximise the way you use time. It will avoid you wasting time and give you more time to enjoy the things you like to do.

Step 3

Organising yourself will also help you to manage yourself and your time better. Here are some practical tips to help you become more organised.

○ Spend solid blocks of time dealing with emails rather than answering them as you go along – if you do the latter, you often lose your train of thought.
○ Use an 'in' and 'out' tray – process the 'in' tray regularly.
○ Manage your diary by planning blocks of time to do specific tasks – master your diary and your time.

- Make sure you file things correctly either on the computer or as hard copy. Using a well-managed filing system saves time.
- When organising meetings, make sure you have an agenda, a chairperson, action points, and stick to a timetable. Ask yourself: is this the best way to communicate the information or could it be done more efficiently using other forms of communication?

Step 4

Master the art of delegation. Sometimes it is all too easy to believe that you are the only one who can do a particular task. But as a supervisor you need to be able to delegate tasks to others. Particularly when you are under pressure, this may be a far better option. Planning delegation is important as the person carrying out the task must be given a clear brief of what to do and how to do it. This should give you more time to do the more important tasks in supervising the work of others.

Step 5

Start today!

HS1

Provide leadership for your team

This chapter covers the following units:

- Level 3 Diploma Hospitality Supervision and Leadership (NVQ)
  HS1: Provide leadership for your team
- Technical Certificate Unit 1: Principles of leading a team in the
  hospitality industry – 1.1, 1.2, 1.3, 1.4, 2.1, 2.2, 2.3, 2.4, 2.5,
  2.6, 2.7, 2.8, 2.9, 2.10, 2.11.

**Working through this chapter could also provide
evidence for the following key skills:**

C.2.1a, C2.1b, C2.2, C2.3.

In this chapter you will learn about:

- effective communication
- reflection and feedback
- objectives
- planning
- leadership styles
- supporting and encouraging a team
- dealing with difficulties.

Likely sources of evidence

1.1. Set out and positively communicate the purpose and objectives of the team to all members.
Witness testimony from colleagues. Narrative of how purpose and objectives are communicated to the team. Minutes of meetings, presentation notes. Observation by assessor.

1.2 Involve members in planning how the team will achieve its objectives.
Minutes of meetings, witness testimony, professional discussion.

1.3 Ensure that each member of the team has personal work objectives and understands how achieving these will contribute to achievement of the team's objectives.
Minutes of one-to-one meetings objective setting, witness testimony, professional discussion, job descriptions, SMART objectives.

1.4 Encourage and support team members to achieve their personal work objectives and those of the team and provide recognition when objectives have been achieved.
Minutes of one-to-one feedback meetings, witness testimony, professional discussion, employee-of-the-week board, emails, telephone conversation.

1.5 Win, through your performance, the trust and support of the team for your leadership.
Witness testimony, professional discussion, emails.

1.6 Steer the team successfully through difficulties and challenges, including conflict, diversity and inclusion issues within the team.
Provide egs via a PD of any difficulties/conflicts you have had to work through with colleagues. Explain how the action you took has ensured that the team stayed on track and performed well.

1.7 Encourage and recognise creativity and innovation within the team.
Minutes of one-to-one feedback meetings, witness testimony, professional discussion, employee of the week board, emails, telephone conversation.

1.8 Give team members support and advice when they need it especially during periods of setback and change.
Minutes of one-to-one feedback meetings, witness testimony, professional discussion, emails, telephone conversation.

1.9 Motivate team members to present their own ideas and listen to what they say.
Minutes of team meetings, witness testimony, professional discussion, suggestion box notes, emails, telephone conversation.

1.10 Encourage team members to take the lead when they have the knowledge and expertise and show willingness to follow this lead.
Minutes of team meetings and one-to-one meetings, witness testimony, professional discussion, emails, telephone conversation.

1.11 Monitor activities and progress across the team without interfering.
Minutes of team meetings and feedback meetings, witness testimony, professional discussion, time sheets, quality checks, smart objectives with measurables, suggestion box notes, emails, telephone conversation.

Introduction

This unit aims to provide you with direction as a hospitality supervisor, motivating and supporting you to achieve the team's objectives as well as your personal work objectives. It has strong links to all other units in the Hospitality Supervision and Leadership suite of standards.

In order to gain evidence for your NVQ Level 3 Hospitality Supervision, you need to be working as a supervisor or training to be a supervisor. It is most important for you to be able to generate real evidence to show that you can do the job. Part of being able to do the job well involves knowing why you do things in a certain way. This will be affected by a variety of factors, including the processes within your own organisation, the particular needs of a situation, and sometimes simply your own style and preferences.

Effective communication

Communication is one of the first things you learn as a supervisor – you will need to organise your staff, hold team briefings, sort out staff problems, attend to quality problems, etc. Communication is rightly termed a 'key skill'.

You need to learn how to be a role model for your staff in order to lead by example, and to motivate the team through your encouragement and your skills. If you lead by example, through your own performance, you will win the trust and support of your team.

Evidence

Think of situations when you have demonstrated your willingness to lead by example. Perhaps, rather than asking someone else to carry out a task and then reviewing it, there was an occasion when you judged that it would be more effective to do it yourself, to set a high standard that they could follow in future. HSL 1.5.

We use our senses in order to understand our surroundings and to communicate with those around us (see following table).

Sense	Percentage contribution to learning
taste	3
smell	3
hearing	13
touch	6
sight	75

Table 1.1 How we use our senses to learn.

Only 13 per cent is understood or learned from the spoken word – effective communication is not just about speaking. When we communicate, we use our eyes most of all, and we learn 75 per cent of everything by seeing and watching. This is why we talk about verbal and non-verbal communication. Our **body language** reinforces what we say – but be aware that body language can also betray us, and communicate the opposite of what we are actually saying.

Definition

Body language: communication that takes place between people through the movements of their bodies and facial expressions.

17

Case study: Body language and its consequences

Negative body language

A customer comes into the hotel, coming through the doors unaided because the doorman is talking to another customer. They walk up to the front desk, but the receptionist is on the phone. As it is a small hotel, there is no one else in the front office area. The customer stands because there is only one seat, which is occupied. The customer has travelled for six hours and is tired. The receptionist, busy on the phone, makes no eye contact. The customer knows the receptionist is busy, but feels

Figure 1.1 Spot the mistakes.

unwelcome. Eventually, the receptionist finishes the call and goes directly to the seated customer. After another ten minutes, the receptionist finally attends to the standing customer, who is now quite annoyed. The receptionist tries to calm the guest down, but realises that this guest could easily complain – the service is not, as it says in the hotel's brochure, 'prompt and courteous'.

Positive body language

A customer comes into the hotel, and the doorman, who was talking to another customer, excuses himself for a minute, opens the door and welcomes the guest. He realises that the only seat in the waiting area is in use, and finds a chair. He then goes back to the other guest and continues his work. The receptionist is on the phone. As it is a small hotel, there is no-one else in the front office area. The customer has travelled for six hours and is tired. The receptionist, realising that the guest is

Figure 1.2 Getting it right first time.

waiting, makes eye contact and smiles, 'Be with you in a minute.' The customer knows that the receptionist is busy, but feels welcome because they have been acknowledged. The guest settles into the chair, content to wait a little. Eventually the receptionist finishes the call and goes directly to the first guest. After a few moments, they finally attend to the new customer, saying, 'I'm sorry to have kept you. You must be Mr Phillips; your room is ready and I'll get the doorman to take up your luggage straight away while we complete the booking forms.' The guest is delighted that they already know who he is, and happily books in at the desk.

Think about the two case studies above. Similar events could happen in any hotel or restaurant. Waiting is part of life, but not being acknowledged is seen to be rude by the customer. In the first case, the receptionist upset the customer by *not* doing things, and it is often the things that are forgotten that upset customers the most.

Good practice

For communication to be effective, you need to think about the following.

o What needs to be communicated? Event information, financial details, skills?

o How urgent is the communication? Is it needed now, today, tomorrow or later?

o Are you the right person to communicate this knowledge to others, or should it be your manager?

o Who needs this information? Manager, colleagues, staff, other departments?

o How are you going to communicate this? Verbal, one-to-one, email, memo, noticeboard, staff briefing, instructions, discussion?

o How will you know you have been understood correctly? Looking at the products, asking people if they understand, asking staff to say how they will put the information into practice, checklists?

Figure 1.3 A staff noticeboard is one way of communicating information to colleagues.

Evidence

Think of all the different types of communication that you use in your job. Which type of communication is most effective for which type of situation? 1.1, 2.1.

What needs to be communicated?

In hospitality, the smooth running of the day will depend a lot on effective communication. As supervisor, you have to make sure all team members, including the manager, are aware of any details specific to that day. The manager must be kept informed of progress made during the day, and of any problems you are unable to resolve as supervisor, given the limitations of your authority.

Take the example of an event being held at your establishment. Event information could be about preparation for the next day – including setting up the rooms, unusual opening or closing times, a change in staff rotas, checking off the stock that will be used (such as screens, tables, stage decking, food, complimentary notepads and other items).

If the staff do not know what to do, or the order in which they should do things, then tasks may be left undone and others may be done twice, wasting time and money. In the end, this could result in serious customer complaints if services they have ordered are not provided because of poor communication.

A lot depends on the team briefing that is carried out at the beginning of each shift. Much of the communication that you need to do will start in this briefing session – for example, rotas for the day, guests' special requirements, information on the standards expected that day. The information communicated to each member of staff must tie in to the duties in their job description, or it must be clearly explained to them in what ways they are being required to work outside their area of responsibility. A good briefing

19

communicates how each person's role will contribute to a successful day for the whole team. Other subjects about which you will need to communicate frequently might include:

- days off for your staff
- order of work for the day, and anything particular to that day
- instructions for carrying out a task
- product or supply orders
- reinforcing good practice by praising and encouraging the staff
- quality indications: things that need to be done better
- information brought up in a training session you have given to a member of staff
- evacuation instructions during a drill or a real emergency.

During your day, you will spend a lot of time working with the staff and issuing instructions as the day unfolds. It is important that you think ahead and communicate with the staff, so that they know exactly what to do and when; this will also avoid unnecessary problems and minimise stress for all involved. You should monitor activities and progress across the team, but you should not interfere; as a supervisor, always aim to support the team, rather than getting too involved in the duties for which your team members are responsible. This shows that you are encouraging and supporting your staff to achieve both their personal work objectives and those of the team. Encourage team members to take the lead when they have particularly relevant knowledge and expertise, and show a willingness to follow their lead. This will instil confidence in your staff, which is vital to a team performing well.

Find out!

Look at the organisational charts of your own business and your own department. How well do you know the structure of your team, and your team members' job roles? As a supervisor, you need to set out and positively communicate the purpose and objectives of the team to all team members. To do this, you will need to know where each team member fits into the overall organisational structure and what their job entails. Write down a plan of how you can effectively communicate objectives to your team members.

Who should do the communicating?

Sometimes it is the manager who communicates information when the supervisor and the team are present together. Often, however, the manager and the supervisor have a meeting, then the supervisor communicates the outcomes to the team; and vice versa, sometimes the supervisor communicates team decisions and suggestions to the manager on behalf of the team.

The different pathways can be represented as:
- manager → supervisor and team
- manager → supervisor → team
- team and supervisor → manager
- supervisor → manager.

Good practice

Who should do the communicating always depends on the information being passed on. As supervisor, you have to know the limits of your authority so that you do not communicate information that is untimely, incorrect, or beyond your authority to disclose. You must not be indiscreet by communicating private or personal information that should remain private and personal; this is called 'professional discretion'. Remember that information about your staff and customers is known only through your working situation, not through any personal right to information.

Who needs the information?

Information is useless if it does not reach the right person. For example, it is ineffective for a team member in the kitchen to complain to one of the housekeeping staff that they are always running out of flour, because the housekeeping staff are not in a position to remedy the situation. It would be better to tell the person who does the order to the stores, because that person can use the information to increase the order and ensure that the kitchen has sufficient flour for its needs. In other words, the recipient of the information must be able to use the data effectively.

Good practice

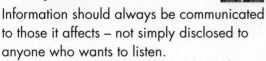

Information should always be communicated to those it affects – not simply disclosed to anyone who wants to listen.

Communicating information is not always a matter of giving orders. Sometimes this may be the case – if your manager asks you to give your team members an instruction, you will sometimes need to do just that. At other times, it gives you an opportunity as supervisor to involve team members in planning how the team will achieve its objectives. Communication in such situations is all about motivation and teamwork.

Good practice

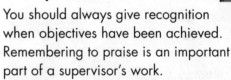

You should always give recognition when objectives have been achieved. Remembering to praise is an important part of a supervisor's work.

Some information that is urgent has to be treated in a special manner. For example, a customer complaint has to be dealt with, not simply filed in the day's report. Similarly, a customer's compliment about food, given to a waiter, should be passed on to the kitchen team so that the compliment reaches the team that was actually responsible.

How to communicate

How we communicate is the most important part of the list of points on page 19. It is choosing the correct and most effective way of communicating information that shows the skills of a supervisor. It may be easy to issue memos – but how many people read them? How can you take into account the very high proportion of non-English speakers working in this industry at the present time? Are your written instructions really clear?

Evidence

Find an instruction booklet for a machine in your work or home, or a recipe you have never used before. Follow the instructions given exactly to the letter. Notice any places where you are not sure what is meant. Think about how it could have been more clearly expressed. For example, would a diagram have helped?

1.1, 2.1.

These machines can be damaged if they are used incorrectly.

Evidence

For your Level 3 Diploma in Hospitality Supervision and Leadership (NVQ) you will have to show the different means you choose to communicate with your staff in all sorts of situations. Good evidence will show why you chose that method and the steps you took to make your decision. You should be able to gather some evidence from, for example, the following situations at work:

o your team briefing sessions
o your agenda notes from meetings with your manager
o presentation notes
o notes from meetings with members of your team.

1.1, 2.1.

To make your notes clear as evidence, you need to make sure that you write down the thought processes that led to your decision. For example, a decision to change a day off for one of your staff will show up on the rota as the original date and then the new date. For your evidence, you might want to show the steps as follows.

1 Chef has to change day off to Tuesday for personal reasons agreed with manager.
2 Sous was off on Tuesday but will now have to cover.
3 Sous will now need to take another day, and the best for cover is Thursday, because there is an event on Friday.
4 Will approach sous early on her shift tomorrow as she is not in today.
5 Sous prefers Wednesday off, so checked cover and it is fine.
6 Agreement made for next Wednesday.

These steps simply show that you have taken into account the wishes of the people involved as far as possible, while being aware of the important days which are too busy for the chef and sous to be off. You also show that you are aware of the importance of cover, and of not just agreeing days off without checking the rota.

Find out!

Gather together examples of communication procedures that you use in your workplace. Most organisations have agreed standards or procedures which, as supervisor, you need to carry out or monitor in the work of your team.

Written communication

Written communication may include:

○ department memos

○ interdepartmental memos

○ suggestion notes to your manager

○ staff rota records

○ procedures for communicating days off and notification of holidays

○ health and safety and food hygiene records

○ machine instructions on the walls or in files

○ work rotas and staff information on noticeboards

○ reports, e.g. events, breakages, maintenance

○ notification of prizes, e.g. employee of the month award.

As supervisor, a lot of your communication will be on the job, giving verbal instructions to your team. But you also need to recognise the importance of written communication. Usually things are written down because they need to be well thought out, or they will form part of records – for example, maintenance, staff rotas, supplies requests. Written communication is taken to be more formal and therefore more binding, so some written communication will have to abide by legal requirements in terms of formatting, such as Hazard Awareness and Critical Control Points (HACCP) recording.

Law and policy

Hazard Awareness and Critical Control Points (HACCP) is one of the systems which you will need to be aware of, and apply, in your work as a hospitality supervisor. For information on HACCP, see Legislation, page 209; also see Unit 4.

Have a look at these two examples of written communication.

Kitchen to stores.
Can we have 2kg onions please?
They are needed for tomorrow
and I forgot to order them

REQUEST NOTE

FROM Kitchen

TO   Stores

ITEM

2kg onions for tomorrow 13.7.09 (forgotten from previous order)

Signature

Supervisor Signature

Figure 1.4 Examples of written communication.

The second example is an official form which carries a date and a signature. This is a better form of communication because it can be traced – if there are any questions as to what type of onion is needed, then the store person can contact the right person. The first example has no name and no date, and could just be ignored by stores as it is not official. If official forms exist in your organisation, it is important to use them; an unofficial note may be ignored and you will not have the onions you need!

Evidence

Writing formal reports on an event, or for deciding budget issues with the manager, may generate evidence for your key skills. For Communication Level 2 you need to write two documents, each of 500 words. Evidence like this will be easy to produce because, in your job role, you will be writing memos to your manager and staff, or sending reports to your manager, for example, a pie chart to express the weekly sales figures, or a graph showing the popularity of a certain dish on different days of the week with recommendations to improve sales on the weaker days.

A smile is positive body language

How you communicate verbally will also be dealt with under 'Leadership styles' (page 32) – how you speak to your manager and staff has a lot to do with your own personal style, as well as the standards required of you in the workplace.

Verbal communication

Verbal communication can include:
- team briefings
- staff appraisals
- meetings with your manager
- individual conversations with staff
- procedures for greeting guests or customers
- training.

As well as what is said, whenever verbal communication is used you need to take into consideration:
- tone of voice
- good use of language
- use or non-use of slang, depending on the environment.

Non-written, non-verbal communication

Communication that is neither written nor spoken may include:
- how staff conduct themselves when they are not directly engaged in service, e.g. how a waiter stands in the restaurant while awaiting customers
- facial expressions – or a lack of them
- speed of service
- how the uniform is worn.

We have to make sure that, when we talk to a customer or a member of staff, our body language (see page 17) communicates what our words say. For example, if you are praising a member of staff, it helps to smile, otherwise they may not believe that you are being sincere. Likewise, if a customer is complaining, you must be serious and not stifle laughter, as they may feel they are not being listened to and their verbal complaint may turn to aggression.

How we wear our uniform and supervise other staff indicates our pride in our work and our self-respect. For example, a cleaner should always have a clean uniform, as a dirty one could indicate that the person is generally careless about their work. Your uniform indicates the company standard and **corporate image**. This image is important for the customer because it indicates branding – the customer should find the same standard, for example, in all hotels of the same chain, as this gives them confidence in the management team and encourages their loyalty to the brand.

Definition

Corporate image: how a corporation is perceived; a generally accepted image of a company's values.

Style of communication

Different styles of communication should be used for different situations. You cannot talk to a VIP in the same way as you would talk to your commis chef. A VIP expects formality and courtesy, and would be offended at overfamiliarity. Communication has its own rules of etiquette or manners, and these rules exist to put people at their ease in different situations because they know what to expect from those around them.

How do you know which form of communication is the best for each situation? The table below summarises some situations and the types of communication you could use.

	Formal	Informal
How?	○ Very polite ○ Use conventional terms of address – Sir, Madam, Mr, Mrs, etc. ○ Body language neat and controlled, even in a busy situation ○ Not engaging the customer in unnecessary conversation	○ Polite but not stiff ○ Use first names if you know them ○ Body language relaxed, at ease ○ Being chatty with the customer
When?	○ Dealing with VIPs ○ Meeting customers in a formal setting, e.g. a fine dining restaurant, a four- or five-star hotel, an event ○ Meetings with your manager or other senior staff ○ Meetings with suppliers ○ An appraisal or discipline meeting with a member of staff ○ Dealing with customer complaints ○ (Team briefing is sometimes formal)	○ Meeting customers in an informal restaurant, e.g. pizza house, chain restaurant, pub ○ When a customer praises the staff ○ Chatting with colleagues at work ○ Talking to suppliers well known to you ○ Instructing the staff in a daily team briefing

Table 1.2 How and when to use formal and information communication.

Briefing versus coaching

A **briefing** may include issuing the day's instructions, setting out the order of work and allotting responsibilities.

Coaching involves working with a member of staff on a task so that they are able to do it confidently. Supervisors often do this, making short comments on a task being carried out so that it can be done better or more quickly. It implies a good, supportive working relationship, so that the person coached does not feel corrected, but encouraged. You should identify opportunities to coach when they arise. Coaching is generally delivered one-to-one, and should be repeated as necessary until the outcome is successful.

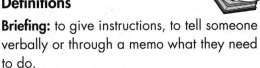

Definitions

Briefing: to give instructions, to tell someone verbally or through a memo what they need to do.

Coaching: to guide someone through a task.

More formal training (see page 39) may be required in the following situations:

○ induction
○ job role training
○ corrective training to improve quality
○ new equipment
○ new company procedures
○ new menus.

As a supervisor you need to be:

○ friendly, but not over-friendly with the team, to allow yourself to be able to reprimand a member of staff when necessary – being overbearing and controlling can make the working day miserable for the staff and usually results in poor customer service, which is always bad for the business
○ aware of when to be formal and when to be informal (see Table 1.2)
○ able to understand that your body language, more than your words, has a lot of influence on your staff and whether or not they can enjoy their day at work and be successful at what they do.

Evidence

Think of three situations in which you needed to use different communication methods for each of the following:

○ involving team members in planning how the team will achieve its objectives
○ setting personal work objectives for members of your team and ensuring that each staff member understands them, and how they fit into the team's objectives
○ providing recognition to a team member, or the whole team, after the achievement of an objective.

These methods may include formal/informal communication, briefing, coaching, running meetings, interaction with guests and training. What kind of tasks did you carry out, and what problems were you called upon to solve? Notes from conversations (face-to-face or by phone), emails, memos, or minutes of meetings from these situations will all provide valuable evidence.
1.2, 1.3, 1.4, 2.1, 2.3, 2.4.

Evidence

Team briefings can generate evidence for Communication Level 2. During a team briefing there could be a discussion (C2.1a) about a pre-prepared topic, for example, when people have been asked to bring suggestions about improving efficiency at the front desk.

Verbal evidence for Communication Level 2 includes a short talk of about four minutes. C2.1b could be covered when you have to brief the team about an event or a change to the booking system. In these cases your communication needs to be very clear, as the information you are communicating is important – it is not just social conversation. Part of the evidence for the talk is feedback from listeners to show that they have understood what you have said. Confirmation of their understanding could be observed by watching them put your instructions or information into action.

Reflection and feedback

A good supervisor is reflective. A reflective person is someone who naturally analyses their success and failures at work and at home, and tries to work out why things happen in order to repeat the successes and eliminate the near-misses and failures.

A good supervisor will always think of their own actions before those of their team when there is a crisis at work. When things don't turn out quite right, we may stop and think, 'Is this my fault because I rushed the briefing, so now the team really are a bit lost?' or 'I can't have explained that procedure well, because no one seemed to follow it.' This

does not mean that we should take the blame for everything – but that we should find out the real cause of something going wrong. On receiving a customer complaint about how a booking was badly taken, we might think, 'I did explain it properly because I asked the team member why he was doing the procedure in a different way and he said that he just didn't like the company way of doing it. I know now that I need to check in some way that my staff are really on board, so that procedures are carried out according to company standards.'

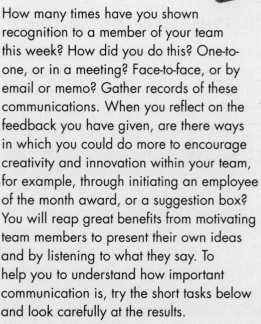

Evidence

How many times have you shown recognition to a member of your team this week? How did you do this? One-to-one, or in a meeting? Face-to-face, or by email or memo? Gather records of these communications. When you reflect on the feedback you have given, are there ways in which you could do more to encourage creativity and innovation within your team, for example, through initiating an employee of the month award, or a suggestion box? You will reap great benefits from motivating team members to present their own ideas and by listening to what they say. To help you to understand how important communication is, try the short tasks below and look carefully at the results.
1.4, 1.7, 1.9, 2.1, 2.6

Make the effort to greet a member of staff whom you find difficult to work with, smiling and using positive body language (relaxed and open). Watch how they respond to you.

Try *telling* someone to do something, and then *asking* the same person to do a different job. How do they react in each case, and what are the results?

27

During a team briefing, try to identify those who dominate the meeting by constantly speaking or interrupting, and those who find it difficult to contribute but still have something positive to say. How do you find yourself reacting when you listen to suggestions you have not previously thought about?

Reflect on this, and try to find solutions to help the meeting run well by including all members of the team, and being confident about unexpected suggestions and how to handle them.

Objectives

Different types of objective

As a team leader, you need to set **objectives** for your team. Different types of objective – business, team or department, and personal objectives – influence not only what we do at work, but how we do it. It is important not to confuse objectives with motivation (see page 35) – sometimes you and your staff will be motivated not by the objective itself, but by personal objectives that help us to attain the larger objective. For example, our manager may set us the task of increasing sales on a certain day. We may find ourselves motivated to work harder, not because we particularly want to increase the sales, but because we want the satisfaction of meeting a challenge.

> **Definition**
> **Objective:** an aim or goal that is being worked towards.

Business objectives are aims the managers set for us. They may include:
- sales targets
- gross profit margins
- customer satisfaction surveys
- growth targets (e.g. open a new spa by next January)
- cost reduction
- new ideas (e.g. introducing special offers).

Good teamwork means a busy restaurant.

Department and/or team objectives will relate to the business objectives, but will usually emerge from the team itself, or from the supervisor and their direct manager, as a way to meet the business objectives. They can include:
- punctuality of team members
- a better service style, which the team should adhere to
- improving the team culture by publicly rewarding good practice
- introducing a reward or bonus system
- attracting more customers
- instigating a training system
- meeting the business objectives.

Personal objectives are specific to each individual member of the team. All of us have personal objectives, and these are often what motivate us and give us satisfaction when we attain them. They can include:

○ meeting a challenge with courage and energy, and not getting unduly stressed by team errors

○ being positive at work to help generate a good working atmosphere

○ increasing sales to earn a bonus

○ improving understanding with a particular member of staff with whom there is a difficult relationship

○ improving training skills so that the team is more fitted to its task (e.g. through a course, observation or reading)

○ completing paperwork on time.

It is important to show team members how their personal work objectives contribute to the achievement of team objectives.

SMART objectives

When setting objectives for your staff, you should ensure that they are SMART:

○ **S**pecific
○ **M**easurable
○ **A**chievable
○ **R**ealistic
○ **T**ime-bound.

Specific

If an objective is not specific, then it is very likely that it will not be achieved. For example, if you think the team is performing poorly in terms of cleaning procedures, and you only tell them they need to clean more thoroughly, then very little may happen – they need to know which part of the department needs attention, and which dirty areas they have not noticed, in order to improve. Personal objectives risk never being achieved if you frame them in such a general way as 'I must have more patience' or 'I will do all my paperwork on time this week'. Framing your goal as 'I am going to be patient today with David during service time and try to encourage him to clear the tables calmly so that he does not upset the customers, or me, like he did yesterday' has a much greater chance of success. Vague, overarching objectives can lead to a constant feeling of non-achievement or frustration, which saps the energy from a team.

Measurable

How do you know if you have achieved the objective? Can you measure the outcome? Can you record the difference (if applicable)? Some achievements can be quantified – for example, an increase in customer numbers or takings. Others are qualitative achievements – such as patience, customer relations, greater motivation and job satisfaction. Qualitative achievements are often the most satisfying, so it is good to know how to reflect on them. They can often be measured by the outcome of the measurable objectives – for example, a happier team will serve the customers more effectively, and often this is shown in an increase in takings or in customers sending in thank-you letters.

Achievable

The objective 'I will always be patient' is not realistic. There will inevitably be situations in which you feel lack of patience. Achievable objectives help us to reach an aim by way of a series of relatively small steps, rather than by one great leap.

More achievable objectives might be:
- 'I will be patient with David at service time.'
- 'Today I will be more patient with Miss Jennings, a regular customer who always complains.'
- 'I will be patient today in the meeting with my manager if I feel she is not listening to me and try to explain my suggestion from different points of view.'

If you set objectives in small steps like this, eventually you will become more patient generally, and you, your team and also your customers will benefit from your small struggles to overcome your impatience bit by bit.

Realistic

To be realistic, an objective has to be within the reach of the team. It is unrealistic to expect the team to cope with building works in the kitchen while trying to increase sales. It is more realistic to have an objective whereby we ensure sales do not drop due to the staff being upset by their working conditions. Realistic objectives become unrealistic when we ask too much from the team – for example, a change of bar menu when we do not have the equipment to cook it, or a change in housekeeping procedures without briefing the staff. Objectives are also unrealistic when the timing makes them

impossible – for example, if the supervisor tells the staff to do some periodic cleaning in a corridor that day, and the staff know that the deliveries will come mid-morning and block the corridor. In this case, they will have to tell the supervisor that it is impossible to finish the cleaning today and ask for it to be rescheduled. If the supervisor insists, then the staff know they will not meet the objective, and will start the work with no hope of finishing; this demotivates and creates bad feeling in the team, which the supervisor will have to deal with.

Time-bound

All objectives have to be time-bound or they are not specific, and therefore are difficult or impossible to achieve. The example given under 'realistic' demonstrates this problem, as does, for instance, a bar manager who plans to refurbish 'some time during the year' but never sits down to start planning when this will be possible. If he does not do a time plan, then he will not refurbish because he does not have a structured year vision and will never take a clear decision. A team that is instructed to speed up will need to know when, otherwise they will have to apply this mandate to the whole day. It will clearly be impossible for them to keep up this momentum unless short-term objectives are in place – for example, 'daily at lunch service' or 'on Fridays when we are very busy'. These short, time-bound objectives help to motivate and to measure improvement, as they help the team to focus. Teams respond to short-term objectives because when they achieve them they are encouraged, and want to take on more objectives which are seen as achievable challenges. In this way the team moves forward and the business and customers benefit.

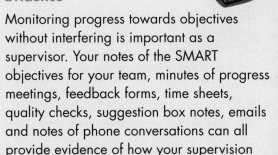

Evidence

Monitoring progress towards objectives without interfering is important as a supervisor. Your notes of the SMART objectives for your team, minutes of progress meetings, feedback forms, time sheets, quality checks, suggestion box notes, emails and notes of phone conversations can all provide evidence of how your supervision of team members contributes to the achievement of team objectives.
1.11, 2.2.

If there is no plan, then it is impossible to control or monitor what is going on. It becomes difficult to check standards and to provide a quality service. If, at work, you find that you are constantly 'fire-fighting' – running behind the challenges of each day and trying just to keep afloat – then you need to:

- STOP!
- plan your SMART objectives: communicate these to your manager and team
- monitor – keep records, and communicate with your manager
- review – analyse, draw experience from good and bad things in the day, and communicate to your manager and staff
- start the next plan – improve and communicate.

(See Unit 3 for more detail on planning.)

Planning

As a supervisor, you will spend a lot of time planning with your manager and with your staff so that they are ready for each day's work.

By planning, you are thinking ahead and developing your leadership skills. Planning can be represented by a circle of actions.

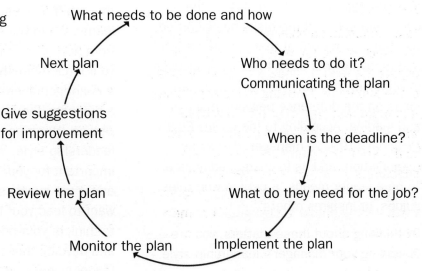

Figure 1.5 The cycle of planning

Leadership styles

Some qualities of a good leader are:

- vision, and the ability to convince others to follow this vision
- patience and justice
- ability to exercise self-control
- strength and resilience, especially in times of difficulty
- honesty about own abilities (but this does not mean arrogance)
- appreciating work colleagues – treating the team members as important people with abilities and expertise which they put at the service of the team and the business
- being observant
- enthusiasm
- willingness to take risks.

You might think that leadership and management are self-explanatory terms, but there are many styles of leadership that have been identified and developed within the past five decades. To be a good supervisor, you really need to use a combination of leadership styles, depending on the circumstances and the tasks being carried out, but it is important that you always lead and motivate your team to achieve success in whatever they do. There are also many ideas on the difference between managing and leading. According to the *Collins English Dictionary 1991*, a manager 'directs an organisation' and 'is in charge, administers'. To be a leader means 'a person who rules, guides, or inspires others'.

By thinking about these matters, you are observing your manager's leadership style.

Evidence

Observe your line manager at work. Look at how he or she gets things done.

- Do they delegate responsibility to you, or just tasks?
- Do they ask your opinion before making decisions?
- Do they shout?
- Do they listen when you speak, or do they interrupt?
- Are they approachable when you have a difficulty with a work objective?

What style of leadership does your manager have?

1.10, 2.5, 2.6, 2.8.

Sometimes you may get on with your manager socially, but find him or her impossible at work. Outside work, they may be relaxed, fun and easy to talk to, whereas at work you may find them bossy and blunt. What you are seeing at work is their leadership style, but not part of their personality. This sort of person may not be good at managing their staff because they are not a convincing leader. When you are very different at work from how you are in other areas of life, then your leadership style could be weak because it is not genuinely 'you'. Being a leader or a manager should be second nature to a person – their personality feeds into their leadership style. Your style of leadership is important for your personal success as well as for the success of the business. If you want to lead your team to success, you need to think of your personal qualities as a leader and develop these so that you become a leader whom people really want to follow.

The race is won through preparation, not just luck on the day.

Hierarchical or autocratic management

A manager who uses this leadership style is someone who simply 'bosses people around' – they give instructions, they control the work environment and they do not involve the staff other than by checking that they have followed their instructions to the letter. The result is that each person knows only about what directly involves them, and not about the aims of the business, or how their department interacts with other departments. This results in a type of dependence on the manager, and a dulling of creativity. Staff will not try to solve problems because they are used to referring everything to the supervisor or manager in case they 'get it wrong' and are disciplined.

Human relations management

This is where the prime focus is on supporting and developing the people in the team. It is a participatory style, where the team contributes to the decision-making process – but it can lead to a failure to achieve the team's objectives if there is a lack of direction and leadership.

Laissez-faire (hands-off) management

This comes from a style in which the supervisor or manager leaves the team to simply get on with the job. This works well with experienced staff, but there does need to be close monitoring by the management, and feedback between management and team. It can fail if there is little managerial control, or where the team is made up largely of inexperienced staff. If the manager is too relaxed then the team can lose direction and become discouraged, and then objectives may not be met.

Servant leadership

Coined by Robert Greenleaf (1970), 'servant leadership' is about leading by meeting the needs of the team – which is different from giving people what they might want, or what they might think they need. Being aware of what people need to do their job well is not just about giving them the right tools, but also about being aware of them as people. It has been shown that someone may work harder if you pay them more, or if you give them a new piece of equipment to aid their task, but research also shows (see the Hawthorne experiments, page 36) that simply showing staff attention at the right moment can increase their output, because people respond to being cared for. For example, there could be someone who is not concentrating at work because they need time to take one of their children to the dentist, and are worrying about this rather than their work. A good supervisor should understand the needs of their team because they know them well, and help to facilitate what the team really needs – rather than giving nagging reminders, just allow a team member to take an hour off one morning.

Transformational leadership

These leaders always have the bigger picture in mind. They inspire their team, and spend a lot of time communicating with team members. As they delegate responsibility, they need to be supported by other managers who attend to the detail of a given job, as these leaders tend to feel tied down by detail. These leaders take risks.

Keeping in control

To be successful, a leader must be natural – even though there is always room for improvement with practice – or they might find that someone else in the team is acting as the unofficial leader. Such an unofficial leader can exert strong peer pressure on the team, and the supervisor must be quick to identify this person and work with them. If the team has what it needs for the job, plus a vision of where it wants to go, then the team leader (practising servant leadership) must lead the way by being a work role model for the team. This involves developing your personality to give you the strength to lead. People will only follow people they recognise as leaders, otherwise they simply do what they are told, leaving the boss to do all the thinking. Staff just doing what they are told is a very frustrating way to work; people should be responsible for their own work, and not just spend their time following instructions. This can cause a lot of friction and an unhappy working environment, even when it is effective in getting the job done.

Often leadership or organisation charts are represented as hierarchical, as follows.

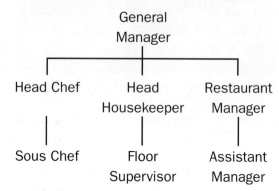

Figure 1.6 Hierarchical organisation chart 1.

Figure 1.7 Hierarchical organisation chart 2.

These organisational charts encourage the attitude that the best is at the top, or that we have to get to the top. This is unrealistic. Not everyone can be a manager – they would have no one to manage! Not everyone has the ability, or the desire, to be at the top of the chart, but this does not make them an inferior person, and they should never be treated as such.

If you are a commis chef or a room attendant, and you are always put at the bottom of organisational charts such as these, you may feel that this is a bad thing and that you should move up a level. However, not everyone will actually be happy making this move: some staff like cleaning rooms or assisting the older chefs in their tasks, and the responsibility that comes with the next step might not be to their liking. Each step has its skills and rewards, and all levels are praiseworthy areas of work.

Sometimes it is good to represent the organisation in a different manner. The 'hanging' organisation chart below gives an impression that people are working together as a team, rather than working 'under' a manager, which can be demotivating.

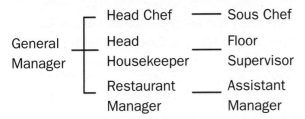

Figure 1.8 A hanging organisation chart.

Another type of organisational chart, which suits the idea of servant leadership, is to turn the triangle upside down.

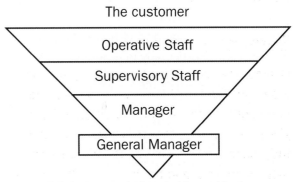

Figure 1.9 An inverted triangle hierarchical organisation chart.

The upside-down triangle takes account of the number of people at each level and their importance. The most important person for the business is the customer, not the general manager. Next come the operative staff who serve the customer directly. Then come the supervisors, who lead teams of operative staff. There are fewer managers who direct the supervisors, and there is usually one general manager who reports to a board of directors.

Not everyone can be a general manager, and there is no need to have more than one per business, so it is important that the other layers of staff are able to work together as well as possible in order that the people they support or serve, ending with the customer, get the best.

Motivation theories

Why do people work? If you ask different people this question, you will get many different answers. Surprisingly, money is not at the top of the list, but towards the middle. Motivation theories help us to understand why people work, and therefore how we can help them to work well and as a team.

Motivation theories come from time-and-motion studies carried out by American industrial psychologists in the USA in the mid-1930s. With increasing mechanisation and industrialisation, people were becoming very expensive to employ, and at times their output was very low, particularly in repetitive jobs.

The Hawthorne experiments were carried out by George Elton Mayo from 1927–32 at the Western Electric Hawthorne Works in Chicago. These were a reaction against 'scientific management', which ignored employees' motivation and behaviour. To see how social factors influenced employees, Elton Mayo raised the lighting level in a factory, and the output went up. Then he lowered the lighting level, and the output went up again. Elton Mayo decided that this was due to the fact that the workers in the factory felt someone was taking an interest in them, not just the product, and they responded by increasing their output. Motivation theory includes the two following theories based on needs.

In the late 1950s/early 1960s, Frederick Herzberg introduced the 'Motivation-Hygiene Theory', based on what he called 'hygiene factors' – that is, the work environment. Herzberg introduced the idea of job enrichment: if someone cannot be promoted, or has been doing a job for a long time, then their job should be enriched so that the employee is given a challenge so they do not become bored and produce poor quality work. He saw that money, cars, gyms, etc. increase motivation a little, but that this increase is short-lived. Motivation concerns the individual, whose worth and capabilities need to be recognised. Employees respond to this recognition by being more productive and delivering higher-quality

work. Job satisfaction comes from job content, whereas dissatisfaction is a negative result of the job context.

Maslow (1943) put forward a theory of individual development based on the hierarchy of human needs. Maslow's theory is often represented by a tiered triangle, as shown below. A higher need can motivate only once the need below it in the triangle has been satisfied, since only unsatisfied needs can be motivators. People strive to achieve each level – for example, being given a promotion at work increases esteem and makes one feel valued. This, in turn, can make getting on with people in the team easier. Reaching your goal of owning a company, or of being head chef, or of simply doing the job you are doing now as well as you can, is self-actualisation.

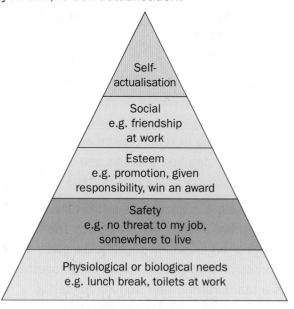

Figure 1.10 Maslow's hierarchy of needs

This theory has practical consequences for the social factors put forward by Herzberg. In much of the hospitality industry, the staff areas of the building are in very poor condition in relation to the customer areas – the so-called 'back-of-house' areas. It is true to say that a five-star hotel does not need to have five-star staff areas, as this would be very costly. But if the back-of-house is in disrepair, the staff food is not good or the staff toilets are a disgrace, then people's basic needs are not being catered for and they will be unhappy at work without necessarily being aware of why. If the staff areas are well looked after, this helps people to look forward to coming to work as they feel respected, and this is a motivator.

Another example is that of hours of work, or breaks during the working day. Hospitality work is usually quite physical and therefore tiring, and it is important that the business provides time for meal breaks during the day, and does not ask its employees to work hours that physically exhaust them. As a supervisor, you are in charge of drawing up the work rotas – it is important to give due consideration for people's lives outside work in order for them to give of their best at work.

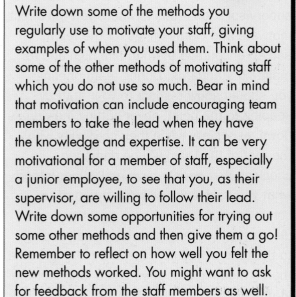

Evidence

Write down some of the methods you regularly use to motivate your staff, giving examples of when you used them. Think about some of the other methods of motivating staff which you do not use so much. Bear in mind that motivation can include encouraging team members to take the lead when they have the knowledge and expertise. It can be very motivational for a member of staff, especially a junior employee, to see that you, as their supervisor, are willing to follow their lead. Write down some opportunities for trying out some other methods and then give them a go! Remember to reflect on how well you felt the new methods worked. You might want to ask for feedback from the staff members as well. 1.9, 1.10, 2.6, 2.8, 2.9.

Supporting and encouraging a team

Recognising achievement, creativity and innovation

Case study

In a busy food service department in a college, you identify a problem which you then share with the team: during lunch service, the beverages area gets congested, staff become short-tempered as they get in each other's way, and the number of breakages is increasing.

A member of staff comes to you with a suggestion about how to rearrange the beverages area so that the equipment is more accessible at peak times. Recently, the manager has asked you to do some staff training on customer service, and also to maximise the use of space for marketing.

The staff member suggests two things.
- One idea involves simply moving the coffee machine so that it is further down the counter, giving more space for the crockery and glasses. This would also mean that the beverages would not be right on top of the cold counter area, which has often become splashed with coffee.
- The second idea involves moving the coffee machine to the back counter, which at the moment has a display of coffees and beverages. There is a water supply at this point and there is a hand-wash basin nearby. If the coffee machine was located in this position, customers would see the person working at the machine, whereas at the moment they are hidden.

From the list of Evidence questions, you may well think that the small matter of reorganising a service counter is a lot of work. What makes it important is that a service counter is a customer contact and sales area, so it is very important for your business that it is well laid out.

The supervisor in this situation should take care to remember that the solution came from the member of staff. Think of ways in which the supervisor could involve them in the project after the suggestion, and recognise their role in the improvement. The supervisor could thank the member of staff individually – but it is also good to be clear to the team who suggested the idea. A supervisor does not lose face by accepting suggestions from team members. Staff respect their supervisor not because they can do everything, and know everything, but because of how they interact with the team to get the job done. Rewarding other people for their ideas, and encouraging them to be creative, should be used to encourage the whole team. It is also true that as a supervisor you may feel challenged by people with a lot of good ideas – but resenting them, or ignoring them just to 'keep them in their place', is poor management. The person may well leave, which would be a loss to the team, or they may make your life difficult. It is part of your job as a supervisor to promote and develop your staff.

Running team briefings

These are a very important part of a supervisor's job – this is where you will direct, motivate and clarify things for the team, and so encourage them to aim high and to maintain standards. During team briefings you should show respect to your staff by keeping to the point, never putting individuals down, especially when their credibility with the rest of the team will be damaged, checking that people have really understood what you have said, allowing the staff to communicate with you by suggestions and discussion where appropriate, and keeping to the time schedule – there is nothing worse than a meeting that goes on so long that the staff have to rush when they get back to their station to make up for lost time.

Evidence

In your job, how do you encourage your team to make suggestions? Can you think of examples of when you have followed suggestions through and put some of them into practice? How do you respond when suggestions are not relevant, or are poor? Writing this down will help you to record evidence and to think the issue through clearly.
1.2, 1.7, 1.9, 1.10, 2.1, 2.3, 2.8, 2.9.

Training

A lot of time is spent by you as the supervisor training the staff, monitoring, analysing performance, coaching and giving '**remedial training**'. As supervisor, you will give a lot of support to staff as you will work alongside each other much of the time. The manager spends more time in the office on the financial and administrative side of the business.

Formal and informal training

Training can be formal or informal. Often, as supervisor, you will be training people informally, for example, when you suggest to someone a quicker way to use the booking programme at the reception desk, which you have learned from experience, or by suggesting a different way of loading a housekeeping trolley, which you found practical when you were busy as a room attendant (see Coaching, page 26). You may also deliver formal training in workplace skills, for example, to an apprentice or a young member of staff who is in their first job and may not have attended college.

For new staff, training is formal and is followed up by coaching – someone on the job will keep an eye on the new member of staff to make sure they know how to do things. As supervisor, you will tend to place new staff with staff you trust and who are good at their job, but you must make sure that you also know yourself how to teach other people to do the job. This is a particular skill. Being able to do a job well is not the same skill as training someone else to do it. You might spend a lot of your time coaching staff so that the company quality standards are met consistently.

Definition
Remedial training: training to correct a fault.

Find out!
Check the most recent training scheme for your department. Re-read your induction notes or employee handbook as a refresher.

Induction

Induction training is the first training an employee receives at work. It is normally carried out in the first day or two of employment in order to introduce the newcomer to the company and to pass on the company's regulations about health and safety and food hygiene, both of which carry heavy penalties if the law is broken.

Here is a summary of possible induction topics:

- health and safety, including food hygiene
- fire prevention and safety
- first aid facilities
- company policies and rules (e.g. smoking policy, reporting accidents, customer care)
- the disciplinary procedure
- terms and conditions of employment (e.g. pay, holiday entitlement)
- company reward schemes (e.g. employee of the month)
- dress code
- uniform supply and laundering.

Law and policy

The laws on health and safety, food hygiene, and fire prevention and safety are covered in Legislation, page 199; also see Unit 4.

In a large company the human resources department will carry out this training, but in a small company it can be the manager or supervisor who gives the induction training.

As supervisor, you will usually give the departmental induction. You will introduce the new employee to their colleagues, show them around the department and explain anything specific – for example, 'Be careful when passing that door, as it opens inwards and it might hit you.'

Often you will then leave the new member of staff with an experienced staff member who performs a similar role, and they will work alongside that person for a few days in order to learn their new job. The supervisor has to support both the experienced and the new member of staff by checking that there are no problems. This system of 'shadowing' or 'work buddies' has to be controlled. The supervisor should outline the task to the experienced member of the team before introducing the new staff member, otherwise the quality of the first days at work for the newcomer may be poor, and a bad start to a new job can be very unsettling.

Analysing training needs

As supervisor, you have the job of identifying staff training needs, as well as sometimes actually delivering the training. This means that you will spend a lot of time 'on the floor' in the department, working with the team. It is important that you do not try to do all the work, but delegate tasks to the team while maintaining an overview. This overall vision will allow you to move people around as the workload demands, and to see where people need to improve in their job, both technically and in 'soft skills' (such as customer and colleague relations). Getting the team mix right is a way of supporting the team. If all the good people work together, then it also means that those who are weaker are together, and this could be very bad for the quality of work produced within the department.

Case study

In a hotel wash-up, the supervisor realised there were problems as the supply of crockery was not quick enough for the restaurant. What drew his attention to this problem was the fact that the porters seemed to be upset when they came to deliver the goods. He decided to watch what was going on in the wash-up more closely by passing through the area more often than usual, and by watching the kitchen porters at the delivery point for clean crockery. He then realised that the working method of the porter working the machine was to let the dirty things pile up and then wash everything frantically. This meant that the drying up and delivery was sporadic and had to be very fast, resulting in an uneven flow of work. The porter running the machine did not seem to realise that his colleagues were suffering because he worked like this.

Good team work.

Evidence

As supervisor, how would you approach the problem described in the case study?
1.3, 1.4, 1.6, 1.8, 1.11, 2.3, 2.4, 2.7.

Good practice

When supporting the team, the supervisor should get the team to work through its own problems as far as possible, so that they take full responsibility for their behaviour at work. Working through a problem also binds teams together as the members learn to understand and appreciate one another more.

In the case study, the supervisor analysed the needs of the porters. It was not a question of training, but of organisation and work methods. In a more complicated situation it may mean that someone needs to update their training in order to change bad habits.

For a supervisor to know what the team needs, they have to be very observant and know how to find things out, not taking the first thing someone says as the whole truth. When a member of staff complains about their work rota, it may take a few questions, maybe over a cup of tea, to find out that they simply don't like working alongside a certain person, or that a particular start time makes it difficult for them to get their children off to school in the morning.

The supervisor's role in training

Analysing the training needs of the team is only one way of showing support. Other ways of supporting your team might include:

○ being on the floor when it is busy (with the team, doing the practical work involved)
○ making sure supplies are delivered on time, which facilitates the work of others
○ not taking sides in an argument
○ being fair when it comes to allocating days off – everyone likes to go on holiday in the summer, but it is not possible unless the business closes!
○ planning ahead so that there are few unhelpful surprises, such as extra bookings in the restaurant, or someone having to cover unexpectedly for a dental appointment of another member of staff
○ organising the workload so that it is evenly spread
○ getting equipment fixed quickly
○ taking suggestions on board
○ dealing with customer complaints
○ helping a team member with a difficult job
○ asking people to do things, rather than issuing orders
○ giving encouragement on busy days when there is a shortage of staff
○ not getting in the way when people are working, and not always taking part in what goes on – sometimes it is good just to observe, as many potential problems may sort themselves out
○ giving people responsibility and trusting them to do their job well.

There are other ways of supporting your team, but this list shows the variety of methods available to the supervisor. The supervisor has to coordinate all the activities, and in doing so it is good practice to give responsibility to other members of the team for their tasks or their areas, to encourage them to perform well. Satisfaction with oneself is a good motivator.

Dealing with difficulties

No matter how well you supervise your team, there will always be difficulties as described in the case study opposite. Read this first before going on to the Evidence task below.

Evidence

Think about the situation in the case study opposite, and put yourself in the shoes of the new supervisor. What do you think are the main problems? What would you do to improve things? How would you relate to the staff and to the manager? How would you increase sales? How would you motivate the team to work together?
1.1, 1.3, 1.4, 1.6, 1.8, 1.11, 2.1, 2.4, 2.7.

As a supervisor, you will need to support team members when they need it, especially on difficult days or during periods of organisational change. Whether dealing with problems confidently through one-to-one meetings, by email or over the phone, this is where excellent communication skills and understanding are most needed. If you can steer the team successfully through difficulties and challenges, including conflict within the team, you will gain the respect of your colleagues.

Case study

A new catering supervisor was appointed to a department store self-service restaurant. She was 24 years old, and it was her first full-time job. She was taking over from a supervisor who was only 19 years old, who was supervising five full-time staff and one part-time member of staff, all female, ranging from about 19 to 64 years old. The team she took on was far from happy. They had a brand new, up-market restaurant but they found it hard to come together as a team. The new supervisor worked for a week with the outgoing supervisor, and her observations of the team during the first week are summarised below.

- The supervisor led by issuing orders, for example, she opened the kitchen door and shouted the orders to the cook.
- She had obvious favourites, shown by special break-time and lunch partners.
- She allowed staff to take breaks whenever they wanted.
- On one occasion she physically pulled a member of staff into the kitchen to talk in private.
- The staff didn't help each other and seemed reluctant to take responsibility for anything.
- The manager visited twice a day and during her visits she shouted at the staff and told the supervisor off in front of the staff, although not in front of customers.
- The supervisor worked hard, but did not delegate very much.
- The staff argued over less appealing tasks, such as washing-up or cleaning the front hotplate.

- The staff were very casual with the customers and didn't 'sell' to them, only to serve them.
- The team were friendly and chatty to the new supervisor, but she felt that they spoke unkindly about her behind her back.
- The part-time member of staff was the oldest and was very experienced at her job.

After a year of real team-building through respect and communication, the team celebrated a 70 per cent increase in sales. Regular customers praised z their friendly and efficient manner.

What the supervisor did was to make the team feel responsible for the whole department, so that it was 'their' restaurant, not just somewhere they worked. This sense of ownership meant that the staff took pride in their work and this, in turn, meant that they worked better. A high standard of work, even in a simple cafeteria, will always attract customers, as they feel they get value for money. Friendly staff, who are genuinely interested in their customers, will usually be able to increase sales, whereas a false, forced smile turns people away.

The supervisor also worked hard to get personal respect from staff, as well as giving them respect. This means doing a lot of listening, being understanding, but not giving way in important matters such as front-of-house behaviour and cleanliness. It also means working hard and motivating people by being a role model who knows how to own up, or at times how to apologise, when you are wrong, and never blaming someone else for your own mistakes.

Evidence

Gather notes on how you worked through a specific staff problem at work, and how the action you took has ensured that the team stayed on track and performed well.
1.6, 1.8, 2.1, 2.7.

How do you know there is a problem here?

Listening and observing

As supervisor, you need to know how to listen to your staff. Often you can learn a lot about staff morale simply by being around and listening. When staff come to complain about one another, which is inevitable sometimes, you have to be careful not to jump in and agree with that person – there are always two sides to a story. Listening to both sides, and then making a careful judgement about a course of action, shows maturity and good leadership skills.

At work, the team often needs time to let off steam or relax a little, especially if there has been a lot of pressure. For example, if reception has been non-stop for a few days

and housekeeping has had a lot of short-stay guests, or the kitchens have had a lot of events on top of their normal workload, then the supervisor will probably see the energy levels of the team dipping a little. Knowing how to lead means knowing that this is the moment when staff problems begin – with small arguments, as people get untidy simply due to tiredness, or too chatty because the pressure is off, and the quality starts to slip.

Supervisors need to know how to lead their team at moments like these. This is where prudence comes in – making the right decision at the right time, no matter how difficult the decision might be. It may be a good moment for a short break for the staff on top of their normal time off – even ten minutes for a coffee will be appreciated. It might also *not* be the moment to introduce new working practices, procedures or systems, as people could easily resent it, making the change even harder to manage.

Remember that 'problems are a deviation from a standard for which we need to find the cause' (Peel, 1993). Good supervision acts on the findings and implements the remedy. Our attitude to difficulties at work has to be calm and positive. It is easy to panic and lose our temper when the pressure is on at work, but this does not show good leadership. Staying calm helps us to think clearly and quickly, so that we can make the right decisions and lead our team through the problems to success.

By knowing the team well, and by trying to be a leader with a solid personality on top of solid work skills, you are likely to lead your team to success.

Test yourself!

1 Name some different styles of leadership. What are their main characteristics?

2 Why should you be a role model for your team?

3 What is the importance of clear, concise, team briefings and meetings?

4 What are SMART objectives?

5 Name some different methods of motivation you could consider using when you are deciding how to motivate your team through a difficult period. What are the advantages of these methods?

6 How do you manage the needs of staff for whom English is a second language when it comes to team briefings?

7 What can you do to recognise a creative member in your team? What are the benefits of such recognition?

8 Why do you need to support your team so that they set up personal work objectives?

9 Why and how do you measure the performance standards of the team?

10 Why should you involve your team members in setting out and achieving the team objectives?

11 Are you aware of the company standards in all the areas you are responsible for? How do you communicate these to your team?

Further information

Elton Mayo, G. (1949) *Hawthorne and the Western Electric Company, The Social Problems of an Industrial Civilisation*, Routledge.

Greenleaf, R.K. (1970) 'Essentials of servant leadership'. See http://greenleaf.org

Herzberg, F. (1968) 'One more time: how do you motivate employees?', *Harvard Business Review*, 46(1):53–62.

Maslow, A.H. (1943) 'A theory of human motivation' *Psychological Review*, 50:370–396.

Peel, M. (1993) *Introduction to Management: A Guide to Better Business Performance*, Pitman.

HS2

Develop productive working relationships with colleagues

This chapter covers the following units:

o Level 3 Diploma Hospitality Supervision and Leadership (NVQ) HSL2: Develop productive working relationships with colleagues

o Technical Certificate Unit 1: Principles of leading a team in the hospitality industry – 1.1, 1.2, 1.3, 1.4, 2.1, 2.2, 2.3, 2.9, 2.10.

Working through this chapter could also provide evidence for the following key skills:

o C2.1a, C2.2, C2.3.

In this chapter you will learn about:

o benefits of developing good working relationships

o roles and responsibilities

o values and culture

o the supervisor's role in promoting productive working relationships.

Likely sources of evidence

1.1 Establish working relationships with all colleagues who are relevant to the work being carried out.
Witness testimony from colleagues. Narrative of how working relationships are formed. Minutes of meetings. Observation by assessor.

1.2 Recognise, agree and respect the roles and responsibilities of colleagues and, particularly in situations of matrix management, their managers' requirements.
Narrative or Professional Discussion. Signpost organisation charts, job specifications, etc. Witness statements

1.3 Understand and take account of the priorities, expectations and authority of colleagues in decisions and actions.
Narrative or Professional Discussion. Signpost organisation charts, job specifications etc. Witness statements. Minutes of meetings. Emails. Function sheets. Briefing events, schedules, daily meetings, informal discussions, oral briefings.

1.4 Create an environment of trust and mutual respect where you have no authority, or shared authority, over those you are working with.
Narrative or Professional Discussion.

1.5 Understand difficult situations and issues from your colleagues' perspective and provide support, where necessary, to move things forward.
Narrative or Professional Discussion.

1.6 Fulfil agreements made with colleagues and let them know.
Narrative or Professional Discussion or witness statement, memos, emails.

1.7 Advise colleagues promptly of any difficulties or where it will be impossible to fulfil agreements.
Narrative or Professional Discussion or witness statement, memos, emails.

1.8 Identify and sort out conflicts of interest and disagreements with colleagues in ways that minimise damage to work being carried out.
Provide examples via a Professional Discussion of any disagreements you have had to work through with colleagues. Explain how the action you took has minimised any likely damage to work.

1.9 Exchange information and resources with colleagues to make sure that all parties can work effectively.
Minutes of meetings, emails, memos, resource requisition sheet.

1.10 Provide feedback to colleagues on their performance and seek feedback from colleagues on your own performance in order to identify areas for improvement.
Debrief at end of a session, appraisals, witness testimony from people receiving feedback. Post-coaching training or feedback forms. Witness testimonies, emails from colleagues giving to feedback on own performance. Minutes of team meetings and inter-departmental meetings.

Introduction

This unit is about developing relationships with the people you work with. These colleagues may be in your organisation, or in organisations with which you do business, for example, they may supply products to you. The success of any organisation is strongly influenced by the people who work there, and how closely they communicate and support each other. It is important for all staff to possess the skills of communicating effectively, and to recognise that everyone has a part to play in ensuring an organisation's success.

There are a number of benefits to developing productive relationships – to you, your colleagues, the department and the organisation. Imagine an organisation where colleagues are disrespectful to one another, fail to communicate important information, and have high staff turnover due to low morale. Contrast this with an organisation where colleagues are supportive and respectful, and there is a buzz of enthusiasm from the staff. Which is the more appealing organisation to work in, given that the working conditions are the same? Most people would select the second organisation, as it offers opportunities for self-development and satisfaction within the workplace.

Good relationships at work are fostered by two main things.

○ The organisation needs a clearly-defined structure, which identifies roles and responsibilities, a hierarchy of accountability, and clear communication channels within and between functions (see page 62). Each individual within the organisation needs to understand the structure and work within it.

○ Alongside the formal structure, an effective organisation must develop a culture that promotes cooperative working. This means that each employee takes personal responsibility for their own behaviour towards their colleagues.

As a supervisor, you have a key role in ensuring that both these requirements are met. You are responsible for ensuring that your team operates efficiently within the organisational structure, and you can help to develop an atmosphere of respect, helpfulness and co-operation.

Find out!
Before reading on, write down a list of all your work colleagues.

Who are your colleagues?

A colleague is someone with whom you work. Colleagues can be within your team or department, within other departments in the workplace, or within the wider organisation – for example, your outlet may be part of a larger company. Additionally, work colleagues may be people working in other organisations with which you have a working relationship.

Find out!
Now re-examine your list of work colleagues – can you add any more names? Even if you can't name people personally, can you add additional job titles or departments with whom/which you have a working relationship?

Benefits of developing good working relationships

Benefits to the individual

Within your workplace, you will be interacting with colleagues with whom you may have little in common. Because you work together, often for long periods, it is important that you establish good working relationships, not only for the benefit of your organisation, but also to enhance your performance at work.

Good working relationships may enchance your performance at work.

Within your department, you and your colleagues will be working towards specific organisational objectives, under the supervision and leadership of departmental heads or unit managers. These work colleagues will probably be the people with whom you spend the majority of your time and with whom you will have the most interaction.

We go to work for a variety of reasons: to enable us to earn money to secure food and accommodation, for companionship, and for the opportunity to further our knowledge, mental abilities and career opportunities. A number of management studies have been undertaken to research what makes people satisfied with their work, and the existence of good working relationships between colleagues has been shown to have a positive impact. In Maslow's hierarchy of needs (see page 36), once our basic physiological and safety needs have been met, social needs are the next priority. At work, colleagues have to relate to one another to ensure the job gets done, to share resources, and within the hospitality industry they tend to spend long periods of time together. The forging of productive working relationships is necessary to achieve these aims.

Additionally, where you feel supported, respected, listened to, and communicated with, and a part of a team working towards a common objective, it will help you to achieve your own personal objectives within the workplace and fulfil the need for social interaction.

In much the same way as you personally benefit by working productively with colleagues, so your colleagues will benefit from working with you. The development of good relationships with all colleagues enables sharing of information and resources, and feelings of belonging, which ensure satisfaction for all within the workplace.

These colleagues may not always be working within the same department – they may not even work within the same building – but nevertheless all will benefit from a culture of high-quality working relationships.

Benefit to the department/ team

What are the benefits of good working relationships to a department? It is important to remember that although a department is classified according to the organisational chart, everyone is part of the larger team that makes up the organisation.

Within the workplace, staff will form relationships based on shared interests, relationships and hobbies. This is known as the informal organisation, and this is how many staff form relationships with colleagues from other departments. The informal organisation is not displayed within the formal organisational chart, but nevertheless an important part of any organisation. As a supervisor, it will be helpful if you are aware of some of the informal friendships between members of your team and others.

When a group of people work together they are often called a team, but that may not be the case. A team has a common purpose or objective, and its members collectively work towards that objective, whereas a group may not have this focus. In order to ensure that the team works together effectively, employees have to develop productive working relationships where individual employees' skills complement those of other colleagues, and team members feel supported and are able to communicate openly and honestly, with compromise and conflict resolution handled constructively.

Tuckman's model of team development (1965) outlines four stages of team development:

1 **forming** – colleagues are brought together and will use this opportunity to find out about others in the group – communication at this stage will be guarded
2 **storming** – this is the period of disagreement and conflict – colleagues will feel more confident at expressing personal views and the team has not yet established a pro forma for working collectively
3 **norming** – at this stage the team has developed a sense of identity – communication is free-flowing, and roles and patterns of behaviour are established
4 **performing** – the team is now fully functioning and working productively together towards shared objectives.

If the team has successfully progressed to the performing stage, colleagues will be working well together, and within the team a number of skills will be in action.

 Find out!
What skills should be exhibited by a performing team?

The benefits of having close cooperation and good working relationships should enable teams to move to the performing stage quickly and facilitate personal and team development.

The problem arises where individual teams become isolated, and great care has to be exercised to build team spirit across all departments. The movement of employees across departments by job rotation, colleagues from different operational areas working on specific projects, and awareness of the importance of all employees within the organisation should encourage the development of productive working relationships throughout the organisation.

Benefits to the organisation

Within the wider organisation, there are a number of benefits to be gained by the development of productive working relationships between colleagues, not least the maximisation of profit. Productive working relationships have a direct impact on the **bottom line**.

> **Definition**
>
> **Bottom line:** the final total in a company's balance sheet.

Attainment of the organisation's objectives

All staff working towards clearly-defined objectives will assist in achieving these through effective and productive working relationships.

Some of the larger hospitality organisations are made up of a number of different brands or outlets. Think of a global hospitality organisation like McDonald's and the number of worldwide units it consists of. Your work colleagues, although working for the same organisation, may be employed in a unit that is based in a different country, with its own unique cultural and ethnic influences. This diversity within many large catering

organisations is often what encourages people to enter this industry. The development of productive working relationships where colleagues are divided by distance, culture, catering brands and products, while still under one organisational umbrella, requires commitment from all employees.

> **Find out!**
>
> How many outlets does your organisation have? Are they all the same, or are there a number of different brands? Are these outlets based in the UK, Europe or worldwide? Are there opportunities for staff to move between these different outlets? What is the procedure within your organisation if you wish to move to another outlet?

Staff turnover

Where staff are satisfied in their workplace, the likelihood of them leaving is greatly reduced. In every organisation, staff turnover is both inevitable and desirable – new staff with fresh ideas are important for organisations to grow. But when staff feel unfulfilled and dissatisfied with colleagues, they will not stay. High staff turnover is a cost to the organisation, and it can also be detrimental to the motivation and job satisfaction of other employees.

Where staff know what they are doing, are given responsibility, and are able to communicate and give feedback, they are more likely to be happy and fulfilled, keeping staff turnover at the right levels.

The organisation's image

The image of an organisation is enhanced if it is known to provide an environment that promotes productive working relationships. This, in turn, encourages new recruits into the organisation, and the staff will feel proud to be working for an organisation that recognises the importance of such relationships.

All organisations have to interact, to a greater or lesser degree, with other organisations to purchase resources. To facilitate the success of these interactions, it is important that staff from both organisations have a good working relationship with each other.

Communication within the organisation

Inherent in fostering productive working relationships is the importance of effective communication, which must be free-flowing and open.

Some principles of effective communication are:
○ listen attentively
○ respect others – and yourself
○ be realistic
○ be direct
○ weigh up relevant factors
○ take decisions – but be willing to think again
○ behave appropriately to the situation
○ use humour – but don't direct it at people.

It is important that colleagues from different departments cooperate and communicate. Often there is rivalry between different departments, where one group of staff may feel that they are more important than the others.

For all departments to work successfully together, supervisors need to develop productive working relationships across all departments and throughout the organisation.

Roles and responsibilities

Organisational structures in hospitality

Even fairly small organisations usually have some sort of organisational structure, which shows how the people working in the organisation relate to each other and work together. In larger organisations, people are grouped together in teams or departments, each carrying out a different function that is necessary to meet the organisation's objectives.

Often this structure is shown in an organisational chart (see pages 34 and 35). The organisational chart includes all the roles in each team, with a hierarchy showing who reports to whom. In a well-run organisation, the responsibilities of each role will be clearly defined, as will be the correct lines of communication between members of a team, and between different teams. This ensures that everyone knows who does what, and whom to contact for information. This is very important for the smooth running of the organisation.

Some organisations will display many layers of management – this is known as a tall hierarchy. This is often the case with large companies that may have a number of different operations. For example, a large hotel chain may have a number of different grades of hotel – luxury, city centre, country and budget – and there will be different levels of management for each grade reporting to a senior management team at head office.

Smaller organisations may only have two or three layers (flatter hierarchies). For example, you may have a small, owner-run restaurant with a manager, supervisors in the kitchen, restaurant and bar, and staff in each area. Supervisors may be required to take on multiple roles: for example, the restaurant supervisor may be responsible for training, the bar supervisor for controlling resources, and the kitchen supervisor for health and safety and hygiene.

Why are organisational structures important?

The formal organisational structure identifies who has authority within each department. Each department will have a specific departmental manager responsible for all the staff in that area. The manager is assisted by supervisors, although in some cases they will be given a technical title, such as head sommelier. Each supervisor has authority over their particular team, and is responsible for the actions of these people.

In turn, the supervisor is accountable to the manager – they will report to the manager and will be held responsible for what happens within their department. As supervisor, you have to take responsibility for your staff, for the work that needs to be done and for standards of performance. The supervisor is the person who is responsible for getting the job done to the manager's satisfaction. A supervisor cannot delegate this responsibility

to employees – if the job is not done, it is the supervisor's responsibility, not the fault of the employee. For example, if the functions manager asks the conference supervisor to set up a conference suite for 1 p.m., and the suite is not set up by the agreed time, the supervisor, being accountable to the manager, has to take responsibility for the failure to achieve this task. It is their responsibility to organise their team to do the work and ensure it is completed successfully.

The manager has authority over the supervisors and sets their objectives. The organisational chart shows all the different levels of responsibility, and whom employees report to. These layers of management are often called the organisation hierarchy (page 34-35).

Patterns of communication

As well as determining lines of authority, responsibility and accountability, the organisational structure influences the **formal patterns of communication**.

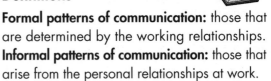

> **Definitions**
> **Formal patterns of communication:** those that are determined by the working relationships.
> **Informal patterns of communication:** those that arise from the personal relationships at work.

Informal communication, often known as the 'grapevine', are not determined by the organisational chart. Staff communicate with colleagues in other departments because they share common interests, for example, they may come from the same country, belong to the company's sports club, or have other things in common. Supervisors need to be aware of the importance of informal communication. Rumours, gossip and misleading information, which may have a negative impact on staff performance, are often the result of informal communication.

Effective communication in any organisation should be a two-way process. Decisions made by the senior management are communicated to the staff through the various levels in the organisation. For example, there may be a change in the menu to reflect new purchasing policies of sourcing food locally. Communication of this will pass vertically down the organisation.

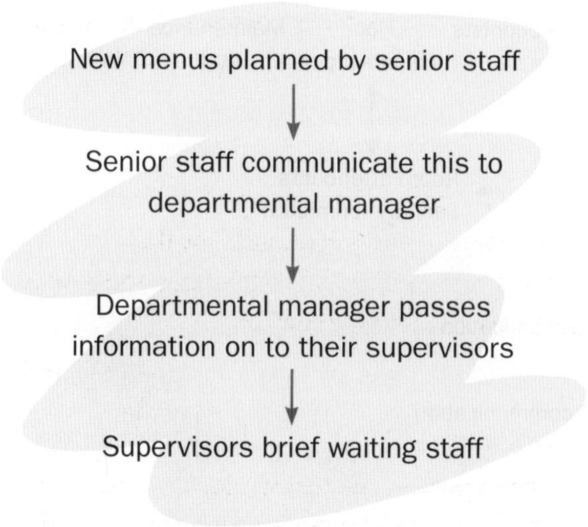

For communication to be two-way, it should also pass vertically up the organisation. Staff may have opinions and views that they need or want to communicate. Customer-facing staff are in a very good position to communicate valuable customer opinions up to senior management. To facilitate this upward communication process, the supervisor should actively seek employees' views through regular communication, for example, via weekly staff meetings.

The exchange of information up and down the organisation ensures that all employees have the opportunity to voice their feelings and opinions, which, in turn, fosters productive working relationships.

New menus planned by senior staff

↓

Senior staff communicate this to departmental manager

↓

Departmental manager passes information on to their supervisors

↓

Supervisors brief waiting staff

Figure 2.1 Vertical communication.

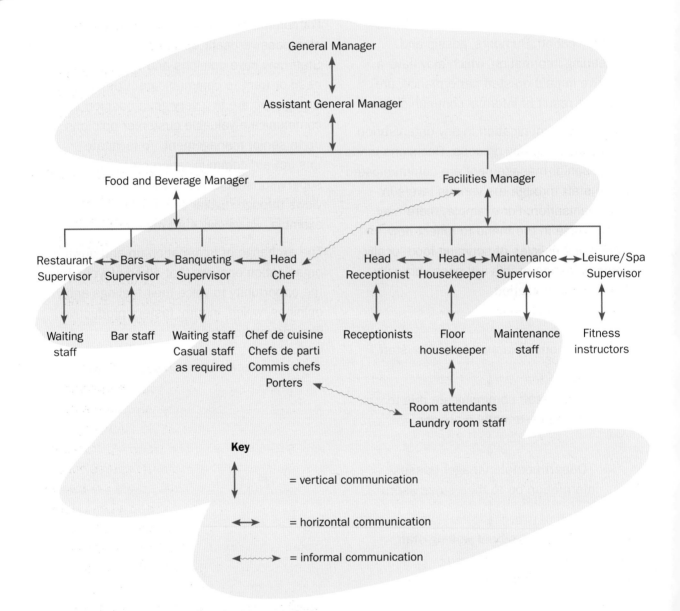

Figure 2.2 Organisation chart showing lines of communication – boutique hotel

If one of your staff was underperforming at work, the first stage would be for you to talk to them and express your concerns, while at the same time communicating the action you have taken upwards to your manager. If the employee's performance failed to improve, you would be responsible for communicating this to the manager, who may start the disciplinary process. Throughout this process, communication should flow up and down the organisation.

It is equally important that communication goes horizontally across the organisation.

This means that communication is fostered between departments, and colleagues communicate formally with their corresponding colleagues in other departments. Information from one department will influence what goes on in another, so information must be shared across the organisation. For example, in a hotel the front office has to communicate horizontally with a number of departments: accommodation, food and beverage outlets, leisure and spa facilities, so that each department can plan and organise itself to be ready for the customers.

Decision-making

Within all organisations, important decisions have to be made. Decisions as to the organisation's objectives will be made by the senior management and directors. To meet these objectives, operational decisions need to be taken. The organisational chart identifies areas of responsibility, who has the authority to make decisions in these areas, and to whom they are answerable. The formal

patterns of communication influence the decision-making procedures.

Areas of authority and accountability will be set out in the employee's job description. As a supervisor, your job description will state your area of responsibility, to whom you are accountable, and over whom you have authority (see the example on the next page).

Within your daily operations you will be required to make decisions – these may be simple decisions, such as who is going to clean which bedrooms, or you may be required to make more major decisions, such as who you are going to recommend for an award for exceptional performance or promotion.

The organisation in which you work will determine to what extent you are involved in decision-making. In a small restaurant, you may be involved in all the day-to-day decisions, such as menu planning, crockery selection, and the recruitment and selection of staff. Larger organisations may not involve you in any decision-making and all decisions may be made by senior management – for example, in large fast food chains all the operational aspects are decided by senior management, who may issue **standard operating procedures** which all staff are required to follow.

Definition

Standard operating procedures: instructions issued by an organisation, which must be followed, covering certain operations that can be standardised across the organisation.

Job description

Job title   Restaurant Supervisor
Department   Garden Restaurant
Salary range   £13,000 – £13,500

Duties and responsibilities

- Assisting the Restaurant Manager in the running of the restaurant.
- Preparing staff rotas to ensure that the restaurant is adequately staffed at all times to cope with projected customer volume.
- Maintaining staff welfare and morale.
- Communicating effectively with staff.
- Leading staff to give excellent customer service.
- Assisting Restaurant Manager in identifying the staff's training needs, and helping with on-the-job training.
- Ensuring that guests are served efficiently with well-presented, good-quality food and drinks in a relaxed environment.
- Handling of customer complaints and compliments.
- Overseeing the cleaning and preparation of the restaurant before service.
- Checking that there are sufficient supplies e.g. crockery, cutlery, glassware, equipment, in the restaurant to serve guests effectively.
- Reporting any maintenance problems to the Restaurant Manager.
- Handling the payment of customers' bills and ensuring that company policy on cash handling is followed.
- Maintaining a knowledge of current legislation and ensuring that all staff follow company procedures regarding relevant legal requirements.
- Assisting the Restaurant Manager in developing and promoting sales in the Garden Restaurant.

Accountable to Restaurant Manager
Responsible for 10 food service staff
Functional contact: The post holder will develop and maintain productive working relationships with colleagues in the bars, kitchen and other catering outlets within the hotel.

Restaurant Manager
Date of job description 1st July, 2009.

Figure 2.3 Example of a job description.

An organisation that values its employees and wishes to encourage cooperative working will encourage open communication regarding decision-making. Where staff are involved in making decisions and contributing to them, they will be more committed to implementing the changes. As supervisor, you may have to make decisions without consulting staff, and you will be responsible for implementing changes that have been ordered by management. Your response to these decisions – for example, through **team briefings** or **team meetings**, and how this information is communicated to your team – will influence their success or failure.

Your own team structure

As a supervisor, you must have a good knowledge of the way your organisation is structured. In particular, you need to be aware of the limits of your own responsibility.

Span of control

The number of people who are accountable to you, and for whom you have responsibility, is called the 'span of control'.

> **Definition**
>
> **Team briefings:** these are not the same as team meetings. Team briefings are intended to convey information.
> **Team meetings:** these are about communication between those present.

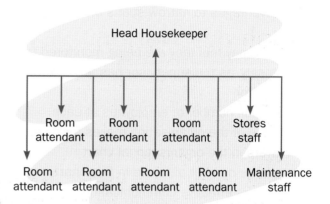

Figure 2.4 Span of control.

The number of employees within your span of control will be determined by the organisational structure.

If a supervisor is responsible for a large number of employees, this is termed a wide span of control. If they supervise only a few employees, this is a narrow span of control. There are a number of disadvantages to both narrow and wide spans of control.

Disadvantages to wide spans of control are that:

- it is harder to supervise a large number of staff
- opportunities for individual staff development and training are decreased due to the supervisor having to deal with more people
- sub-groups or 'cliques' may form that develop patterns of behaviour out of line with the overall departmental ethos
- personal communication between supervisor and employees is not as easy due to the supervisor having to communicate with more staff.

Disadvantages to narrow spans of control are that:

○ staff may feel they are being monitored too closely, as the supervisor has few staff to monitor

○ a small number of employees at each stage of the organisation makes for more layers in the organisational chart

○ a large number of layers in this chart hinders effective communication

○ the team may not consist of enough staff, with different aptitudes and knowledge, to be effective.

The responsibility you have for staff as a supervisor will therefore depend upon your span of control, and this will vary depending on the organisation. In some organisations the supervisor will have a lot of responsibility and will actively participate in planning and decision-making; in others there will be clearly-defined areas of responsibility. It is important to know exactly what these are, and that staff are aware of them. Decisions regarding pay and conditions of service are likely to be part of a management role, but as a supervisor you may be responsible for planning the staff rota.

The roles and responsibilities of each person in your department

An important part of the supervisor's job is to ensure each member of their department knows what their role involves. This involves a combination of forward planning and day-to-day management of circumstances.

When an employee is recruited, they will have been selected to fill an operational role, as detailed in their job description. However, no job description will cover every aspect of the operational role, so it is the supervisor's task to ensure that the employee knows in detail exactly what the job involves. This should be covered during the employee's induction, but will also involve ongoing communication, clarifying job responsibilities and expectations as the employee does their work.

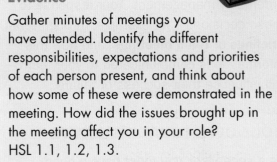

Evidence

Gather minutes of meetings you have attended. Identify the different responsibilities, expectations and priorities of each person present, and think about how some of these were demonstrated in the meeting. How did the issues brought up in the meeting affect you in your role?
HSL 1.1, 1.2, 1.3.

There will often be occasions when an employee is unsure about what they are expected to do in a particular situation. In these cases, the supervisor has to ensure that the job is being completed by the right person. Sometimes it will be necessary for an employee to step outside their normal job role – for example, if a colleague is absent. The supervisor should encourage a degree of flexibility within teams so that employees are able and willing to take on different responsibilities when necessary. If an employee is being asked to carry out work beyond their normal role, then the supervisor must ensure they are given adequate support via mentoring, coaching, training or supported supervision. It can be very motivating for a staff member to be asked to take on different work, if it is presented by the supervisor as an opportunity for career development.

For an effective team, working employees should be selected to fulfil an operational role and a team role. Meredith Belbin (1993) identifies nine roles that an effective team should possess, where each individual team member possesses specific skills and qualities that enable the team to function productively. Each role is given a name that relates to the skills the individual is likely to contribute to the team:

- **plant** – creative skills
- **resource investigator** – extrovert communicator, good at developing contacts
- **coordinator** – good chairperson, clarifying objectives and promoting decision-making
- **shaper** – possesses drive and courage to overcome difficulties
- **monitor evaluator** – skills of objective assessment and accurate judgement
- **teamworker** – good listener and diplomatic, helps avert friction
- **implementer** – turns ideas into practical actions
- **completer finisher** – conscientious, ensures objectives are achieved on time
- **specialist** – provides specialist knowledge.

Belbin's research was based on management teams, but the principles of selecting staff who possess different skills can be used by the supervisor. The supervisor should recognise their staff's skills and qualities, and try to develop these skills in their jobs to help ensure team effectiveness.

As supervisor, you will fulfil the role of chairperson, clarifying objectives and ensuring all staff are listened to and their contributions acknowledged. Staff members who are willing to contribute ideas should be encouraged to think about better ways of completing the job, for example, by coming up with a better way of organising the tables in the restaurant to create more space. When difficulties arise and the team become frustrated, they need someone who can encourage them to go forward. The staff member who is positive and well liked by all is useful in ensuring good relationships within the team. This person usually takes the initiative, and will probably be the one who organises a team social event, for example.

As supervisor, you should be aware of both the operational and personal skills of your individual employees so that you can place the right person in the best job for them, while meeting the needs of the organisation. You should consider creatively how to get the best out of people. To ensure you are getting the best from your staff, it is important to be aware of current ideas and techniques for supervising people from the hospitality and management literature. There is ongoing research in many organisations regarding people management and human resources. A good supervisor will be aware of this by reading about current good practice in catering and human resource publications and try to implement creative and novel ideas as appropriate. (See Further information, page 82.)

Communication lines in your department

Within an organisation, communication has to go vertically up and down through the different levels. As a supervisor, you will be communicating directly up to your manager, and passing on communications from them to employees. It is important that all employees are made aware of the correct procedures for communication, and it is up to you to ensure these communication channels are known and followed by all within the department. Staff should know when and where to contact you, either verbally, or by written or electronic means. Time needs to be assigned for regular staff meetings, with agendas and minutes circulated to all the team. The supervisor must ensure the meeting is chaired professionally, with all items on the agenda being discussed. All employees should be given the opportunity to speak, and issues should be actioned within realistic timescales.

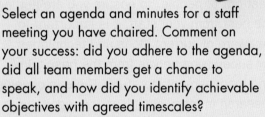

Evidence

Select an agenda and minutes for a staff meeting you have chaired. Comment on your success: did you adhere to the agenda, did all team members get a chance to speak, and how did you identify achievable objectives with agreed timescales?
1.1, 1.2, 1.3, 1.4, 1.5, 1.6, 1.7, 1.8, 1.9, 2.1, 2.2, 2.3, 2.4, 2.5, 2.6, 2.8.

In Unit 1, a number of communication methods are identified (see pages 21–25). For communication to be effective, as supervisor you have to select the most appropriate method for the message you are sending. You can pass on information verbally, making sure you talk to each team member, but noticeboards, memos, staff newsletters, emails and letters can also be used to circulate information as appropriate.

Within your department, communication has to pass horizontally between all colleagues, and systems must be put in place to ensure this happens. Take the example of a well-known guest staying the night, who always requests extra pillows. The room attendant who usually cleans the guest's room may know this, but fails to communicate it to the room attendant on whose floor the guest is staying on this occasion. The customer arrives to find that not only are they not in their usual room, but that their expectation of extra pillows has not been met, and they complain. The communication of this piece of information between colleagues would have prevented the problem arising in the first place. It is up to the supervisor to encourage all employees to communicate important work-related information between themselves and to set up means of doing so, for example, by having briefing sheets that employees can fill in with client information.

Find out!

What methods does your organisation use to communicate information within your department, and between different departments? Collect examples of these methods, such as emails and newsletters.

Communication lines and links with other functions

The effective operation of any organisation depends on all employees having productive working relationships throughout the organisation. No single department can function without interacting with other departments, and it is the supervisors in each department who influence the success of these relationships. A supervisor who displays a good working relationship with colleagues in other teams is a good role model for their team.

Each supervisor should be communicating regularly with their colleagues in other departments. This communication should be planned both to ensure relevant information is being passed on, and to find out what is happening in other teams. In some organisations, supervisors meet daily to discuss what is happening on that day so that everyone is aware of what is happening in other departments and how that will influence their department. A large conference being held will have an impact on the catering and beverage facilities in a hotel; a promotion being implemented by the marketing department will affect the other departments. Meetings between supervisors and their line manager should also be planned on a regular basis, although day-to-day informal communication should be ongoing.

Each departmental supervisor needs to know how other departments function and what their roles are, and should communicate this information to their employees. In small organisations, employees may be required to rotate between different departments. In these circumstances, supervisors have to establish which employees they are responsible for, and let the member of staff know to whom they are answerable. It is very confusing for an employee who works in a number of different areas to be given conflicting instructions by different supervisors. Communication between supervisors is needed to avoid this problem, especially in the hospitality industry, which is often composed of many small and medium-sized organisations that rely on employees working between different departments/functions.

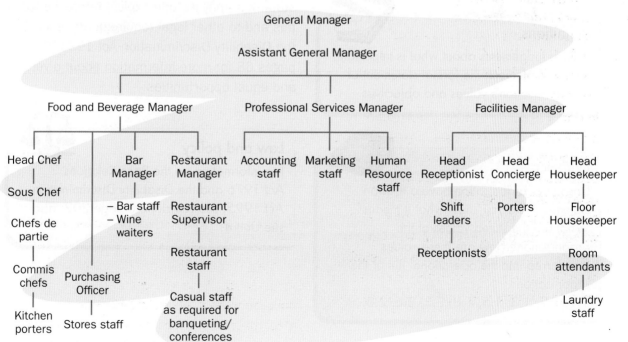

Figure 2.5 Example hotel organisation chart.

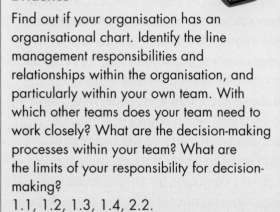

Evidence

Find out if your organisation has an organisational chart. Identify the line management responsibilities and relationships within the organisation, and particularly within your own team. With which other teams does your team need to work closely? What are the decision-making processes within your team? What are the limits of your responsibility for decision-making?
1.1, 1.2, 1.3, 1.4, 2.2.

Find out!

Find examples of mission statements from other organisations. McDonald's mission statement is:

> "McDonald's vision is to be the world's best quick service restaurant experience. Being the best means providing outstanding quality, service, cleanliness, and value, so that we make every customer in every restaurant smile."

Values and culture

The **values** and culture of many organisations are often expressed in the company's **mission statement**. This may be a simple slogan, which is often used for advertising, or it may be more detailed, outlining its values more fully.

Definitions

Values: judgements about what is important.
Mission statement: the formal statement of an organisation's values and objectives.

Evidence

Does your organisation have a mission statement? Do you know what it means? What are the stated values of the organisation? How are these values transferred into the operational life of the organisation?
1.1, 1.2, 1.3, 1.5, 1.8, 2.3, 2.6, 2.8.

It is not always the case that the values an organisation publishes actually happen in practice in the workplace. For example, an organisation may claim to be an employer offering opportunities to all, but may in fact discriminate against potential employees of a different religion or race. Discrimination on the grounds of race is illegal (Race Relations Act 1976), and an organisation's mission statement may include explicit reference to this and to other legal requirements, such as the Disability Discrimination Act 1995. See pages 68 for more information about diversity and equal opportunities.

Law and policy

For information on the Race Relations Act 1976 and the Disability Discrimination Act 1995, see Legislation, page 202; also see Unit 4.

The importance of shared values

Hospitality is an industry which relies on people working effectively in teams. As we have seen, the organisational structure can help with this, but just as important is the way that individual people relate to each other.

Within an effective team, the roles and responsibilities of each employee should be clear. Staff should know what they are expected to do, when they should be doing it, where they should be, and how the work should be completed. The team should be able to rely on fellow members. Where employees cannot rely on their colleagues, the team cannot move to the performing stage (see page 51). Team members may feel frustrated and angry with colleagues who are stopping them performing efficiently at work.

Role of the supervisor in promoting company values

It is important to make sure your staff know what is expected of them in the workplace. You are the link between the employees and the management, and you are central to achieving productive working relationships within the organisation and communicating the organisation's values. This will require that your own professional behaviour is a model for staff to follow.

As a supervisor, your role is to ensure everyone knows what is expected of them, and that this is clear and unambiguous. Staff should be given specific tasks and realistic timescales in which to achieve them, and checks should be made that their performance is up to the required standard. Professional behaviour of all employees in the workplace ensures a pleasant working environment for all. This professional behaviour is developed by you as supervisor, and should apply to all staff, who must pay particular attention to the following.

○ Punctuality and time-keeping. Staff should be informed of the times at which they should start work. This is not the time they *arrive* at work, but when they should be *ready* for work, in their uniform, with everything they need. A member of staff who is constantly late will have a negative effect on other staff. Poor timekeeping will also affect the customer.

Case study

A chef was never ready for lunch service at 12 noon. The chef was often late, and this caused problems for the restaurant staff, who were then frustrated. Customer service – both internally (other restaurant staff) and externally (customers) – was then negatively affected, as the staff were upset and this was reflected in the standard of their work.

○ Courtesy and politeness. When staff are dealing with customers, they should be polite and courteous. The same attention should be paid to these qualities when staff are communicating with each other, and as supervisor you should ensure that employees are aware of the importance of treating each other with respect. It should be common practice for staff to greet each other politely and say 'please' and 'thank you'.

○ Shouting. Despite the media image of high-profile chefs shouting and screaming, this behaviour is not acceptable. You should not allow staff to shout at colleagues, and supervisors themselves should not shout at staff. Shouting at staff is not good for morale, and a culture of fear does not foster productive working relationships.

Case study

A waitress could see that a customer's dinner was wrong, but she was so terrified of being shouted at by the chef, she served it to the diner, who then complained.

○ In high-pressure situations, there may be occasions when people will shout. However, you should try to ensure that shouting is not the normal pattern of behaviour for staff.

Lending a helping hand.

○ Staff helping each other. Staff need to work as a team, and that means helping each other as required. You need to draw staff members' attention to when their colleagues are struggling, and ask them to help. Encouraging staff to help each other should be welcomed within the organisation. Supervisors and managers can lead by example, by helping colleagues in other departments and team members. The movement of staff helping other colleagues in other departments helps to develop productive working relationships. It is also an effective use of resources for the business.

○ Keeping promises and honouring commitments. To gain the loyalty and respect of staff, it is important that they see that promises and commitments within work are honoured. Where supervisors fail to honour commitments to their team, colleagues or line managers, staff will have little confidence in them. This will lead to feelings of being let down, staff not believing formal communications, and feelings of frustration, which demotivate staff and can distract from achieving the organisation's objectives. You should ensure that you, personally, and your staff honour commitments by communicating their importance and by being seen to help staff to do so.

Diversity issues

There are many benefits to be gained by developing productive relationships with colleagues, but thought has to be given as to how this can be achieved. In today's multicultural organisations, many employees have very different backgrounds. To form productive working relationships, it is necessary to recognise and acknowledge different cultural backgrounds, as they will influence colleagues' behaviour. Colleagues who come from different cultures will vary in their language and dialect, body language, clothes, religious beliefs and educational background. The hospitality industry is multicultural, whether manifested by internal or external customers, cuisine or décor. Staff need to reflect this in behaviour, style, methods and their approach to service and the product.

This may mean that, at a basic level, we have difficulty understanding what some staff say. Even within the UK, there are differences in regional dialects and what items are called – for example, a pillow case or a pillow slip? Communication has to be carefully planned so that there is common understanding. Verbal cues differ among different cultures: tone of voice, speed of speech and eye contact are all dependent on cultural influences, and it is important not to make assumptions that someone is being disrespectful because they do not behave in the same way that we do.

Evidence

It is helpful to carry out exercises with staff to encourage them to imagine the feelings of customers with special needs, such as blindness, deafness or another physical disability. Perhaps some staff can be asked to role-play as a blind customer while wearing a blindfold.

1.1, 1.5, 1.9, 2.3, 2.4, 2.7.

A high percentage of communication is through a person's body language. This will be influenced by their cultural background. Europeans are generally more expressive than the British. How close a person stands to you is also dependent upon culture, and the traditions of different countries and religions (Pease, 1981). Understanding these differences will help as you try to build relationships with employees and colleagues from different cultures.

You must ensure staff are not prejudiced against those from different backgrounds – since this is a legal requirement – and aim to build bridges between all staff. This can be done formally and informally. Formally, the issues of cultural diversity can be covered in staff training and briefing, and within the organisation, policies should be in place to cover diversity issues.

Law and policy

For information on the diversity legislation, see Legislation, page 218; also see Unit 4.

If the supervisor is aware of some of their staff's hobbies and interests, this can be used to encourage informal relationships between employees that will benefit team spirit. For example, one employee may have a passion for football, so perhaps as supervisor you could let other team members know this, and a common interest may be forged between staff from different backgrounds. Positive relationships outside work will have an impact on staff interactions in the workplace, and when staff get to know a fellow team member personally, cultural differences become insignificant. Informal or team activities may also encourage staff to see their colleagues in informal settings and to see another side of their personality.

You must make yourself aware of any discrimination towards team members because of their cultural/religious beliefs, their age, gender and sexual preferences, and deal with this immediately. This may involve formal disciplinary procedures. The importance of open communication and professional behaviour of all staff needs to be emphasised by the supervisor. No member of staff should be discriminated against because they are different. A team that is composed of people from a variety of backgrounds is to be welcomed. Respect and professional conduct should include all in the organisation, notwithstanding their background.

Equality of opportunity

Discrimination may:

- prevent individuals getting chances they deserve
- limit productivity within the business
- portray to others a poor image of the company/organisation
- break the law
- contravene internal equality of opportunity policy.

An organisation's workforce may comprise people from a variety of cultural, educational, social and religious backgrounds, who will all interpret the organisational culture and values differently. It is up to you as supervisor to communicate to employees the organisation's values, to be aware of the legal requirements and to ensure all employees share and relate to these values.

Evidence

Conduct a survey of your colleagues from different cultures and countries. Staff should feel comfortable discussing this with you. In order to do this, staff must be aware of the company's equal opportunities policy. They should know what is acceptable in terms of speech, behaviour and the provision of facilities. They should also know what will happen if the equal opportunities policy is not followed. Use the Internet to discover the different ethnic groupings in the UK. Find out how welcome these colleagues feel within the organisation. Ask them what could be done to help them feel more comfortable in the organisation. Produce a short report for management with your recommendations for improving integration of staff from different cultures.

1.4, 1.5, 2.2, 2.3, 2.7.

Modelling good behaviours

As supervisor, you should lead by example – it should not be a case of 'do what I say, not what I do'. There may be occasions when supervisors work alongside staff to help guide and support them. You should be approachable and supportive to all staff, and communicate openly and honestly. Formal communication should be planned and regular, using a variety of methods that ensure all staff and line managers receive the correct information (see pages 21–25).

You should follow the correct channels of communication and ensure all staff know to whom they are answerable. When talking to staff, you should be open and responsive, and even under pressure should not engage in shouting, but try to remain calm.

Informal day-to-day communication with colleagues, staff and line managers helps to build interpersonal relationships. As a supervisor, you should not be seen to spread tales or gossip, and sensitive personal information must not be repeated in or outside the workplace.

When dealing with staff, you must be fair to all – it is not acceptable to favour individual members of staff (for example, always giving one member of staff the weekend off). The courtesy and respect shown to staff by the supervisor will greatly influence the manner in which staff relate to one another. All staff, no matter what their background, should feel they are important to the organisation, and you should give professional commitment equally to all. Staff should understand how their individual efforts contribute to the organisation's business values and mission.

You should lead the way in making sure you are punctual for work, and that their appearance conforms to company policy. All staff represent the organisation they work for to the public, so it is up to you to set a positive image for staff to aspire to. A good supervisor can be a very motivating influence for employees, who may be inspired to strive towards this objective.

When dealing with difficult situations as supervisor, you should try to exhibit assertive rather than aggressive behaviour. Aggressive behaviour, where the person shouts, reacts defensively and gets their own way by intimidation, is unacceptable and unprofessional. Your behaviour should be calm and reasonable, asking questions to find out what the problem is, and proposing solutions that are acceptable to both yourself and the employee.

An employee storms into your office, shouting about having not been given the time off they requested. An aggressive response would be, 'I'm the supervisor, I'll do what I want, how dare you shout at me.' An assertive response would be, 'I'm sorry that you are upset about the duty rota. If you would like to discuss this, we will see what we can sort out.' Two very different responses to the same situation, but the assertive response ensures both parties get the opportunity to discuss the situation and agree a solution. It is important for staff to see that the supervisor is able to handle difficult situations calmly and professionally.

As a supervisor, you have authority over your team, and will lead your team to achieve set objectives. You will direct staff in their roles and should encourage them to achieve their personal objectives.

Staff will learn from your experiences and will be watching to see how you perform at work and how you form productive working relationships with colleagues throughout the organisation.

Giving constructive feedback

As staff carry out their roles, they will need support, guidance and feedback on their performance. Within the organisation, formal **appraisals** will take place, where all staff are given the opportunity to discuss their progress and to develop realistic personal objectives.

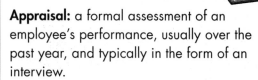

Definition

Appraisal: a formal assessment of an employee's performance, usually over the past year, and typically in the form of an interview.

The appraisal is usually between the employee and their line manager, but other staff may contribute or provide information to feed into the appraisal. The results of the appraisal will be recorded, with specific objectives and timescales being noted. These objectives will be reviewed at the follow-up appraisal. You may be required to participate, and will certainly be asked to comment on your staff's daily performance. You will also be appraised by your own line manager, when you will discuss together the development of your supervisory skills.

The manager and employee will meet at a pre-arranged time to discuss the employee's performance, highlighting weaknesses and reinforcing strengths that the employee may possess. Where improvements are required, a remedial action plan can be agreed. Positive feedback can be given for good performance. Future training and development will also be discussed, either internally within the organisation, or outside the organisation through colleges or training providers.

As a supervisor, you will be giving staff feedback on their performance and behaviour at work. To be effective, it is important that the feedback is immediate and constructive. If a member of staff is late, this needs to be discussed on the day, not a week later. Staff should not be 'told off' in front of colleagues. If you need to draw a member of staff's attention to a job performed badly, or to unprofessional behaviour towards customers or colleagues, it is important that you have evidence to back up what you are saying.

When giving constructive feedback, staff should be asked to comment. Open questions will help staff to identify the problem, such as:

- Why did this happen?
- How do you feel that went?
- What could you have done differently?
- What do you think?

Two-way, open communication between supervisor and staff can ensure the feedback is constructive. Negative feedback, such as 'You're useless, that dish is only fit for the dustbin!' is demotivating, and the chef has not been told specifically what the problem is. A more constructive approach would be to ask the employee, 'What do you think of this dish? Would you like to eat this dish? What could you do to improve it?' In this way the chef identifies the problem and the potential solutions.

Feedback should also be given for positive behaviour that reflects productive working relationships and achieving departmental objectives. Pay attention to your staff helping each other, doing good-quality work, and give positive feedback – 'Thanks, that's great', 'Well done'. Positive feedback is good for staff morale and building employees' confidence.

As a supervisor, you will both give and receive feedback. Your response to constructive feedback should be to view it as an opportunity for developing your supervisory skills. Colleagues can be a valuable resource in identifying skills and qualities, of which you may be unaware, that could be developed further. They may also highlight areas of weakness that can be improved. You need to be open to objective comments and assessment by colleagues and line managers to continue with your professional development.

The supervisor's role in promoting productive working relationships

Making reasonable agreements within and between departments

Within the workplace, each department will have their own set objectives, and all staff need to be aware of these objectives and working to achieve them. It is the supervisor's job to ensure all staff are aware of their individual objectives, and how they each contribute to achieving the departmental and organisational objectives.

When setting objectives for individual staff members and their team, supervisors should make sure they are SMART (see page 29).

In daily operations, the supervisor must be realistic in what they want to achieve, and take account of both their staff's capabilities and conditions in the workplace. It would be unreasonable to expect the highest-quality food from a head chef who was working in cramped conditions, with poor-quality equipment and inexperienced staff. The pursuit of high-quality food may be the head chef's long-term goal, but at the present time a more realistic goal may be to serve good-quality food within the prescribed time constraints.

By ensuring staff get the opportunity to voice their opinions, the resulting open communication should help everyone to agree what can be reasonably achieved. These agreements should be formally recorded and communicated to all staff so that everyone knows what has been agreed, and their individual commitment should be noted in individual staff records.

Within the organisation, departments have to work cooperatively, and you should aim to work productively with your colleagues in other departments.

Taking account of priorities of others

When developing interdepartmental agreements, it is necessary to be aware that each supervisor will have their own objectives and priorities. For example, the priorities of the hotel's head receptionist will be to let customers check into their rooms on arrival and to keep customers happy, while the floor housekeeper's priority will be to ensure all rooms are cleaned to the specified standard without putting their staff under too much pressure. With such conflicting priorities, agreement has to be reached between these two departments so that each can fulfil their function, perhaps by agreeing the number of cleaned rooms that can be issued to customers by certain times.

Open communication ensures everyone gets a chance to voice their opinion.

Supervisors should know what happens in each department so that they can understand their colleagues' viewpoints. As a part of staff training, all staff should spend time in each department so that they can understand the priorities of that department. Chefs moving into the marketing department, and responding to customers' queries on function menus, may gain a better understanding of why it is important to get the functions menu to the marketing department on time.

The agreements between departments have to balance the needs and priorities of each. Each department has to feel that their requirements have been met, and that a win-win solution has been achieved. This requires communication and negotiation skills. Each supervisor must try to ensure their department is not being pressurised by the demands of another, and that they are protecting their team from unacceptable agreements that would be difficult to fulfil.

Evidence

Collect an example of an agreement that you made with a colleague or colleagues from another department, in which you needed to balance different priorities. Were there any difficulties in fulfilling this agreement? How did you communicate these difficulties to your colleagues? Think about how you were able to deliver on the agreement, and what supporting evidence can back this up (e.g. emails, memos, minutes of meetings).
1.1, 1.4, 1.5, 1.6, 1.7, 1.8, 2.1, 2.2, 2.3, 2.4, 2.5, 2.6, 2.8.

Internal politics and power struggles

Organisations should aim for a situation where all staff are highly motivated to achieve the prescribed objectives, communication is free-flowing, and the formal organisational hierarchy ensures effective decision-making. In practice, this is sometimes difficult to achieve. Individuals and departments may have their own agendas which they are pursuing. Staff may have their own personal objectives which are contrary to those of the organisation.

It is part of the supervisor's role to be aware of these, and to find ways of ensuring these different agendas do not obstruct the achievement of the organisation's or department's objectives. This can sometimes call for great skills of tact and diplomacy!

Case study

James is head barman in a medium-sized hotel. His objective is to achieve the Wine Sommelier of the Year award. He would like the hotel to stock quality, expensive, specialist wines to taste and sell. The hotel's objective is to maximise profits during a time of recession. They want to limit the value of wine stock and concentrate on selling low-cost, popular wines.

As supervisor, you need to be aware of individual objectives and aspirations. If you were James's supervisor, what steps could you take to keep him motivated while still working within the organisation's objectives regarding profitability?

It is important when making agreements to be aware of the organisation's internal politics. Being aware of the informal communication and the workplace gossip ensures that discussing agreements, you have background knowledge about what is underlying another person's viewpoint. A member of staff who feels aggrieved that they have been passed over for a promotion will probably not be as happy to agree to decisions as someone who is satisfied in their work.

Managing conflicts of interest

Conflict occurs when people behave in a way that obstructs the achievement of objectives. There are a number of ways in which conflict is displayed in the workplace – conflicts between members of staff, conflicts between departments for resources, conflicts between team members. In managing conflict, it is important to consider what or who is causing the problem, and what can be done to solve it. Clear communication between you, as supervisor, and your staff is necessary to ensure conflicts are solved quickly and professionally.

Consider the scenarios in the following two case studies.

Case study

In a restaurant, there is conflict between staff as there is a shortage of teaspoons, and some members of staff have started to hide the teaspoons at their service points so that they always have them for their customers. There are two problems here: first, there are not enough teaspoons, and a request for more needs to be communicated to the manager; second, the staff are not working as a team. The supervisor needs to give attention to developing team cohesion, either formally in the workplace, or by organising a social event for all the team to attend where personal relationships can be strengthened.

Case study

In the wine bar, there are two staff members who are in conflict because, although they are being paid the same, one employee feels that they are expected to do more than their colleague. The supervisor can minimise conflict by ensuring the job descriptions of both staff members clearly outline their roles and what their job involves, and that this reflects what actually happens in the workplace. Clear communication between the supervisor and the two employees, where each employee is given the opportunity to voice their feelings and to propose solutions to the problems, will help resolve the conflict.

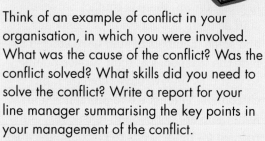

Evidence

Think of an example of conflict in your organisation, in which you were involved. What was the cause of the conflict? Was the conflict solved? What skills did you need to solve the conflict? Write a report for your line manager summarising the key points in your management of the conflict.
1.5, 1.8, 2.3, 2.5, 2.6.

Managing expectations

You will have expectations about how your staff should perform – and your staff will have expectations of you. They will expect you to behave professionally, communicate openly, and be their link to the upper layers of the organisational hierarchy. They will expect you to be able to direct operations successfully within their department. It is important that staff know you have the capability and experience to do all the jobs which you are supervising them to do, otherwise they will

not respect you. The staff's expectations of you are implicit within your role as supervisor. If you fail to realise these expectations associated with the role, this will cause difficulties with your staff, who may choose not to communicate with you, instead going directly to the departmental manager.

You have a key role to play in managing other colleagues' expectations of your department. You must be sure that any promises you make are ones that you know your department can fulfil. It is important to be honest and admit that you cannot, or may not, be able to deliver something, rather than promising something you are not sure you can deliver.

Case study

In a hotel, the coffee shop supervisor has asked the supervisor of the on-site laundry to launder all the coffee shop's tablecloths nightly and return them in the morning. The laundry supervisor knows this will be a problem, as the laundry staff finish work before the coffee shop sends down the tablecloths, so there will be no staff to get them laundered. However, the laundry supervisor says, 'I'll see what I can do'. Next day, one of the laundry staff takes a phone call from an angry coffee shop supervisor demanding to know where the clean tablecloths are. They have not been told anything about this requirement.

What expectation does the coffee shop supervisor have, following her conversation with the laundry supervisor? How will the laundry staff member feel during the telephone call with the coffee shop supervisor? What actions could the two supervisors have taken to avoid this situation occurring? What could they do to put it right now?

Don't agree to unreasonable requests

When colleagues request you to undertake a task that you feel is unreasonable, you must communicate this to them. It is unreasonable for a colleague to ask you to request on numerous occasions that your staff do overtime without pay to serve customers. As a supervisor, you are the spokesperson for your staff, and it is your responsibility to ensure they are treated correctly and professionally.

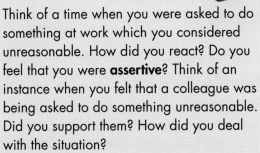

Evidence

Think of a time when you were asked to do something at work which you considered unreasonable. How did you react? Do you feel that you were **assertive**? Think of an instance when you felt that a colleague was being asked to do something unreasonable. Did you support them? How did you deal with the situation?
1.2, 1.3, 1.4, 1.5, 1.7, 1.8, 2.2, 2.3, 2.5, 2.6.

Definition

Assertiveness: behaviour in which a person is not afraid to speak his or her mind or of trying to influence others, but does so in a way that respects others. Being assertive is being neither passive nor aggressive.

Ensuring agreements are met

As a supervisor, it is your job to ensure what you have agreed to do is actually carried out. This requires that all staff know what their job is, and that they work as a team to support each other and are given feedback on their performance.

Ensure that all relevant parties have all the necessary information and resources

In directing staff, you must ensure that all staff know what their role in the team is. This role may be straightforward if they work only in one area, for example, on the counter, taking and assembling customer orders. In small organisations, an employee's role may well be more complex, and they may be required to work in a number of areas. In a small hotel, for example, a staff member may start the day serving breakfast to guests and then clean and service bedrooms, and finish their shift serving drinks at the bar. As a supervisor, you must communicate with the staff member to explain their role in the organisation, answering any queries and questions staff have and solving problems as they arise.

Communicate clearly and concisely what needs to be done

In order to get the job done, staff need to be given specific instructions. In some organisations, each job will have a formal job schedule detailing the exact way in which the job is to be completed. For example, in many popular restaurants there will be very specific instructions for the completion of each dish on the menu so that all dishes conform to company standards.

Where the job is complex, for example, setting up the banqueting suite for a formal dinner, it needs to be divided up so that each member of staff is given a specific task. Two members of staff may be asked to polish the cutlery, two to put on the tablecloths and fold the napkins, and two to polish the glasses.

Once all the individual tasks are complete, the tables can be set up. The amount of direction and supervision you need to give will depend on the experience and capabilities of your staff, but as supervisor you are responsible for ensuring the banqueting suite is set up to the expected standard.

Where the job is not formally detailed, for example, in servicing a bedroom, you need to tell the room attendant what needs to be done. They should be given specific instructions so they know exactly what has to be accomplished. It is also important to tell them *why* a job is being done in a specific way, so that they can understand the reasons. For example, a room attendant has been told to vacuum each bedroom before dusting. Why? If the vacuuming is completed after dusting, more dust is created – doing it before dusting ensures that the room is cleared of dust. Try to involve each member of staff in explaining why a job is done in a specific manner, for example, 'What are the benefits of doing it like this?'

Check that everyone has understood what needs to be done

You need to check that members of staff understand your instructions completely. This requires effective communication skills, and the skilful use of open questions that prompt an active response, rather than closed questions that only need a 'yes' or 'no' answer. Take the scenario in the following case study.

Case study

You have asked a member of your staff to prepare a fresh fruit salad, and have asked them if they can do that. They have said they can. At the start of service, you check the fruit salad and discover there is tinned fruit in it. The staff member has not clearly understood what you wanted – a fruit salad made with *fresh* fruit. By asking a closed question, you have not been able to check that they fully understand your instructions.

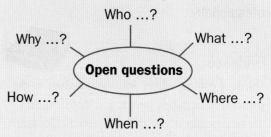

Figure 2.6 Open questions.

When checking that the staff member was clear about making the fresh fruit salad, you could have asked them instead: 'What fruits are you going to use in this dish?' or 'How are you going to cut up these fruits?'

Where you are supervising staff for whom English is a second language, or a staff member who is unfamiliar with your organisation's way of working, it is very important to check understanding. Effective communication requires that the person sending a message always checks understanding; this is often the part of the communication process that people forget.

Never assume that your instructions are going to be completed in the way you expect! Check that all staff know exactly what needs to be done – but be careful that you do not make staff feel foolish or stupid by being patronising.

Check that everyone has the resources to do the job

To perform the job, staff need the resources to complete it. To service a bedroom, a room attendant needs equipment, detergents, laundry, beverage and snack supplies, and promotional materials. If they do not have any of these resources, they will be unable to do the job. To produce sandwiches in the coffee shop, staff need food and the equipment to make the sandwiches.

It is up to you to check that staff have everything they need to do the job. Providing a checklist for different jobs can help staff check that they have the necessary resources. If there is a problem, it is up to you to direct the staff to where they can get the missing items.

If resources are in short supply (for example, towels in the leisure complex), the supervisor needs to communicate this to the line manager so that this situation can be remedied (see Unit 3, page 87).

Monitor team performance

To develop and support productive working relationships within the organisation, you need to monitor both individual staff members and your team as a whole.

You are the spokesperson for your team, and responsible for ensuring all team members are contributing equally. You need to observe carefully how team members behave towards one another, and towards other teams. You must also be aware of personal relationships outside the workplace and their impact on the team.

Case study

Two staff on one team were involved in a personal relationship. The supervisor started to notice that these two staff members were increasingly working on their own, sharing their own private jokes, and not interacting with the rest of the staff. This was causing problems within the team and needed to be dealt with. How would you deal with this situation?

Make time available to support the team

Spending time with your team will enable you to monitor their performance. As a supervisor, you will have opportunities to talk informally with your team, perhaps at staff breaks, when they arrive for work and at social events. But you should be careful not to become too friendly with your team – it is very difficult to supervise staff with whom you are over-friendly. Your role is to support and direct your team; to do this you need to be approachable and professional in your interactions with them.

As supervisor you must also plan to allocate time on a regular basis to meet with your team formally. This can involve meetings with the team, as discussed previously in the correct communication lines in your department. Individual meetings with team members to discuss their jobs and roles can be used to reassure, support and give advice as appropriate. Team members need to see that you are available to support them and you need to plan for this when organising your workload.

Figure 2.7 Meeting the team.

In a crisis situation – for example, when staff are facing redundancy, or when changes are being implemented regarding new working patterns – it is very important that you are there to communicate decisions being made by the senior management, and that you support your team.

Hold people accountable

Your staff are accountable to you for performing the tasks you set them. If you are sure the objectives you have set are achievable and have been communicated clearly, then you should have an absolute expectation that they will be carried out. This is very important in motivating staff to perform well – they need to know that you trust them to do what you have asked of them.

Evidence

Find any work schedules that you have drawn up, allocating tasks to particular members of staff. Were these tasks allocated on the basis of the job specification, or was the staff member being asked to carry out something outside their job description? Were the tasks carried out satisfactorily? If not, what action did you take, and what feedback did you give to the staff concerned?
1.2, 1.9, 1.10, 2.10.

By setting high expectations of yourself, you will also encourage individual staff members to have high expectations of themselves and of each other. Within an effective team, all members must contribute equally to achieving the departmental objectives. As the supervisor, you must ensure that this happens by distributing the work fairly to team members. If one team member fails to complete their job successfully, this will have a negative impact on the team. For example, if one team member has been asked to assemble the cheeseboard for dinner service and fails to do so, all the team will be affected by it not being ready. It is your responsibility to deal with the employee whose job it was to prepare the cheeseboard. They are accountable to you, and must be made aware of the consequences of failing to do what they were asked. Your team has to be reassured that you will hold people accountable for what they have been asked to do, and that you will not allow staff to neglect duties.

Recognising and dealing with disagreements

Within every team and organisation there will be disagreement. All teams have members who can sometimes exhibit challenging behaviour, and there will be occasions when disagreements occur due to personality clashes. As supervisor, you have to recognise disagreement and deal with it promptly so that it does not interfere with achieving the department's objectives. Disagreements may also occur between different departments.

Recognise disagreements

Disagreements within and between teams will be displayed by a change in the behaviour of team members. A team that has previously worked well together and then has a disagreement will stop communicating positively, members may become isolated and form sub-groups, and there may be little cooperation between the team members.

Disagreements between departments will be apparent when one department fails to honour its commitments. For example, if there has been a disagreement between the purchasing department and the kitchen over the time at which food stocks are delivered to the kitchen, this disagreement could lead to the purchasing department deliberately keeping the kitchen waiting for its food stocks.

Dealing with disagreements and damage limitation

Having established that there is disagreement, as a supervisor you have to deal with it promptly. Failure to sort out the problem will affect working relationships and the achievement of objectives. If there are disagreements between individuals that are affecting the team, you will have to talk to each staff member and resolve the problem. You will need to judge whether it is best to speak to staff individually, or get them together. Using open questions (see page 76) will make communication more productive and help you to appreciate both sides of the argument. Ask staff to suggest solutions themselves. Don't take sides. Make clear to them the impact their disagreement is having on the team. If you can end the discussion by agreeing a firm outcome, all parties will be able to move forward positively. It is a good idea to follow up the meeting after a short period of time, perhaps after a week.

Disagreements between departments will involve the supervisors in both areas solving the problem by discussing the causes and probable solutions. Again, you will have to plan the best way to discuss the problem, whether a meeting is held between yourself and the relevant supervisor in the department concerned, or whether it is more of a team meeting, at which several staff are present. A neutral person might be appropriate, to act as a 'referee' if conflict is likely to become a problem and obstruct finding a solution. Open questions will again promote an open discussion, and will encourage a flow of ideas to solve the problem. The important thing for you as supervisor is to ensure that disagreements in work do not adversely affect achieving the organisation's objectives. If you are unable to solve disagreements with your department, or with another department, it may be necessary to bring the matter to the attention of your line manager.

Keeping everyone informed

There will be times when plans that have been made will have to change due to internal or external circumstances. An example of internal circumstances changing might be that the line manager is replaced, and the new manager wishes to try something different from what was previously agreed. Changes to external circumstances could include the supply of resources, financial considerations or market forces that will affect the organisation and agreements that have been made – for example, if a regular supplier goes out of business, or is taken over by a larger organisation.

Whatever the reason for the change of plan, it is important that you keep everyone informed. The team needs to receive regular communication regarding changes to planned agreements. Regular communication ensures that staff feel involved in the changes, and prevents misunderstandings and wasted time and resources.

Case study

A hotel was hosting a large conference party. The guests were expected at a specific time, but this time was changed. The reservations supervisor communicated this information to the front office supervisor. Unfortunately, the front office supervisor failed to inform their team of the change of plan. This meant that the reception team who were expecting to book in a large conference party at the arranged time were left waiting for the party, who arrived an hour later. The result was frustrated receptionists who had wasted time waiting for the party, and had changed their work patterns to ensure there were enough staff on the front desk to check in the guests efficiently.

What effect could this have had on:
- the reception the customers eventually got at the desk;
- the work output of the receptionists during that day;
- the willingness of the receptionists to accommodate extra requests in future?

Communication to inform members of staff may be verbal and/or written, depending upon the urgency of the change. You may want to tell your team about the change of plan, then follow this up with a memo to individual team members to ensure your communication is effective.

Obtain and use feedback from colleagues

Once agreements have been made, it is necessary to seek colleagues' feedback as to how successful you have been. It is never good practice to assume that if you hear nothing, everything is fine. It is good practice to ask your colleagues in other departments for feedback:

○ Was the job completed in the way you expected?

○ Were there any problems that we should know about?

○ How can we improve?

○ Was there any member of my team who gave excellent service?

This feedback can be obtained formally in meetings, or informally over a cup of coffee.

There is no point in obtaining feedback unless it is used constructively. Comments, observations, criticisms and praise should be passed on to your team. Problems that have occurred should be analysed to see what could be changed on the next occasion. Good practice should be adopted as standard procedure. Feedback should not only be negative – where the feedback is good, congratulations and thanks should be extended to your team.

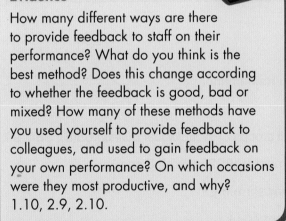

Evidence

How many different ways are there to provide feedback to staff on their performance? What do you think is the best method? Does this change according to whether the feedback is good, bad or mixed? How many of these methods have you used yourself to provide feedback to colleagues, and used to gain feedback on your own performance? On which occasions were they most productive, and why? 1.10, 2.9, 2.10.

Test yourself!

1 What are the benefits of productive working relationships for the individual?

2 What does the formal organisational chart show?

3 Why is it important to recognise and value different personalities within a team?

4 What is meant by horizontal communication? Give some examples from your own organisation.

5 List some examples of professional behaviour in dealing with conflict.

6 Why is it important for the supervisor to be aware of the informal organisation?

7 How can a supervisor ensure that staff know what needs to be done?

8 Why is it important to seek feedback from colleagues in other departments?

9 What skills should a supervisor possess in order to develop productive working relationships?

Further information

Belbin, M. (1993) *Team Roles at Work*, Butterworth-Heinemann.

Pease, A. (1981) *Body Language*, Sheldon Press.

Tuckman, B. (1965) 'Development sequence in small groups', *Psychological Bulletin* 63(6): 384–99.

The Chartered Institute of Personnel and Development (CIPD), www.cipd.co.uk

The Society for Human Resource Management, www.shrm.org

People Management Online, www.peoplemanagement.co.uk

Institute of Hospitality, www.instituteofhospitality.org

Investors in People (IIP), www.investorsinpeople.co.uk

HS3

Contribute to the control of resources

This chapter covers the following units:

o Level 3 Diploma Hospiitality Supervision and Leadership (NVQ)
  Unit HSL3: Contribute to the control of resources
o Technical Certificate Unit 1: Leading a team in the hospitality industry
  – 3.1, 3.2, 3.3, 3.4, 3.5; Unit 2: Supervision of operations in the
  hospitality industry – 2.1, 2.2, 2.3, 2.4, 3.1, 3.2, 3.3, 3.4, 3.5.

**Working through this chapter could also provide
evidence for the following key skills:**

o C2.2, C2.3, N2.1, N2.2, N2.3.

In this chapter you will learn about:

o identifying the resources you need
o availability of resources
o your responsibility for acquiring resources
o purchasing resources
o receiving and issuing resources
o storage
o stock control
o health and safety
o using resources effectively and efficiently
o presenting recommendations to decision makers.

Likely sources of evidence

1.1 compare the resources available to them with the resources they need for their work
organisation charts, staff rotas, equipment inventory, diary, budgets, stock records, supplier lists, computerized stock records.

1.2 follow the correct procedures to obtain additional resources needed for their work
staff schedules, job schedules, equipment inventory, diary, booking lists, stock turnover records, order forms, requisition forms, consumption records.

1.3 deal with any problems in obtaining resources following agreed procedures and keeping relevant people informed
staff schedules, job schedules, equipment inventory, diary, booking lists, order forms, requisition forms, emails, records of telephone conversations, professional discussion, observation, witness statement.

1.4 check the quality, quantity and suitability of resources before they are needed for use
emails, records of telephone conversations, professional discussion, observation, witness statement.

1.5 make sure that equipment and materials are correctly stored and maintained
stock records, equipment inventory, temperature records, health and safety records, HACCAP records, accident records, notes of meetings/conversations with colleagues, professional discussion, observation.

1.6 encourage their colleagues to make efficient use of resources and minimise waste
emails, records of telephone conversations, professional discussion, observation, witness statement, posters, training notes, environmental policy documents, energy bills.

1.7 monitor the use of resources in their area of responsibility
booking lists, stock records, equipment inventory, temperature records, health and safety records, HACCP records, accident records.

1.8 make sure that resources are used effectively, efficiently and in line with organisational and legal requirements
stock records, equipment inventory, temperature records, health and safety records, HACCP records, accident records, risk assessments, emails, records of telephone conversations, minutes of meetings, professional discussion, observation, witness statement, posters, training notes, etc.

1.9 keep records about resources up-to-date, accurate and in the specified place
professional discussion, could signpost stock records, staff rotas, schedules, booking lists, etc. observation

1.10 recommend ways of making better use of resources following organisational requirements
emails, records of telephone conversations, professional discussion, witness statement

Introduction

This unit is about ensuring you, and the staff for whom you are responsible, use resources effectively and efficiently, without undue waste. All organisations use resources to achieve their objectives. They have to be purchased, controlled and monitored to ensure they are being used productively, safely, and for the maximum benefit of the organisation and the wider environment.

Identifying the resources you need

Your department is likely to need some or all of the following:
- staff
- supplies
- equipment
- time
- finance
- energy.

> **Evidence**
>
> Gather documents about the resources that are available to you. Examples might include organisational charts, staff rotas, budgets, stock records (including computerised records) and supplier lists. HSL 1.1, 1.2, 2.1, 2.14.

Staff

The number of staff who you will be responsible for supervising depends on a number of factors.

The organisation and its objectives

A fast-food restaurant relying on prepared, purchased food that is reheated and served will not require as many members of staff in the kitchen as a restaurant serving high-quality, gastronomic meals.

The organisation's formal structure and spans of control

The organisation's human resources policy may, for example, be to employ only key staff full-time and to employ other staff as and when needed. This is often the case in function catering, where it makes good business sense to have a small number of permanent staff, with banqueting staff employed on a casual basis.

Staff skills

If the staff are highly skilled and productive, fewer staff will be needed than if they are less well trained. For example, a highly-skilled waiter/waitress will be able to serve 20 customers at any one time with plated service. However, an inexperienced member of staff would only be able to manage about 10 to 12 customers.

Staff turnover

The hospitality industry is well known for high staff turnover. Staff move jobs very frequently, and this may be reflected in your department.

As well as temporary staff, there are a lot of part-time staff working in the industry, and turnover may be higher for part-time employees.

As supervisor, you are responsible for making sure you have the right number of staff – including the right balance between full- and part-time staff – with the right skills, in the right place to do the job. In order to do this, it is necessary to know:

○ what you have to do
○ when do you have to do it – dates, times
○ where are you doing it – in single location (e.g. a restaurant) or in multiple locations (e.g. serving meals to guest bedrooms).

For example, reception will know the level of business from the bookings, and will need to communicate this to all departments so they can prepare suitable staffing and supplier levels. From this information, you need to plan your staffing requirements. To plan effectively, you will need information from colleagues in your department and colleagues in other departments. This information may be discussed with your line manager at planning meetings, or it may be communicated by written reports – for example, function sheets or room changeover lists – regarding projected customer numbers and their specific requirements. Past experience will also influence your staffing requirements – for example, in city centre restaurants, Friday and Saturday nights are usually the busiest.

Case study

The head receptionist in a hotel catering for business customers has a large conference party due to check in on Friday afternoon. Normally they might plan to have only one member of staff on reception, as Friday night is usually very quiet, but in this case they will need to have more members of staff on duty to check in the conference party.

Case study

The head housekeeper in a 50-bedroom country hotel specialising in weekend breaks learns that the marketing manager has booked a mid-week wedding party who will all be staying in the hotel. They usually plan to have only two staff working mid-week, as the hotel is normally not that busy, but on this occasion they will need to schedule more staff for this period, as all the hotel bedrooms will need servicing.

Evidence

Find out how staffing schedules are planned in your organisation. Find an example of a staffing schedule for your department for last week. Did you have enough staff for each shift, and if not, why not? Did you have too many staff, so that the staff on duty did not have enough to do? Why did these problems arise? What recommendations could you make to solve these problems? Collect examples of rotas, emails, records of telephone conversations or some form of written report that indicates why you have had to increase staffing levels to accommodate business levels.
1.3, 1.10, 2.1, 2.2, 2.3, 2.4, 2.22.

Supplies

The supplies that you and your staff need will depend on the job. It is obvious that chefs need food, bar staff need drinks, and housekeepers need cleaning products and laundry. However, there are more resources that you will need to think about. Restaurant staff need crockery, cutlery, glassware, tableware, serving dishes and implements. As supervisor, you will be responsible for identifying the supplies that are needed in your department and making sure staff know how they are going to be used.

When supervising staff, you may use documented job schedules. The job schedule gives instructions about how the job is to be completed, and what supplies staff need to use. Where a formal job schedule is not used, you will have to ensure the staff know what supplies they need to complete the job, and you may choose to have a checklist for each job.

Find out!

Are there formal documented job schedules in your organisation? Where are these schedules kept? Do staff follow these schedules? These documents will help you to identify the resources you need for your work.

Job schedules

Job schedule for setting table in bistro

Supplies needed

Cutlery – knife and fork for each cover
Place mat – 1 place mat per cover
Napkin – 1 napkin per cover
Glasses – 1 small wine glass per cover
Salt and pepper – 1 cruet set per 4 covers
Table numbers – Each table needs a number
Clean dishcloth and antibacterial spray

Procedure

1   Spray each table with antibacterial spray and wipe table top.
2   Place a place mat down for each cover on the table, so that place mat is 1 inch in from the edge of the table.
3   Place knife, blade side in towards mat, on right-hand side of place mat.
4   Place fork on left-hand side of place mat.
5   Fold napkin in half and place in middle of place mat.
6   Place glass on right-hand side of place mat above the place mat.
7   Put cruet set and table number in middle of table.
8   Check that each cover is uniform in appearance.

Figure 3.1 An example of a job schedule.

Equipment

You will need to know what equipment is available to use within your organisation, and you may be required to identify equipment that is needed for specific jobs. For example, to offer **gueridon service** in your restaurant, you need to have trolleys and flambé lamps. The functions supervisor, when planning a function, will need to identify the number of tables and chairs needed, and compare this with the number in the functions area – if there is a shortfall, more furniture will need to be arranged.

Definition

Gueridon service: food partially prepared or cooked within the restaurant itself, usually on a trolley beside the guest's table.

When planning a job, staff need to be told what equipment to use and trained to use it properly. You will need to ensure this equipment is working properly and safely. Where there is a shortage of equipment, this will negatively affect staff's productivity; for example, if there are not enough vacuum cleaners in housekeeping, room attendants will have to share, and this will affect how quickly they can vacuum the rooms.

Advances in technology affect the performance of equipment, and you need to keep up to date with developments in your area so that you can identify the best equipment and suggest that it is purchased. However, new equipment requires financial commitment, and the available budget will influence its replacement.

Evidence

Conduct a review of the equipment in your area. If there is an inventory of equipment in your department, check through it to make sure nothing is missing. If you need to obtain some new or replacement equipment, what are the right procedures? Is it all working effectively, or does it need replacing? Take one piece of equipment and research whether there are newer models that are more effective and energy-efficient. Prepare a report for your manager using three examples of similar equipment, and justify the purchase of each: cost versus time-saving, features, etc.
1.1, 1.2, 1.5, 1.6, 1.8, 1.10, 2.1, 2.25.

Time

Time is a resource, and although everyone has the same amount, some people seem to be better at using it than others. As a supervisor, you will have to determine the amount of time you need to do your job, and adhere to time limits imposed upon you. For example, in a restaurant serving lunch you will have to be set up ready for service at noon; guest bedrooms in a hotel usually have to be ready for occupation at 2 p.m.

You will need to manage your time carefully to achieve your different objectives. When planning your day, it is a good idea to set down all the different jobs that you have to do and prioritise these within the time constraints. Be realistic about what you can achieve, and plan for interruptions and the unexpected. When making agreements with colleagues in different departments, it is necessary to consider the time you will need to fulfil this agreement, and communicate this to them (see page 62).

Not only do you have to manage your own time, you will also be responsible for planning your staff's work time. When planning a job, you need to consider its complexity. In some organisations there are clear time limits prescribed for specific jobs – e.g. servicing a bedroom (25 minutes), cleaning a bedroom (35 minutes). So the housekeeper can plan how much time would be needed to clean and service ten bedrooms and allocate the appropriate number of staff.

Some staff will work more quickly than others, and you need to be aware of this: an experienced **barista** will serve hot beverages much more quickly than an inexperienced member of staff; experienced staff working in the sandwich bar making customers' sandwiches to order will be faster than a new

> **Definition**
>
> **Barista:** a person who serves in a coffee bar.

employee. As supervisor, when planning a job, you need to give thought to the time you and your staff will need – wasted time is an expense to the organisation.

Finance

The main aim of most businesses is to be profitable. The money that is generated pays staff wages and helps in the reinvestment

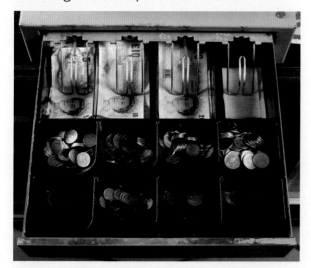

It is important to keep a close eye on finances.

needed to sustain the business and hopefully enable it to grow. Prudent financing is required to make sure all aspects of the business work together to maintain not only the revenue, but also the profit levels.

Most sizeable organisations prepare a business plan – this sets out the organisation's objectives and how it plans to achieve them – the business strategies. It may include information about the market, and critically it is a financial forecast.

A typical plan may include:

○ an executive summary – an overview of the business
○ marketing and sales strategy – why people may want to buy and how the business plans to sell to them
○ the management team, indicating the team's skills
○ operations – premises, product facilities, IT information systems
○ financial forecast, detailing projected costs and revenue.

It is important to understand that in order to keep all staff employed, a business needs to be successful and to keep a tight rein on the budget. This is why, especially in large organisations, careful control is kept on, for example, suppliers of both equipment and commodities. Well-run businesses will also have set procedures for how orders are placed, for maintaining stock levels, and to limit authorised spending by staff within the organisation by setting spending limits.

As a supervisor, you will control resources in a number of ways and for a number of reasons: to avoid waste, to be cost-efficient, and to help manage the revenue – often called the bottom line (page 52) – the amount of profit made after all costs have been taken out.

To be a good supervisor, you need to know:
○ the limits of your authority when purchasing
○ the importance of good staff
○ how to increase efficiency
○ how to improve/maintain customer service and/or products.

You need to manage your own resources efficiently to contribute to the business plan, and know the procedures that are in place to control costs. This will help you to work within agreed spending limits in most cases, and if you do spend more than has been agreed, ideally you should first obtain agreement from your line manager and be ready to identify where costs could be reduced in the future to try to stay within budgets.

Energy

Energy is a resource that all organisations use. You need to be aware of the ways in which energy is used in your department. It is not usual for supervisors to have to identify their energy requirements, but you should take account of your energy consumption, how much this costs, and if energy is being wasted. The head chef will use ovens, but does not have to switch them on first thing in the morning if they are not going to be used until later in the day.

You need to educate your staff in using energy wisely, switching off lights, switching off equipment when not in use, and not wasting water by letting taps run. When planning work, thought needs to be given to the most effective use of energy. For example, instead of using the oven for just one dish, use it for two. Explaining to staff the importance of reducing energy consumption should be part of your role, and you should monitor staff to check that they are adhering to any directives that exist.

Availability of resources

The resources that you need to do the job have to be available when needed, and you will need to check that the right resources are accessible at the right time. If you have identified specialist food ingredients needed for a dish on the à la carte menu, you need to make sure the chef has these ingredients when the dish is being prepared. You may also need to be prepared with contingency plans for when things go wrong, for example, in the event of equipment failure.

Checking resources are available

As a supervisor, you need to ensure you and your staff have the resources to do the job at the right time. Delays in staff receiving the equipment and supplies that they need will hinder them in doing their jobs, affecting customer service and products, and having a negative impact on the business. There are a number of checks that you can do to ensure resources are available as required.

○ **Stock checks** – supplies should be checked regularly to ensure you have enough food, beverages, crockery, cutlery, glassware, linen, stationery and cleaning materials. Stock checks ensure stock levels are controlled, inform the projection of future sales, and indicate expenditure as part of the budget of the business.

○ **Equipment inventory** – within each department, an inventory should be kept on the equipment in that area. This inventory should detail each piece of equipment, its service record, and where it is positioned or stored. For example, in function catering you may store extra equipment in a store room. If you are planning a function and need 20 tables, you can go to your equipment inventory and check how many tables you have. The equipment inventory will also have an impact on the control of costs, so that accurate costs can be calculated on damaged, stolen or broken equipment. Within large organisations, other departments may have equipment that you need, and this information needs to be available to all supervisors. In small organisations, there may not be a formal record of equipment, and it is important that you know what equipment is available and check it is all in good working order.

○ **Staff rotas** – to successfully complete a job as supervisor, you need to have the right number of staff with the right skills available when you require them. This means knowing which staff are going to be available. Staff may be unavailable due to sickness, training or holidays, or because they have worked their contracted hours of work for that week. The staff that are available must have the right skills to do the job. For example, if you are planning a Valentine's night dinner dance and want silver service, you need to ensure your staff are trained in silver service. In some cases you may have to employ casual staff to meet your specific requirements.

Checking the suitability of resources

You need to ensure that the available resources are suitable and 'fit for purpose'. This will depend on the organisation's objectives, and how they are reflected in your department's objectives, which should be set out in policies, procedures and the business plan.

For example, in a five-star hotel there is a restaurant offering a high-quality meal experience. As a part of this experience, the table settings use fine bone china and crystal glasses. The head waiter in charge of setting up the restaurant needs to check that there are enough glasses, that each place setting has three glasses, and that they are clean, free from chips, and the right size.

The floor housekeeper needs to ensure the staff have enough linen to change the beds, checking that there are enough sheets to change both the top and bottom sheets, and that the sheets are the correct size.

Staff have to possess the technical and interpersonal skills that are needed for the specific job – for example, staff interacting with customers will need good communication skills and should have good product knowledge. As a supervisor with two staff available to serve aperitifs at a drinks reception, you may select the staff member who has the technical expertise to serve drinks efficiently and in a friendly manner, as opposed to someone who is technically competent but is not good with customers.

Find out!

What systems are in place in your organisation for checking the availability and suitability of resources? Whose responsibility is it to keep records on resources? Collect this information and keep it for your portfolio.

Your responsibility for acquiring resources

Your responsibilities for acquiring resources will be determined by the organisation in which you work, and will be detailed in your job description. For example, as head chef in a small, independent food outlet, you may have the responsibility for acquiring all the supplies you need. Alternatively, as head chef of a fast-food unit of a large organisation, your responsibility would be restricted to ordering supplies from a central supply point. Your choice of supplier in a large business will often be set by the organisation.

Awareness of the organisation's financial targets

All catering organisations can be classified into two main categories:

- profit-making – catering outlets whose objective is to make money
- non-profit-making – catering outlets where the catering is a service and will not be seeking to make a profit over and above the money it needs to sustain itself.

Whatever the type of organisation you work in as a supervisor, you will need to have knowledge of its financial targets. These targets may include:

- gross profits – the profit achieved after food/beverage costs have been taken off
- food/beverage costs – the cost per dish/beverage
- average room revenue – room sales divided by number of rooms
- average spend per customer
- room revenue – average spend per room
- staff costs – usually expressed as a percentage of sales
- equipment costs – including maintenance and replacements
- energy costs
- net profit – profit achieved after all costs have been taken off.

These organisational targets are set by the organisation's senior management, and each department will be given sales targets and/or a budget for expenditure in their area.

Working within agreed budgets

You will need to know the **budget** for expenditure in your area, as this will determine spending on supplies, equipment and staffing. To ensure you keep to this budget, you need to record of expenditure and plan carefully to ensure you spread the expenditure over the allocated period.

For example, as head receptionist you may be given a budget for stationery for the whole year. You need to plan how much you will spend on stationery each month by looking

at past records of expenditure and thinking about future stationery needs, as some months you may need more than others.

In the kitchen, the head chef will be given a **gross profit** that they will be expected to make on each dish. So when planning dishes,

the head chef has to consider both the cost of raw ingredients and the price to charge, to make sure they achieve the agreed profit.

As housekeeper, you need to be aware of the costs of laundry. If you are exceeding your budget, you may need to reconsider how you can get the laundry done within the agreed budget. Perhaps in this case you may choose to use another laundry service.

Procedures for exceeding budget

As a supervisor managing a budget, there will be occasions when you will need to exceed the stated budget, and you need to be aware of the correct procedure in your organisation. In some organisations, you may be given the flexibility to exceed your budget on a short-term basis as long as the yearly budget is maintained. Therefore in one month you may spend more than the budget, but this is balanced out by a reduction in spending in the next month. Perhaps you may be allowed to exceed your budget up to a certain percentage, such as two to three per cent.

In most organisations, you will need to seek permission from your manager for exceeding your budget. They will probably expect you to explain why you have failed to stay within your budget, and to justify your reasons for increased expenditure.

It is important that you know and follow the correct procedure within your organisation to stay within the overall budget.

Purchasing resources

Purchasing refers to the buying of products necessary for your business to function – food, linen, porters' trolleys, stationery, etc. Resources need to be purchased to fulfil the organisation's objectives. Purchasing should be monitored constantly to ensure both you and the customer are achieving value for money. Your main aim is to provide goods and services within a given budget. You need to be aware of the organisation's purchasing policies and procedures to ensure resources are available in sufficient quantity and of the specified quality when needed. It is useful to have a good idea of normal consumption levels.

Purchasing policies

Every organisation will have its own policy regarding the purchasing of resources. This is influenced by a number of factors.

○ **Size of the organisation** – larger organisations will have a specialist department dealing with purchasing, which will prescribe to individual units how purchasing of resources is to be conducted. For example, a multinational company such as McDonald's will purchase resources centrally, and units will be told when, and from whom, they should order resources.

○ **Organisation's objectives** – the values and objectives of the organisation will influence the purchasing of resources. Perhaps the owners of a restaurant wish to use only locally-grown products, in which case their purchasing policy will reflect this. They may use this as a part of their marketing strategy – 'We use local producers.'

○ **Senior management** – the personal preferences of the senior management may dictate the purchasing of resources. For example, maybe the senior manager thinks that Egyptian linen is superior and dictates that all linen sourced is Egyptian.

○ **Personal contacts** – in small organisations, resources may be purchased from people who are known to the organisation's owner, or who are good customers, and the policy will be to favour these suppliers.

○ **Ethical and moral influences** – the use of child labour in producing goods (e.g. clothing), the environmental damage caused by producing the resources (e.g. through transportation), and the use of packaging are all ethical issues that will influence purchasing policy.

○ **Financial considerations** – if the suppliers of resources offer preferential discounts and/or payment terms, so that the organisation benefits financially, this may determine purchasing policy.

○ **Availability of supplies** – there may be a number of suitable suppliers; or there may only be one supplier who can fulfil your specific need, in which case you may be obliged to use that one supplier.

> **Evidence**
> Read and refer to the purchasing policy when collecting relevant evidence, to help you prepare for the professional discussion. 2.12.

You need to have a knowledge of the purchasing policy to make sure that you contribute appropriately to the business plan. This will include a knowledge of procedures within the organisation.

Organisation procedures and responsibility for purchasing

Your responsibility for purchasing resources will vary depending on the organisation and the scope of your responsibilities. The questions to ask, as supervisor, are:

- What resources are you responsible for purchasing?
- Who is responsible for sourcing suppliers?
- Who is responsible for ordering?
- Who is responsible for paying?
- What is the procedure in your organisation when purchasing resources?

In larger organisations, this may include a request form that is sent to the purchasing department, who will then process your requirements. In smaller businesses, you may be directly responsible for purchasing resources. For example. the head chef may order the food they need and the housekeeper may purchase cleaning materials. Where resources are used in a number of areas, you and your colleagues should decide who will do the purchasing.

It is first necessary to produce a purchase specification for each item. A purchase specification should detail exactly what qualities are required from that item, so that the supplier knows the standard you require. This then allows you to compare prices/quality between different suppliers.

Standard purchase specification
Fresh whole prawns (cooked)

Appearance – The prawns must be uniform in size
The prawns must display the characteristic colour of the species
Black spot or any other abnormal colouration is not acceptable
The prawns should have an odour characteristic of the species.
Objectionable odours such as sour, putrid or smelling of ammonia are unacceptable

Size of product – They should be of a size to give a count of 25 to the kilo

Eating quality – The flavour of the cooked product should be sweet and characteristic of the species
The texture should be firm
The colour should be pink
Sour/ bitter or rancid flavours are not acceptable
A soft texture is not permitted
A very slight cold storage flavour is acceptable
The salt content in the prawns should not exceed 2.5per cent

Packaging – Prawns should be wrapped to provide protection from contamination and physical damage and may be packed in ice. Products should be packed in units of 1 kg

Temperature – The temperature at time of delivery should be in the range of 0°C–4°C

Figure 3.2 Example of a purchase specification.

Evidence

What is the procedure for purchasing resources in your area? Produce the documentation that is used in your organisation for purchasing resources. Produce a purchase specification for an item used within your department, or place an example of one in your portfolio.
2.13, 2.15.

Consumption levels

Resources that are being stored are an expense to the organisation. Too much food being purchased leads to waste, and the purchasing policy should reflect the point at which resources are purchased.

This will be done by examining past records of consumption and estimating future use. Busy periods of trading will mean high levels of consumption of food and wine in a restaurant, for example, so higher quantities of food and wine need to be purchased. In quiet periods, there will be less purchasing of food and wine to avoid food waste and too-high levels of stock.

In larger organisations, where resources are monitored electronically, the computer will automatically process orders based on predetermined stock levels. However, as supervisor you still have to monitor these orders to ensure your purchasing reflects projected sales.

Just-in-time purchasing

Just-in-time purchasing is a policy that relies on ordering resources as needed – only limited stock is held within the unit. This purchasing policy requires you to monitor stock turnover closely, noting how quickly resources are used. It is also necessary that the supplier will be able to fulfil your order within the specified time period. This policy is used by large organisations, which can monitor consumption levels very accurately and guarantee supplies as needed. Just-in-time purchasing reduces resources being stored, wastage, and the opportunities for fraud within the unit.

However, when suppliers fail to deliver resources as required it can have a negative effect on service.

Case study

A chain restaurant had a pre-set menu: due to failure of the vegetable supplier to deliver lettuces on the day, the salads, making up 20 per cent of the menu, could not be served.

Suppliers

There are a number of different types of supplier from whom resources can be purchased. The choice of suppliers may be determined by the purchasing policy of a large organisation, or it may be influenced by the resources being purchased – it may only be possible to buy the item from one type of supplier. Your suppliers should be regarded as colleagues, and productive working relationships should be fostered with them so that the objectives of the organisation can be achieved (page 52).

Manufacturers

The manufacturer is the company that makes the product, and will have its name on the product (e.g. Hobart ovens, Hoover vacuum cleaners). You will be aware of brand-name products that are used in your area, and you may wish to purchase their items directly. A brewery could be described as a manufacturer supplying public houses in its area. Some breweries own public houses, while others just supply pubs with their products. Some manufacturers do not sell directly to catering outlets; others offer sales, distribution and servicing facilities.

Do not assume that the manufacturer will be the cheapest. Other suppliers may have purchased in bulk and be able to pass discounts on to customers, and the items may actually be cheaper than buying direct. For example, when buying a new dishwasher you may find the manufacturer is more expensive than a wholesaler or equipment distributor.

Wholesalers/distributors

A wholesaler will have purchased resources in large quantities for supply to individual organisations. Food wholesalers may specialise in meat, fish, dairy, pastry, or frozen or dried goods. Beverage wholesalers may supply beers, wines or soft drinks. Equipment distributors may have a showroom where you can go and physically look at the different manufacturers' equipment.

The wholesaler will have a sales team, which will advise you on new products, discounts and special promotions. In some cases, a sales advisor will contact you to take your order for resources on a daily, weekly or fortnightly basis, so that an order is secured.

Many hospitality organisations use specialist catering wholesalers to purchase resources.

Nominated suppliers

As a supervisor purchasing resources, you may be told to order from a nominated supplier. This is a supplier who has secured the contract to supply items to all the units within the organisation, and because of this commitment by the organisation, is able to offer preferable financial terms. If you are a supervisor working in a non-profit-making organisation (e.g. hospital or schools catering), or in a large organisation, you will probably purchase resources from a nominated supplier.

Cash-and-carry/market

In smaller catering organisations such as small hotels and restaurants, resources may be purchased from a cash-and-carry. As the name suggests, the purchaser has to go to the cash-and-carry premises and physically walk around, selecting the commodities they need. Having purchased and paid for the goods, it is up to the purchaser to transport the resources back to their outlet.

Cash-and-carry outlets offer benefits to small organisations – resources can be purchased in the quantities needed, and they are often better value than alternative suppliers. However, it takes time to travel to and from the cash-and-carry and to select and purchase the goods, which is an extra cost to the organisation.

Specialist food markets are the forerunner of the modern cash-and-carry, where the purchaser visits the market to select what they need and transport it back to the outlet.

As a head chef, you may visit a meat market, for example, to see what products are good value on a particular day.

Specialist suppliers

A specialist supplier is one which specialises in a particular product, such as wine or stationery, from whom you purchase because they are able to offer you something unique. For instance, as head sommelier you may have a number of specialist wine suppliers who each offer wine from a different region. These suppliers will be very knowledgeable about their products, and will be able to advise the organisation as to the best products to buy for its customers.

Retail outlets

As a supervisor in a small catering outlet, you may purchase resources from high street retail outlets. The proximity and convenience of these stores means that resources are purchased as needed and in small quantities. The cost of resources from these outlets is usually higher than from other suppliers, and in the case of equipment, care has to be taken that the items are suitable. For example, a domestic microwave does not have the capacity and power of a commercial one; in the same way, a domestic washing machine will not have the capacity of a commercial one. There are health and safety issues with using domestic products in a commercial unit as the products will not be as durable and may disintegrate, which could cause injury.

Local suppliers

The purchasing policy of the organisation may favour purchasing from local suppliers. Many head chefs may source food produced locally that reflects the specialities of the area, such as meat, cheeses, pork or fish. The supply of local produce may influence the menu and beverage choice offered to customers.

As a supervisor, you may purchase from just one of the types of supplier listed here, or from a number of different suppliers. Whichever one you choose, it is important that you are confident they can deliver the resources you need at the specified quality and price, within agreed financial budgets.

Ethical and environmental issues in purchasing

The purchasing of resources needs to be completed in line with the organisation's purchasing policy, and a part of this may be to take account of the environmental impact of your purchasing practices. As customers are becoming more aware of environmental issues and will judge organisations on their responsiveness, these issues will be of greater importance when making purchasing decisions.

Food miles

Food miles is a term that reflects how far the food you are buying has travelled. Purchasing from local suppliers and retail outlets that are based near the outlet will be more environmentally friendly than buying food that has been transported long distances from manufacturers and wholesalers. Increasingly, menus reflect this by stating where food is sourced.

Packaging

Packaging needs to be disposed of, and the organisation may have to pay to have its rubbish removed. You can reduce the cost of disposing of packaging by purchasing from suppliers who use limited packaging, or who supply goods in packaging that can be re-used (e.g. milk bottles, beverage bottles). Some suppliers may even reimburse you for recycling bottles and will take away packaging for you (e.g. wooden crates, pallets). The environmental impact of disposing of rubbish to landfill can be minimised by the reduction of packaging, and as supervisor you need to be aware of how you can do this.

Disposal of obsolete equipment

When you purchase new equipment, you need to be careful to dispose of the obsolete equipment in a way that causes least damage to the environment. The supplier may be able to give guidance and the local council should also be able to advise. If the equipment being replaced is still working, you may be able to sell it at auction or donate it to charity, although legal advice may be necessary here because it needs to work correctly. You should know what your organisation's procedures are for disposing of all waste, including equipment.

Receiving and issuing resources

Responsibility for the receipt of resources will depend on the organisation. If it is a large hotel, there may be a purchasing officer who will take responsibility for all resource purchasing, receipt and control until it is issued to the individual department.

In smaller organisations, it will be your responsibility as supervisor to receive the resources you have ordered. For example, the head chef will be the person who takes delivery of their order; the housekeeper will be responsible for the delivery of cleaning materials.

If you are responsible for the receipt of resources and are unavailable – perhaps it is your day off or you are busy – it is important that this duty is allocated to a responsible member of your team who has the necessary skills to perform this task, and who understands the returns policy and the checks that need to be made.

In order to cause minimum inconvenience, you may allocate a particular day and/or time for the delivery of orders, so that you can plan for this.

Checking quality and quantity

When resources are delivered, it is vital that a number of checks are completed by the person receiving them.

- Resources should be in the quantity required. They will need to be counted – do not assume that because you have ordered 40 oranges, 40 oranges will be delivered, despite what the delivery note may say.
- Resources should be of the quality required – check goods against your purchase specifications and physically examine goods for damage.
- The temperature of food items should be checked.
- The packaging of equipment should

be checked for damage to the goods enclosed.

○ The standard of cleanliness of the delivery vans should be checked (for food deliveries).

○ All purchases should be accompanied by a delivery note or invoice/receipt in the case of cash purchases.

As supervisor, you need to take action immediately if you have a problem. Resources that are not of the required quality should be rejected. Frozen goods that are thawed could cause food poisoning. Dried goods that are past their sell-by dates, beer kegs that are leaking beer, and substitute non-brand cleaners instead of the brand cleaners requested are all examples of sub-standard quality and should be returned.

Deficiencies in quantities should be noted on delivery notes and suppliers informed immediately so that you are not being charged for resources not received, and so that you have actioned what is needed to make up the order.

You need to take great care when receiving resources. Failure to ensure you get exactly what you purchased will affect the achievement of the organisation's financial objectives in the business plan.

Invoice checking, delivery notes and credit notes

This is a very important part of the purchasing process. An invoice is the bill a supplier sends, often with the goods, which asks you for payment. An invoice has to follow certain legal requirements (page 102). If the invoice is not sent at this point, the

supplier will send a delivery note, which looks almost the same as an invoice except that it does not ask for payment. The delivery note has to be signed, which means that the goods have been accepted, and after this point it becomes difficult to return something if it is damaged (unless the damage cannot be seen until the packages are opened, for example, mouldy biscuits in a closed tin). This may mean a cost to the organisation, which will affect the bottom line.

If the items are damaged, this is recorded on the delivery note or invoice, the supplier keeps a copy, as do you, and the goods are replaced. If the goods are not replaced immediately, a credit note is sent or issued there and then, which discounts the value of the damaged goods from the total on the invoice so that you pay the correct amount. The credit note must make reference to the right invoice!

You have to check that the invoice has the following information, which is a legal requirement.

○ The full company name of the invoicing company (e.g. The Beer4U).

○ Your business name and address (e.g. The Fish Inn, 14 Regent Road, Norwich, NL5 2PL).

Find out!

Find an invoice from a supplier to your company, or from your company to a customer, and look at the format of the invoice.

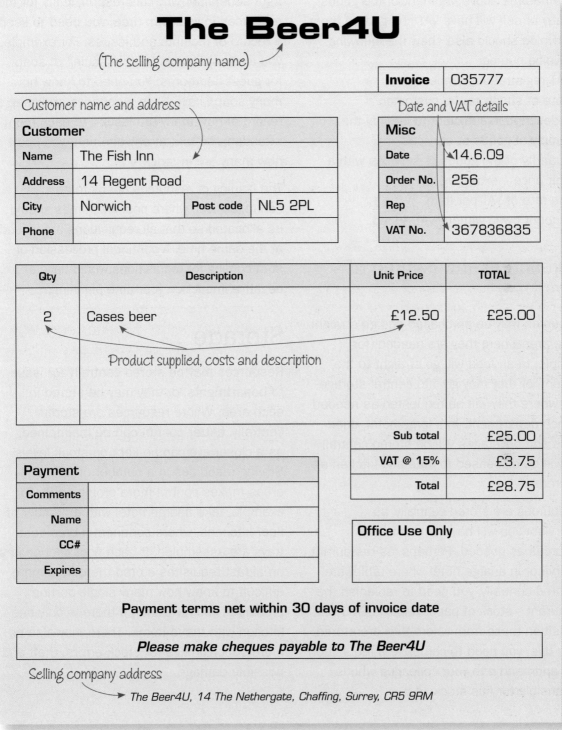

The Beer4U

(The selling company name)

Customer name and address

Date and VAT details

Customer	
Name	The Fish Inn
Address	14 Regent Road

City	Norwich	Post code	NL5 2PL
Phone			

Misc	
Date	14.6.09
Order No.	256
Rep	
VAT No.	367836835

Qty	Description	Unit Price	TOTAL
2	Cases beer	£12.50	£25.00

Product supplied, costs and description

Sub total	£25.00
VAT @ 15%	£3.75
Total	£28.75

Payment	
Comments	
Name	
CC#	
Expires	

Office Use Only

Payment terms net within 30 days of invoice date

Please make cheques payable to The Beer4U

Selling company address

The Beer4U, 14 The Nethergate, Chaffing, Surrey, CR5 9RM

Figure 3.3 Example of a supplier invoice.

As well as the above, as many of the goods you buy or sell will have VAT charged on them, the invoice should also show the following:

○ invoice number
○ VAT registration numbers
○ date of supply to the customer
○ a description sufficient to identify the supply of goods or services
○ quantity of the goods or services with a unit price – excluding VAT
○ the rate of VAT per item
○ amount owed without VAT added.

Requisition and issuing of resources

Resources may be purchased and go straight to the area where they are needed (for example, fresh food will go straight to the kitchen), or they may go into central storage, from where they will be requested as needed by each department. In a large hotel, dried goods and beverages will be stored centrally and will be dispensed to bars and kitchen as required.

If resources are stored centrally, as supervisor you will have to requisition resources as needed. Perhaps, as restaurant supervisor in a large hotel where tableware is stored centrally, you need to replenish the restaurant's stock of paper napkins. You will requisition these from where they are stored. To do this, you need to complete a requisition form and hand it to your colleague who is responsible for this stock.

As a supervisor who has responsibility for the resources in your own area, you need to keep a record of receipts and issues. For example, you are responsible for the issuing of soap for guest bedrooms. You need to know how many soaps have been purchased and keep a record of how many are issued to each room attendant, so that at any one time you know how many are in stock.

The issuing of resources needs to be controlled and, where possible, times should be allocated so that all requisitions are issued at the same time. A continual procession of staff coming for requisitions would have a negative impact on your time planning.

Storage

Resources may be stored centrally for issue to departments, or they may be stored in each area. Where resources are stored centrally, better control can be maintained, as a closer eye can be kept on stock levels. Storing resources in a number of different areas makes control more problematic. For example, take a large hotel with a number of floor kitchens, where continental breakfast trays are assembled. If each floor kitchen has breakfast requisites stored there, it is more difficult to know how many single-portion preserves you have than if there is only one kitchen with these items. There may also be more opportunities for stock errors, theft and possible damage.

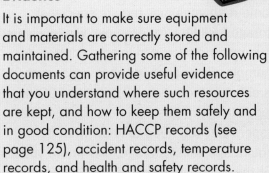
As a supervisor, you need to know the optimum storage conditions for all the resources used in your area. Stores need to be well designed to ensure the security of resources, with no access to unauthorised personnel or other individuals. Shelves, floors and wall surfaces should be of the correct specification in line with hygiene and health and safety legislation. The stores should be arranged in such a manner that goods are easy to find, and the placement of items should follow the layout of the stock record sheets, as discussed later (page 106).

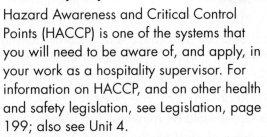

Law and policy

Hazard Awareness and Critical Control Points (HACCP) is one of the systems that you will need to be aware of, and apply, in your work as a hospitality supervisor. For information on HACCP, and on other health and safety legislation, see Legislation, page 199; also see Unit 4.

Frozen, chilled and room temperature storage

Resources need to be stored at the right temperature, and as supervisor you have to know the temperatures of the different types of storage.

Frozen storage

Here the temperature should be -18°C, and should be monitored carefully to make sure it remains constant. Where staff are working in frozen storage rooms for replenishing stock and stock-taking, protective clothing (e.g. gloves) has to be provided as a legal requirement (see page 132).

Chilled storage

Fresh food and some wines and beverages will be stored under chilled conditions of between 3 and 5°C. The chilled storage may be a walk-in chilled room or a refrigerator in the kitchen. The hygiene and safety of chilled foods is very important, and you need to ensure that all staff are trained when storing food in chilled conditions. For example, raw meat should never be stored above cooked meats, as the blood from raw food could drip onto the cooked meats, which could cause food poisoning. Chilled storage facilities need to be cleaned with an antibacterial cleaner frequently, and all food should be dated to ensure it is used in rotation.

Good practice

To ensure stock is used in rotation, use the FIFO rule: first in, first out.

Room temperature storage

Stationery, equipment, dried food goods, vegetables and fruit, beverages, crockery/ glassware, linen and cleaning fluids are all stored at temperatures of 16–18°C. Dried food items may be stored in stainless steel containers to prevent contamination. Goods in bags, such as flour, should never be left on the storeroom floor.

As supervisor, you need to make regular checks that equipment is being maintained and stored properly.

Where staff are responsible for lifting large quantities of packaged goods, for example, tins, or for lifting heavy items of equipment, they need to be given the appropriate training and provided with the necessary lifting equipment and protective clothing, including footwear. Staff must practise safe lifting techniques to avoid injury, especially back injury (page 108).

Risk assessment

You need to be aware of the health and safety risks that staff may encounter when using any of the different storage areas, and ensure a risk assessment is carried out for each area. Having identified the risks, you have a duty of care to ensure all staff are informed about them and trained to deal with them, and that reasonable attempts are made to minimise the risks. For example, when chairs are being stored in stacks, the number of chairs that can be stacked on top of one another should be specified to prevent the chairs falling over and hurting someone. A trolley needs to be provided for staff to guard against injury when lifting and moving chairs.

Specialist storage

Some resources may require specialist storage facilities, for example, wines, cigars, toxic materials used in leisure centres, for example, water purifying chemicals, such as chlorine (see page 132 on the COSHH Regulations) or gas canisters for beverage dispensing. You need to know what items require specialist storage, and where you can get the information you need to store these resources properly. One London restaurant stored all its expensive wine in a specially-made wine cellar off the premises and requested bottles as required.

Advice may be sought from the Fire Authorities, the Health and Safety Executive and Environmental Health if you need advice on specific questions related to storage of resources.

Security of resources

The security of resources is important to prevent stealing by staff and customers. From the point of delivery, all resources should be kept secure and not left unattended; when resources are delivered they should be stored immediately and not left unattended in corridors, open-access areas or stairwells. All resources should be kept securely, ideally under lock and key. Storerooms should be kept locked and should be accessed only by authorised staff. The number of key-holders should be minimised to prevent large numbers of staff having access. Freezers and refrigerators should be locked when not in use and during quiet periods.

Unfortunately, fraud and stealing happen in every organisation, and as supervisor you should lead the way by being seen to protect the organisation's resources. Staff should be aware of the serious nature of stealing, and where a member of staff is caught stealing, disciplinary action should be taken. Where the security of resources is causing concern, the installation of closed-circuit television (CCTV) to monitor activity in storerooms may be considered, and frequent physical stock-takes should be introduced.

Stock control

'Stock control' is a wide-ranging term which covers:
○ setting stock-holding levels
○ keeping stock records
○ physical stock-taking.

As a supervisor, you need to have knowledge of each of these areas. Stock control is a vital measuring tool for how your department is operating.

Setting stock-holding levels

To have too much stock of a resource is a waste of space and is not cost-effective. If stock-holdings of some resources are too high, there is always a danger of perishable items deteriorating before they can be used – for example, food and beverage products have an ideal shelf life or use-by date. This may cause profit loss.

Too low a stock-holding of resources can lead to negative customer service. Also, having to make frequent purchases is time-consuming and not always cost-efficient;

if you need products quickly you may be obliged to pay more for them if you have not had time to negotiate on price. For example, as supervisor of a sandwich bar, if you do not have enough eggs in stock to make the egg mayonnaise filling, you may be forced to buy eggs from a local retailer which is more expensive than your normal egg supplier. The time to go to collect the eggs will also cost money.

What then is the ideal stock-holding level? This will depend on many factors:
○ menu/beverage range
○ extent of your services – limited trading hours, or open for longer periods
○ forecasted trading figures – number of expected customers
○ suppliers that you use and their delivery schedules, if appropriate
○ available storage space – you may have limited space and therefore be unable to store extra stock
○ shelf life
○ financial considerations – cashflow, favourable trading terms that make larger purchases more profitable
○ price movements and anticipated market conditions – if you know the price of a resource is going to rise, or it is going to become scarce, you may purchase more.

Each organisation will determine its stock-holding levels. As a supervisor in a large organisation, you will probably be told this information; in small organisations you will need to find it out. Accurate stock control and stock-taking are vital in order to monitor your department's productivity.

Stock records

In order to control the movement of resources in and out of the organisation, there should be stock records for all resources. These may include the use of the following.

- Ordering books – where all purchases ordered are noted, with the date of order.
- Goods received book – when goods are received, all the details are noted as printed on the delivery note or invoice. Where the delivery note does not include prices, this information should be taken from the invoice on its receipt.
- Stock cards/**bin cards** – each resource is allocated its own stock card, on which the purchases, issues, price and re-order points can be recorded. In larger organisations each item will have a pre-printed stock card; smaller organisations may not have these as stock is used almost immediately.

Item: Tomato and herb sauce		Size: 2.25 kg			
Supplier: Brake		Price: £3.95			

Date	Ref	In	Out	Bal
22.2.09	Bal B/F			3
24.2.09	Brake	6		9
24.2.09	Main kitchen		5	4
26.2.09	Brasserie kitchen		2	2
1.3.09	Brake	6		8

Maximum holding – 12 Minimum holding – 2
Reorder point: 4

Figure 3.4 Example of a bin card.

- Stock summary sheets – these should list all the resources in each area, and will be completed when a physical stock-check is completed with the total number of each item, its cost price and a total of all resources. This is used for financial calculations such as gross profits and stock turnover.

Computerised stock records

Technological advances and increasing use of computers within hospitality organisations mean that there are now a range of computer software programs for resource control. These computerised control packages use databases that are customised for different areas (such as reservations, reception, restaurant and beverage sales, accommodation, resource control).

The computerised control system is used for stock control in the same way as described above. Purchases are entered for each stock item, and when these items are issued or sold, the stock is adjusted accordingly. Pre-set stock levels will automatically generate a purchase order, and at the end of trading periods the stock-holding level and its financial value will be readily available.

The advantages of computerised stock control include:

○ pre-set stock levels ensure resources are ordered as needed
○ levels can be easily accessed, although you will need to verify this with a physical stock-check
○ the financial value of stock can be quickly obtained
○ you can track the issuing of items to each department
○ fraud can be highlighted
○ trends in usage can be tracked so that you can adjust stock levels or identify problems.

However, any computer package is only as good as the data entered, and staff need to be trained in using the software. The system needs to be backed up regularly, and contingency measures need to be in place in case the system fails – if the system goes down, you may have to revert to a manual stock-control system.

Physical stock-taking

A physical stock-take of all resources should be carried out frequently. If you suspect that there is fraud, stock-takes of expensive items – such as meat, expensive wines or spirits – may be carried out daily to compare stock used with sales recorded in order to monitor sales and stock levels.

Resources should be held in central storage with their own bin cards. Each item should be counted or weighed and compared with the quantity recorded on the **bin card**. If bin cards are not used, the items should be counted and listed on stock record sheets. A computerised stock package will have a record of what stock should be in each department, and this needs to be verified by physically checking each item.

In some organisations, an independent stock-taker will be employed, and you will be expected to ensure this person is able to conduct the stock-take effectively and efficiently by having the necessary records up to date and readily available. This system is particularly used in public houses.

Evidence

Collect or identify records used in your department to control resources, and identify any deficiencies. Produce a flow chart of the control process that identifies the appropriate record for each stage a resource item passes through, from ordering it to using it in your organisation – this can be a food item, beverage, stationery, linen, equipment or cleaning product.
2.22, 2.26.

Health and safety

Unfortunately, within the hospitality industry, accidents and injuries happen in all departments. Slips and trips remain the single most common cause of major injury in UK workplaces, the occupations most affected being kitchen assistants, chefs and waiting staff. Manual handling accounts for the second-highest cause of accidents resulting from lifting and carrying loads, pushing, pulling and handling materials, and injuries from sprains and strains (source: www.hse.gov.uk).

Dermatitis (see page 120) is one of the main causes of ill health for catering staff (chefs, cooks and catering assistants). If you are the head chef supervising kitchen staff, or the housekeeping supervisor, you need to attempt to minimise staff contact with cleaning products, food and water where possible, for example, by using a dishwasher rather than washing up by hand, and by advising staff to use utensils and/or wear protective gloves rather than their hands when dealing with food.

As a supervisor, you have to be aware of all the dangers your staff may encounter at work. In kitchens, cuts and burns are a problem. Customers becoming aggressive and violent can also be a problem for many frontline staff, especially in bars and nightclubs. In leisure centres, the use of chemicals can pose dangers. The Health and Safety Executive is the government department that deals specifically with health and safety issues, and it produces a number of publications to help you deal with dangers in the workplace (see page 121).

Legislation

The main legislation covering health and safety in the workplace is the Health and Safety at Work Act 1974 (for more information see Unit 4, page 122).

Using resources effectively and efficiently

Resources within the organisation have to be used effectively and efficiently to achieve the business objectives. You should monitor your team's use of resources to make sure they are being used properly and as efficiently as possible.

Case study

A restaurant supervisor finds that a computerised restaurant system with hand-held terminals to take customer orders has been installed while she was on holiday. On her return to work, she discovers that the staff are still taking customers' orders manually, so this expensive resource is not being used effectively or efficiently. She needs to take action to ensure staff are confident using the new system.

She arranges a staff meeting to discuss the benefits to them, and to the organisation, of using the computerised system. She asks them what problems or worries they have about using the system. Having identified specific problems, she can arrange training to address these issues, including one-to-one training for staff who need more support. She then appoints some team members to take orders using the new system, and asks other members to shadow them, building up a 'buddy' system. She is available to support staff during the 'bedding down' of the new system. She then sits down again with the team to review how it has gone.

Why is it important to monitor?

Resources are a cost to your organisation, and these costs need to be monitored to ensure financial targets are reached and the business plan is achieved. As a supervisor, you need to know the budget for your area, and you need to be aware of costs in your area. The head chef has to monitor the costs of food production, and the restaurant supervisor has to monitor the costs of supplies used to serve customers.

Energy costs, staff costs and equipment costs all have to be monitored to ensure that you can identify patterns of usage and note unusual patterns.

Case study

The housekeeper has received details of energy costs in her area, and discovers that they have risen sharply over the past month. When she investigates, she discovers that the heating system has been left on all the time, and that the automatic thermostats are not working properly. The first thing she does is to get the automatic thermostats fixed. Secondly, she identifies when the heating is needed, and communicates that to staff. She appoints one or two people to be responsible for the heating. Finally, she lets all staff know about the cost to the business of wasted energy, and issues notices reminding staff to switch off appliances.

Evidence

You must make sure that resources are used efficiently and effectively, and that you and your staff know how to use resources in line with your organisational and legal requirements. Equipment inventories, stock records, health and safety documentation, health and safety posters, accident records, risk assessments and minutes of meetings are all useful evidence of your knowledge.
1.6, 1.8, 1.10, 2.19, 2.23, 2.24, 2.25.

The efficient monitoring of resources also includes the monitoring of waste in each area. In the kitchen, much of the food is perishable, and if not stored and cooked properly it is wasted. Overcooking or burning food is a waste, and as the food cannot be served to customers there is a cost implication that will need to be monitored and accounted for.

Waste also occurs in all areas of hospitality organisations, from wasting paper to cleaning staff wasting cleaning products by not measuring out exact quantities (this may also result in poorly cleaned areas).

You must monitor resources to ensure that theft and fraud is not happening.

Case study

A head receptionist notices that her photocopying costs have risen sharply. By monitoring use over a timed period, she notices that the photocopier is being used more when one member of staff is on duty. When the staff member is questioned, it emerges that they are doing photocopying for their friends. This is stealing of the organisation's resources, and the staff member is disciplined.

How do you monitor?

How monitoring is carried out will depend on which type of resource is being examined. Monitoring is important in all areas of the business.

Food and beverages

Monitoring of the efficient use of food and beverage resources is carried out as follows.

○ Assessment of financial results – was the projected gross profit achieved? Were the food costs within budget?

○ Customer satisfaction surveys – were customers happy with the food and beverages they received? As a supervisor, you may carry out formal customer surveys to gain customer feedback, such as short questionnaires. Staff need to be trained to ask customers about their satisfaction with their meals, and this information needs to be recorded. Both complaints and compliments received will give you information about the quality of the food and beverages.

○ Assessment of waste – kitchen waste and plate waste all needs to be recorded. If there is a lot of waste in food production, this may indicate that the food is poor quality and attention needs to be given to purchasing, storage and stock turnover, or it may indicate a problem with production. Plate waste can indicate that portion sizes are too large.

○ Drink/bar waste – wastage will occur when beers and ales are dispensed from kegs and barrels, through pipe cleaning and at the start of service periods; care has to be taken that staff are trained to minimise this waste. Opening wine before service is another form of waste in the bar, and you should train staff not to open excess bottles of wine. It is also important to train staff not to throw away drinks that have been wrongly dispensed; keeping a waste log is a useful record to allow analysis of the reasons and to pre-empt stock shortages.

○ Staff assessment – your staff should be asked about the food and beverages they are using: are they happy with the supplies they are receiving and the production of meals and beverages? For example, staff in a coffee shop were unhappy with the quality of the coffee being purchased. Coffee sales started to fall, and when the financial results indicated a loss of profit, the staff were quick to point out that they had voiced concerns to their supervisor over the coffee. As a supervisor, you need to communicate with your staff about the resources they are using.

○ Stock turnover – the movement of stock in and out of the organisation indicates how efficiently food and beverages are being used. Where a food item is not being used, this indicates that there is a problem with this product and it may need to be replaced. For example, if you have had a quantity of one soft beverage in stock for over a year with low sales, this indicates low customer demand, and future ordering of this product should be reviewed. In some such cases, this stock is '**written off**'.

Definition

Write off: remove or disregard a worthless asset from an account.

Equipment

Equipment costs money to purchase and run, and therefore has to work efficiently and effectively. So how can you monitor this?

Evidence

All the points on the previous page can be used to gather evidence to monitor the use of resources in your area of responsibility. Write a report in which you discover ways of making better use of resources according to your organisational requirements.
1.7, 1.8, 1.10, 2.1, 2.2, 2.24, 2.25.

○ Ask staff for their opinions about the equipment. Do they find it easy to use? Does it save them time, or is it too difficult to operate so they do not use it? For example, you may have a food processor in the kitchen, but staff may not use it because it takes too long to assemble or to clean after use.

○ Record the frequency of equipment usage – for equipment stored centrally, you can look at the bin card and work out how often the equipment is being used. For equipment stored in your department, you can keep a note of how often the equipment is being used.

○ Analyse the accident book – one piece of equipment may be responsible for causing more accidents than another. For example, the gravity feed slicer for cutting meats may be causing cuts if the blade is stiff and staff are pushing it with their hands.

○ Repair manual – as supervisor you need to keep an inventory of all equipment in your area. This inventory record should also show details of servicing and repairs. By examining these records, you may identify that a piece of equipment often breaks down or needs parts changed frequently. For example, as housekeeping supervisor you notice that one brand of vacuum cleaner needs replacing before another brand you use. This indicates that there is a problem with this brand and that it is not suitable for your needs.

○ Computer system failure – the amount of time that a computer system is non-functional should be recorded.

○ Assess energy usage – equipment's energy usage can be monitored to assess its efficiency in comparison with that stated by the equipment manufacturer.

Evidence

Keep records about resources up to date, accurate and in the specified place. Check that all staff know where to find them.
1.9.

Catering sundries, stationery, laundry and ancillary items

The use of these resources can be monitored by the following means.

○ Financial targets – was expenditure in these areas within the agreed budget?

○ Wastage and damage – stationery is often wasted by not being stored properly and by only using one side of the paper for printing. Using paper napkins instead of cloths to mop up spills is another form of wastage. Damage to glasses, crockery and cutlery, where the item cannot be used due to poor handling and/or carelessness, is inefficient.

○ Replacement of items – you need to know which items are being replaced frequently. In many restaurants, cutlery often needs replacing because it gets thrown into the bin with the waste food.

○ Stock-takes – to enable you to see which goods are being purchased, and whether this is in line with expectations, stock-takes of non-food resources need to be done. For instance, you may do a stock-take of detergent for the in-house laundry and discover that more has been used than you would expect for this period. This may indicate that the detergent is not being used efficiently, and instead of being measured accurately, is just being thrown into the washing machines. As a supervisor, you need to know why stock is being used.

○ Fitness for purpose – the right resource has to be used for the right job. White wine glasses should be used for white wine and not for the service of soft drinks, which should be served in tumblers. You need to check that staff are using the correct item for the job, and you can monitor this by checking staff as they carry out their duties. Training of staff is also very important.

Energy

With the rise in the cost of energy prices and the environmental awareness of energy wastage, you need to know how to monitor energy consumption.

○ Financial targets – is expenditure in your area within the agreed budget?

○ Benchmarks – how does your energy consumption compare with industry standards? For example, water consumption per guest can be calculated and compared with figures from similar hotels.

○ Wastage – being aware of wastage by staff can help you monitor efficiency. Using the dishwasher a quarter full is inefficient, and wasteful of water and energy.

○ Meters – water, electricity, oil and gas meters allow use to be monitored in between invoices received by the organisation.

○ Computer software – specialised computer programs can be used to monitor energy consumption, and these allow you to identify trends in energy consumption.

Monitoring how resources are used is a necessary part of the control process that you, as a supervisor, have to oversee in order to meet the organisation's objectives.

Evidence

Find out how resources are monitored for effectiveness and efficiency in your area. Are there any other ways in which you could monitor these resources? How difficult is it to calculate this information?

1.7, 1.8, 1.10, 2.22, 2.25.

Environmental impact

The purchase and use of resources has an impact on both the organisation and the environment. This impact starts with the resources that are going to be used, and how and where they have been produced. Customers are used to having a wide choice of goods, many having been transported long distances, and organisations have to decide whether to offer these goods to customers. These choices may be influenced by financial considerations. For example, it may be cheaper to purchase soaps produced in China than soaps made in the UK.

Some catering outlets purchase from local suppliers or grow their own food, seeking to minimise environmental damage (see page 98 for more information on food miles). The purchase of equipment that is effective and efficient will mean that it will last longer and will not need replacing as often, and will have an impact on equipment disposal. Your choice of supplier for resources may be influenced by environmental considerations, such as where the supplies have to travel from.

You need to know about the environmental impact of disposing of waste, and consider the most efficient means of doing so. Your organisation is very likely to have policies on recycling, but all staff can make suggestions to management to improve these policies, and everyone can do their bit to recycle. Recyclable packaging should be separated out and disposed of in the correct manner (glass bottles to bottle banks; paper should be shredded if confidential; tins and cans; cardboard; batteries and printer cartridges can all be recycled). Food waste should ideally be composted, oil from fat fryers can be recycled, and many catering outlets are now selling their cooking oil for road fuel. Boxes can be compressed to make them more compact while they are waiting for disposal.

Does your organisation recycle?

Energy use in your organisation has environmental consequences. Water is becoming a scarce resource, and global warming and the shortage of natural fuel sources means that everyone ought to conserve their energy resources.

Communicating with staff

As a supervisor you need to educate staff and customers about the consequences of wasting energy and try to reduce energy consumption when possible. Staff should be involved in discussions about using energy efficiently and encouraged to propose changes that can be made to help save energy. By involving staff in developing environmental policy-making, staff will be more committed to putting these changes into action (see page 38).

Once these changes have been agreed, staff may need training so that these energy-saving measures can be practised as they undertake their duties. Cleaning sinks by using plugs and not letting taps run are two very simple measures that can quickly be adopted by room attendants. Not keeping all the computers on standby, and shutting down computers while they are not being used, saves electricity at reception. Turning down heating, as opposed to opening windows, in the restaurant can cut the restaurant's heating bill.

As supervisor you lead by example, and you should be seen by staff to be aware of the environmental impact of using resources effectively and efficiently. When energy resources are monitored and recorded, staff should be informed about the results and congratulated if energy expenditure is decreased.

Technological innovations

Technological innovations in the production of equipment reflect environmental concerns – for example, energy star ratings on electrical appliances reflect the equipment's energy efficiency.

As a supervisor purchasing resources, you need to conduct some background research on the technical innovations for that product, so that you are aware of the latest developments and their benefits before making a decision. Purchasing low-energy light bulbs instead of normal bulbs is an effective way of saving energy, as the higher cost of such bulbs is quickly recouped. Technological innovations in food production can mean that some frozen food items are

nutritionally superior to fresh (frozen peas, for example, are excellent and may be purchased as a replacement for fresh ones).

The area in which technological innovation has been greatest is in computer systems and software packages which allow monitoring of resources to be carried out with greater speed and in more detail, which helps with analysing the results.

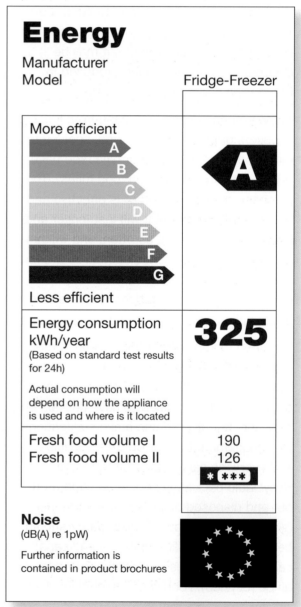

Figure 3.5 Example energy label for a fridge-freezer.

Presenting recommendations to decision-makers

As a supervisor who is responsible for using resources effectively and efficiently, you will need to make recommendations about the resources you need, their purchase, control and use to those who make decisions in the organisation.

You need to know who these decision-makers are, and the formal channels of communication you need to follow within your organisation. In a small organisation your manager may be the decision-maker and you can communicate your recommendations in a meeting. In a large organisation you may be required to present your recommendations in writing to your departmental manager, who will forward them up the organisational hierarchy.

Recommendations need to be presented with justification. Is there a business case for making the recommended changes? Is it going to result in cost savings, reduce staff time, enhance customer satisfaction, be environmentally friendly?

As a supervisor, you will play an important role in achieving the objectives of your organisation, and the control of resources is a fundamental part of this. It is your responsibility to ensure you and your staff use resources effectively and efficiently.

Good practice

Recommendations may be presented verbally to decision-makers, and as a supervisor you need to be aware of the importance of preparing for such meetings with all the necessary facts and figures. Where staff are involved in proposing recommendations, they should be acknowledged and informed as to the final decision.

Test yourself!

1 What resources do you, as supervisor, have to control?

2 Why is it important to manage your time effectively?

3 What influences the purchasing policy of an organisation?

4 What is just-in-time purchasing, and what are its advantages and disadvantages?

5 What are the different types of suppliers from whom you can buy food and beverages?

6 Why is correct and secure storage important?

7 Identify the different types of stock records used for control of beverages.

8 What are the two key requirements of the Health and Safety at Work Act 1974?

9 How would you monitor the effective and efficient use of equipment?

10 How can hospitality organisations minimise the effects of their use of resources on the environment?

Further information

Health and Safety Executive – www.hse.gov.uk

HS4

Maintain the health, hygiene, safety and security of the working environment

This chapter covers the following units:

- Level 3 Diploma Hospitality Supervision and Leadership (NVQ) Unit HSL4: Maintain the health, hygiene, safety and security of the working environment
- Technical Certificate Unit 1: Leading a team in the hospitality industry – 3.1, 3.2, 3.3, 3.5, 3.6, 3.7, 3.8.

Working through this chapter could also provide evidence for the following key skills:

- C2.1a, C2.1b, C2.2, C2.3, N2.1.

In this chapter you will learn about:

- health and safety legislation
- Hazard Analysis and Critical Control Points (HACCP)
- Control of Substances Hazardous to Health Regulations 2004 (COSHH)
- Reporting of Injuries, Diseases and Dangerous Occurences Regulations (RIDDOR)
- Fire Regulatory Reform (Fire Safety) Order (2005)
- emergency procedures
- food safety
- security.

Likely sources of evidence

1.1 make sure you have information on the health, hygiene, safety and security procedures that apply to your area of responsibility
Find documents relating to the above.

1.2 make sure colleagues have relevant information on the health, hygiene, safety and security issues within your area of responsibility
Have relevant information in a readily accessible place.

1.3 make colleagues aware of the importance of following health, hygiene, safety and security procedures
Induction/initial training records for staff for all of the above. COSHH product sheets for all chemicals used in your department – signpost where they can be found. Make reference to this when doing a PD. Reference to any internal procedures and policies relating to security. Reference to your job description.

1.4 check that colleagues follow the health, hygiene, safety and security procedures in your area of responsibility
Records of H&S checks e.g. temperature checks, hygiene checks etc. or PD discussing with your assessor how you monitor this in your area of responsibility. Equipment safety checks.

1.5 monitor your area of responsibility for risks to health, hygiene, safety and security
Risk assessment documentation. Evidence of dealing with reporting equipment faults to e.g. a line manager or a supplier. Health risk e.g. a torn tile. Hygiene risk e.g. checking whether a product will still provide hygienic cleaning if used in cold water. Reports of breaches of security. Accident book entry.

1.5 deal with risks and accidents promptly, following organisational and legal requirements for safeguarding customers and staff
Dates on documents that show risk was identified and actioned promptly or accident dealt with quickly – an audit trail.

1.6 record or report risks and any health, hygiene, safety or security action taken, following organisational procedures
Hazard analysis records. Reporting of risks of the above. If low-level risk could be a minute of a meeting or orally by telephone in which case evidence may be a witness statement or a memo. Hygiene audits. Temp records. Equipment checklists. Reference to either org policy or/and a PD.

1.7 pass on information about how health, hygiene, safety or security procedures are working
Safety data sheets accessible. Minutes of meetings. Witness testimonies from colleagues including those who are non-English speaking. Training records.

1.8 make suggestions as to how health, hygiene, safety or security procedures can be improved
Memos or witness statements. Emails. Minutes of one-to-one and team meetings. Production of charts for use of chemicals. Production of posters for safety or security procedures.

Introduction

This unit is about maintaining health, safety, security and hygiene standards relevant to your area of responsibility, and also knowing what is outside your authority, and how and to whom to report it. Maintaining these standards is essential in protecting staff and customers from harm.

As a supervisor, you will be involved in monitoring procedures to maintain health and safety, and in the training of staff, particularly within your department. It is usually the managers, in fact the senior managers, who draw up the policies and procedures, and it is down to the supervisors to ensure they are followed correctly and that the recording systems are kept up to date.

Every business will have its own way of distributing the responsibility for health and safety. As long as the legal requirements are met, an organisation can allocate responsibility as it sees fit – for example, in a small organisation the manager may be the one to collate health and safety information, whereas in a large hotel the supervisors may play a major role in this.

For a business of five or more employees, a health and safety policy must be written down (see page 122). If you are the supervisor in a three-person kitchen, you still need to train the staff about health and safety issues, and you must abide by the law (see page 124).

You may also have a role in investigating why certain things have gone wrong, and like all employees you have a responsibility to suggest improvements and to notify the management of things that contravene, or almost contravene, the law (such as badly-stored stationery, bare wires on a piece of equipment, flooring that is becoming a trip hazard) (see the Health and Safety at Work Act, page 122).

As a supervisor, you will be involved in training staff in health and safety, and possibly also food hygiene and security issues. Staff will expect you to answer their queries about health and safety, as you are their first port of call when it comes to notifying the management of health and safety issues.

Your responsibilities are summarised as:

o Monitor health and safety in your department by dealing with and/or reporting hazards, collate information on health and hygiene procedures (e.g. fridge and freezer temperatures) and make sure these procedures are being followed by the staff you supervise.
o Organise or carry out **risk assessments**, keep records of accidents, collate cooking temperature information, and/or report equipment failure.

Definition

Risk assessment: an assessment of risk that supposes the worst can happen and tries to identify any uncertainties.

o Train staff to comply with health and safety and other regulations, such as food hygiene, provide induction of new employees, provide refresher training when skills are rarely used; food safety and security, and organise emergency procedures. Check that these regulations are being followed.

○ Pass on information relating to how health, hygiene, safety and security procedures are working and how they can be improved.

○ Develop good working relationships: be aware of staff abusing alcohol and/or drugs, both of which can lead to serious accidents and sometimes to dismissal.

○ For security reasons, you may control the issuing of keys to staff, keep staff records, open up and close down the booking system on the computer or in the kitchen, do stock-taking, etc.

Why is health and safety so important?

In 2007–08, 3.5 million working days were lost due to accidents at work: that is, 1.5 days per year per worker. That means 30 million days off due to work-related ill health, and 6 million due to workplace injury. Maintaining the health, hygiene, safety and security of the working environment is one of the most important parts of a manager or a supervisor's job, because accidents can cost lives.

All industries in Britain are governed by different **legislation**. The hospitality industry has to comply with many laws, not only those dealing with health and safety, but also weights and measures legislation, financial laws, employment law, working-time regulations and the Data Protection Act, to name just a few.

Definition

Legislation: a set of laws concerning a particular area or activity.

Accidents

According to data from the Health and Safety Executive (HSE):

○ accidents cost one company 37 per cent of its profits in 2006–07

○ there were four reported fatalities in the hospitality industry in 2006–07

○ in 2007, 1,863 people received an injury that kept them off work for more than three days

○ 640 employees in hotels and catering suffered a major injury (many resulting in broken bones)

○ in 2006–07, 52 per cent of major injuries to employees in hotels and catering were a result of slips or trips; handling, lifting or carrying accounted for around 15 per cent

○ the only ill-health condition that occurs at a markedly higher rate, compared with industry in general, is **dermatitis**.

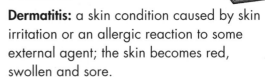

Definition

Dermatitis: a skin condition caused by skin irritation or an allergic reaction to some external agent; the skin becomes red, swollen and sore.

Good practice

Remember, accidents don't just happen – they can be prevented.

In the hospitality industry, most accidents at work are caused by:

o slips, trips and falls
o handling, lifting and carrying
o exposure to steam and chemicals (harmful substances)
o being struck by moving or falling objects or machinery
o ill health from chronic **musculoskeletal** disorders and dermatitis.

Definition

Musculoskeletal: relating to the muscles and skeleton together.

This unit looks at how to prevent workplace accidents, which have the potential to cause permanent injury and even death. The health of employers and employees is paramount.

Health and safety legislation

As a supervisor, you need to know some laws more fully than others, as they are the ones that fall under your responsibility at work. For example, you may have to monitor fridge and freezer temperatures, or comply with the Data Protection Act when storing customers' private data when they book into the hotel. You are also responsible for the staff under your care, and any customers your department deals with.

The Health and Safety Executive

The HSE is the body responsible for the promotion, regulation and enforcement of workplace health, safety and welfare, and for research into occupational risks in England and Wales and Scotland. Laws relating to health and safety are entrusted to the Health and Safety Commission (HSC), appointed by the Secretary of State for Transport, Local Government and the Regions.

The HSE and local government are the enforcing authorities that support the work of the Commission. The mission of the HSE is to enforce the health and safety laws in order to protect people's health and safety by ensuring risks in the changing workplace are properly controlled (source: www.parliament.uk).

It is important to understand the difference between an **Act of Parliament** and **Regulations**.

Definitions

Act of Parliament: creates a new law or changes an existing law (primary legislation). Once implemented, an Act is law and applies to the UK as a whole, or to specific areas of the country. An Act may come into force immediately, on a specific starting date, or in stages.
Regulations: (secondary legislation), made up of Statutory Instruments, often referred to as 'regulations' (source: www.hse.gov.uk).

A significant amount of primary legislation that affects the hospitality industry is owned by the HSE.

The HSE also owns a significant amount of secondary legislation.

The law is split into two types:
○ **civil law** deals with disputes between individuals, and with claims or agreements – this is where one person takes another to court over a particular issue
○ **criminal law** protects society and aims to punish as a deterrent – here it is the State (e.g. the HSE) that takes a person or a business to court because the law has been broken.

Health and Safety at Work Act 1974 (HASAW)

The Health and Safety at Work etc. Act 1974 exists to protect people at work and the general public. Under the Act, everyone at work has a legal duty to uphold certain standards of health, safety and welfare. This includes:
○ employees
○ employers
○ the self-employed
○ suppliers and importers
○ those who control premises.

This Act is designed to make work healthier and safer. Specifically, it aims to:
○ secure the health, safety and welfare of persons at work
○ protect the general public against risks
○ control the possession, storage and use of dangerous substances
○ control the discharge of certain substances.

Duties of employers

Under the Act, employers must ensure the health, safety and welfare of their employees, so far as is 'reasonably practicable'. This means that your employer must:
○ ensure the health and safety of their employees and those (such as contractors and customers) who might be affected by their activities, so far as reasonably practicable
○ prepare a statement of safety policy and the arrangements for achieving the policy (written if you employ five or more people).
○ consult employees, through a safety representative if the workplace is unionised, or if it is not unionised, through an employee representative, or directly
○ appoint someone competent to assist with health and safety
○ assess which workplace risks are significant
○ make effective arrangements to control these risks
○ carry out health surveillance where appropriate (e.g. in catering, for dermatitis or musculoskeletal risks).
○ set up emergency procedures, including those for temporary workers (in hospitality these are only likely to be for fire and gas leaks)
○ inform and train employees on the risks present and the arrangements in place to control them – record this training
○ coordinate procedures and work safely with others (in hospitality these are likely to be landlords, maintenance staff and catering engineers)

○ provide protective clothing, equipment and safety devices

○ have all relevant information in a readily-accessible place for you and your staff, including displaying the official HASAW Notice (see below).

Figure 4.1 The Health and Safety Law poster.

Evidence

Walk around your workplace to observe where the information on health, hygiene, safety and security is displayed. Can any improvements be made in the positioning of posters or folders? Do staff know where to look to find the health and safety information they need? Pass on any information about how the display of information or procedures can be improved.
HSL 1.1, 1.2, 1.9, 2.6, 2.7, 2.9, 2.10.

Duties of employees

Employees should take reasonable care for the health and safety of themselves and others affected by their actions or omissions while working. This means you are responsible for what you do – and what you don't do. This means you must:

○ cooperate with your employer's procedures or equipment put in place for health and safety purposes at work

○ never treat things provided for health and safety purposes disrespectfully (horseplay)

○ be aware of potential health and safety hazards

○ attend training provided during work hours by the employer.

Role of health and safety representatives

Full details of their role are set out in the Safety Representatives and Safety Committees Regulations 1977. In a small business, the supervisor, after receiving appropriate training, may also be the health and safety representative for the department.

As they then represent the workforce, apart from their normal monitoring duties, they should actively promote worker involvement by:

o participating in activities (e.g. employer/employee/enforcing authority discussions)
o communicating effectively and regularly with the wider workforce
o cooperating with managers to ensure workers' concerns are acknowledged and responded to, as well as being consulted by managers over health and safety issues
o championing health and safety by setting a good example.

Implications of breaking the law

The local authority **Environmental Health Officer** (EHO) and the HSE inspectors have the same role, but they inspect different types of premises. The hospitality industry is inspected by the local authority. This means that if the law is broken, it will be the EHO employed by the local authority (borough council) who will take the business to court. If your organisation is within a public sector building, then it may be inspected by the HSE.

Definition

Environmental Health Officer: representative of local government who advises on and enforces public health standards.

When an inspector visits your premises, he or she will inspect it for health and safety, food hygiene and food standards. The inspector may arrive without prior notice, and could do any of the following:

o follow up complaints and investigate outbreaks of food poisoning, infectious disease or pests
o collect samples for laboratory testing, take photographs, talk to staff
o enforce environmental health laws, look at working practices, the workplace, your management of health and safety, your legal compliance
o investigate accidents at work
o advise the business about related topics
o keep records and write a report.

If the inspector finds a breach of the HASAW at a workplace, they have the right to:

o serve an improvement notice – this means an employer has to take action to put things right within a specified time (e.g. install a light in a dark area at a workplace to minimise the risk of an accident)
o serve a prohibition notice – this means an employer has to stop a hazardous operation if there is an immediate risk of danger to workers or to the general public (e.g. a meat slicer without a working guard will be labelled 'do not use' and have a yellow and black tape stuck round it, or could be removed from the premises by the inspector if he or she feels the employer will simply remove the sign and continue to use it).

Penalties

In the event of non-compliance with the legislation described, or in the case of a severe breach of the law, the EHO may prosecute (take an organisation or an individual to court). Failure to comply with an improvement or prohibition notice could result in a fine of up to £20,000 or six months' imprisonment, or both. Unlimited fines can be imposed by the High Court.

Apart from the HASWA, there are other Acts that apply to the hospitality industry with regard to safety and security, including the Food Safety Act 1990.

As a supervisor, you may accompany the EHO on their visit around your work area. Make sure you know the answers to their questions, or at least where to get the answers; you are in charge of others, and it is within your role to know the basic requirements of health and safety, and food hygiene at work.

Hazard Analysis and Critical Control Points (HACCP)

According to the **Hazard** Analysis and **Critical Control Points** regulations, every employer has to make a suitable and sufficient assessment of:

o the health and safety risks to which employees are exposed while at work

o the **risks** to the health and safety of persons not in his employment arising out of, or in connection with, the conduct of his [or her] undertaking.

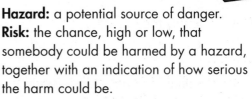

Definitions

Hazard: a potential source of danger.
Risk: the chance, high or low, that somebody could be harmed by a hazard, together with an indication of how serious the harm could be.
Critical control points: those points at which things must be controlled in order to prevent something going wrong.

The assessment is needed is so that the employer can identify what they need to do to comply with the law. All the health and safety, food safety and fire laws require risk assessments to be carried out by the 'responsible person'.

Controlling risk

Identifying risks, and putting steps in place to minimise them, is something that you will be involved in as a supervisor. The main business risks will be dealt with by the health and safety officer for the organisation, but you may well be involved in drawing up a risks document for a new piece of equipment, or after working methods have been changed in your department. Your organisation will have forms for risk assessment; a sample form is on the HSE website (www.hse.gov.uk, go to 'Catering and Hospitality').

Risks are a normal part of life, but what you are trying to do is identify the seriousness of a risk and take steps to minimise it, or display a notice warning people when the risk cannot be eliminated (e.g. a sign saying 'Very Hot Water' near the water boiler).

Steps to controlling risk

The five steps of risk assessment:

○ Step 1 Identify the hazards.
○ Step 2 Decide who might be harmed, and how.
○ Step 3 Evaluate the risks, and decide on precautions.
○ Step 4 Record your findings and implement them.
○ Step 5 Review your assessment, and update if necessary.

Step 1: Identify the hazards

Look again at the main cause of accidents in the hospitality industry (page 121). These show you the main risks we face at work.

○ Slips, trips and falls (e.g. floors wet with water or oil are very slippery; if you are carrying something that blocks your vision, you may trip if something is not left in the correct place, like a box or a flex).
○ Handling, lifting and carrying (e.g. carrying loaded trays, heavy bottles of chemicals, housekeeping supplies, picking up vacuum cleaners, twisting at a till point when handling money).
○ Exposure to steam and chemicals (harmful substances – e.g. steam ovens in kitchens, coffee machines, cleaning stores, when carrying out cleaning tasks – oven cleaner is caustic).
○ Being struck by moving or falling objects or machinery (e.g. items falling off shelves if stacked incorrectly).

○ Ill health from chronic musculoskeletal disorders and dermatitis (e.g. not using personal protective equipment (PPE) such as rubber gloves on the wash-up; repetitive strain injury from using a computer at the front desk; arm problems from continual use of a knife; leg and back problems from pushing heavy trolleys as a porter).

Step 2: Decide who might be harmed, and how

Different people may be harmed by different things in your workplace. You need to think of staff and customers, as well as maintenance workers and suppliers or visitors to the establishment. The risks will differ not only depending on the hazard, but also on the person. For example, cutting yourself with a knife is a serious risk for a new starter in the kitchen, but much less of a risk for an experienced chef, so the new starter needs specific training to minimise the risk. A person in a wheelchair on the fourteenth floor of a hotel will need special help in an evacuation, which is why this risk is minimised by providing rooms on the ground floor for the blind and wheelchair-users.

Step 3: Evaluate the risks, and decide on the appropriate precautions

This means that you decide whether something is of low, medium or high risk. It makes sense to minimise the risks according to their seriousness.

Remember that although the likelihood of an accident may be slim, if the outcome could be devastating, it is graded as high risk. For example, slipping on a non-slip floor is less likely than on a slippery floor, but the result could be a serious back injury, putting a hand in hot liquid on attempting to break the fall, or hitting your head on a sharp object when falling.

Step 4: Record your findings and implement them

This must be done when there are five or more members of staff. A written assessment is also useful for small businesses because it helps to clarify the risks and keep track of the solutions put in place. These records will need to be shown to the EHO when they visit.

Step 5: Review your assessment, and update if necessary

This is important when things change, for example, if new equipment is introduced to an area. The supervisor usually checks the risk assessment on a regular basis (e.g. once a month) to make sure staff are kept up to date with safe working practices.

One example of a risk assessment recording form is shown below.

Company Name: Denby Café   Date of Assessment: 14th June 2009

Step 1	Step 2	Step 3
What are the hazards? Spot hazards by: • walking around your workplace • asking your employees what they think • visiting the Your industry areas of the HSE website • calling the Workplace Health Connect Adviceline or visiting their website • checking manufacturers' instructions • contacting your trade association Don't forget long-term health hazards.	Who might be harmed and how? Identify groups of people. Remember: • some workers have particular needs • people who may not be in the workplace all the time • members of the public • if you share your workplace think about how your work affects others present. Say how the hazard could cause harm.	What are you already doing? List what is already in place to reduce the likelihood of harm or make any harm less serious.

1	Slips and trips in back of house	Staff working in area and those passing through to get to front corridor could slip on water and trip up on boxes if not flattened properly Medium risk of slipping but high risk of injury through slipping	**A** Non-slip floor recently installed
			B Good housekeeping – work areas kept tidy, goods and waste stored suitably, etc.
			C Kitchen equipment maintained to prevent leaks on to floor.
			D Notices on doors to warn through-traffic
			E Staff issued with uniform non-slip shoes
			F Staff clean up spillages (including dry spills) immediately and leave the floor to dry
2	Hot water in sink taps	All staff and customers could be scalded High risk	Warning signs in public toilet areas
4	Gas appliances	Staff and customers if there is an explosion Medium risk	New central gas cut off switch installed June 07 All gas equipment serviced annually
5	Fire	All staff and customers at risk especially disabled customers Medium risk	Fire risk assessment carried out and action duly taken Equipment serviced regularly. No-smoking policy

Step 4

What further action is necessary? How will you put the assessment into action?
• You need to make sure that you have reduced risks 'so far as is practicable'.
• An easy way of doing this is to compare what you are already doing with good practice. If there is a difference, list what needs to be done. Remember to prioritise. Deal with those hazards that are high-risk and have serious consequences first.

	Action	Action By Whom	Action By When	Done (date)
1A	None			
1B	Remind staff in team briefings about being tidy	Supervisor	1st Monday of the month	15.8.08
1C	Will add a warning note to customers' information pack in rooms	Housekeeping manager	31st Sept 08	1.10.08
1D	Repair damaged floor tiles by the entrance			
1F	Draw staff attention to reporting of leaks and damaged equipment	Supervisor	Team meeting 26th Sept 08	Team meeting 26th Sept 08
1G	Sort out who is responsible for area cleaning materials with housekeeping manager	Manager	14.9.08	12.9.08
2	Add note about hot water in the guest information packs	Manager	27.9.08	26.9.08
4	Make sure staff know how to operate this switch in emergencies Remember new staff	Supervisor	Team meeting 26th Sept 08	Team meeting 26th Sept 08
5	None			

• Review your assessment to make sure you are still improving, or at least not sliding back.
• If there is a significant change in your workplace, remember to check your risk assessment and where necessary, amend it.

Step 5 Review date:

Signature _____   Manager _____

Figure 4.2 Example risk assessment recording form.

Flow charts can also be used to identify the critical control points (CCP), which you then have to decide how you will control. The example below shows CCP where temperature control is necessary to prevent food spoilage or contamination.

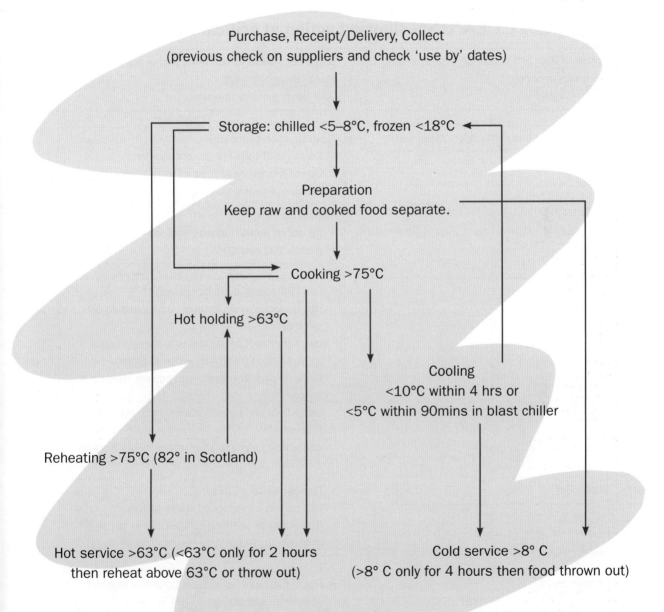

*Flow Chart representing suggested stages of HCCP (Critical Control Points) in a catering business. Adapted from Cook**Safe** Food Safety Assurance System (Food Standards Agency)*

Below is a simple HACCP flow chart for housekeeping staff, showing what to do at certain critical control points and why. The table is the result of a risk assessment carried out by management.

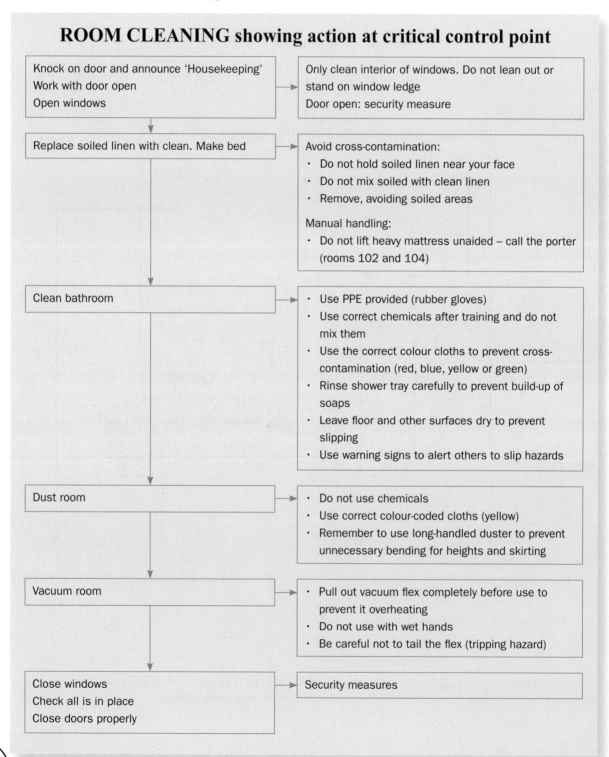

ROOM CLEANING showing action at critical control point

Knock on door and announce 'Housekeeping' Work with door open Open windows	Only clean interior of windows. Do not lean out or stand on window ledge Door open: security measure
Replace soiled linen with clean. Make bed	Avoid cross-contamination: · Do not hold soiled linen near your face · Do not mix soiled with clean linen · Remove, avoiding soiled areas Manual handling: · Do not lift heavy mattress unaided – call the porter (rooms 102 and 104)
Clean bathroom	· Use PPE provided (rubber gloves) · Use correct chemicals after training and do not mix them · Use the correct colour cloths to prevent cross-contamination (red, blue, yellow or green) · Rinse shower tray carefully to prevent build-up of soaps · Leave floor and other surfaces dry to prevent slipping · Use warning signs to alert others to slip hazards
Dust room	· Do not use chemicals · Use correct colour-coded cloths (yellow) · Remember to use long-handled duster to prevent unnecessary bending for heights and skirting
Vacuum room	· Pull out vacuum flex completely before use to prevent it overheating · Do not use with wet hands · Be careful not to tail the flex (tripping hazard)
Close windows Check all is in place Close doors properly	Security measures

Figure 4.4 HACCP flow chart for critical control points.

The Health and Safety (Safety Signs and Signals) Regulations 1996

If a risk cannot be eliminated, then it must be controlled, and that is where safety and hazard signs are used. Placed near equipment or on a wet floor, etc., they draw people's attention to the hazard. Care must be taken when there are non-English-speaking staff or customers. Most signs are common across Europe for colour, but the text will not necessarily be recognisable.

Signs can be categorised into the following groups.

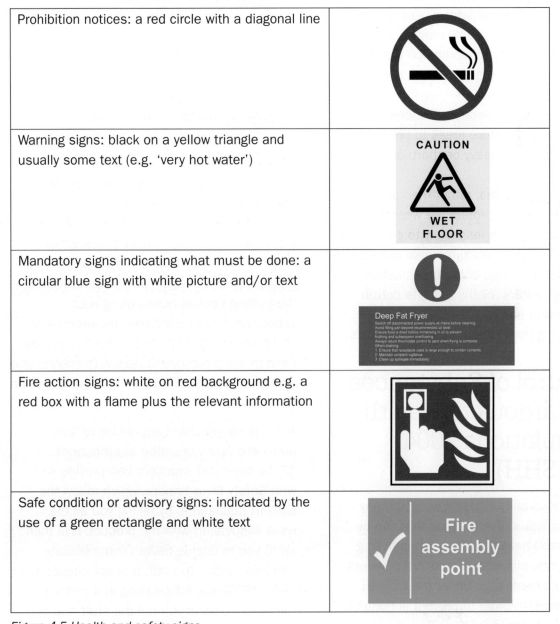

Prohibition notices: a red circle with a diagonal line	
Warning signs: black on a yellow triangle and usually some text (e.g. 'very hot water')	
Mandatory signs indicating what must be done: a circular blue sign with white picture and/or text	
Fire action signs: white on red background e.g. a red box with a flame plus the relevant information	
Safe condition or advisory signs: indicated by the use of a green rectangle and white text	

Figure 4.5 Health and safety signs

Personal protective equipment (PPE)

Where a hazard cannot be eliminated, and signs have been put up but more protection is needed, then personal protective equipment (PPE) is issued. In hospitality, this usually means:

○ wearing rubber or latex gloves (which, however, some people may be allergic to)
○ wearing waterproof aprons on the wash-up
○ wearing eye goggles to clean ovens, and sometimes a mask
○ wearing steel toe-capped shoes in kitchens and store areas to prevent damage from heavy or sharp objects falling on to feet
○ wearing uniforms, rather than personal clothes, which protect the wearers' own clothes and are less likely to get caught in machinery – uniforms also express the corporate image of the organisation
○ using waiters' cloths or white cotton gloves to handle hot dishes
○ wearing thick jackets to enter freezers.

Control of Substances Hazardous to Health Regulations 2004 (COSHH)

In the hospitality industry, we use many different types of substance that can be considered hazardous to our health (e.g. detergents, oils, insect repellent powders, cleaning chemicals). Under the COSHH regulations, in order to prevent ill health or injury to people at work, employers must:

○ assess the risks
○ decide what precautions need to be put in place
○ prevent or adequately control exposure
○ make sure control measures are used and maintained
○ monitor/check exposure
○ carry out appropriate health surveillance (e.g. for dermatitis and musculoskeletal risks)
○ prepare plans and procedures to deal with accidents, incidents and emergencies involving hazardous substances
○ ensure employees are properly informed and trained.

In practice, this means that as a supervisor you need to use the HACCP system to establish the risk each substance poses to those working with it. You also have to establish whether health surveillance (monitoring) or exposure monitoring is necessary, as well as assessing the training needed before using each substance. You may not have the experience or the knowledge to do this yourself, and may need to ask a competent person (someone who is knowledgeable) to do the risk assessment on your behalf.

The risk assessment should be written down and communicated to employees. All the chemical suppliers can provide you with Safety Data Sheets, which follow the COSHH regulations by telling you all the risks associated with the product. It is then up to you to decide how to communicate this information to staff; it is not enough to simply leave the information in a folder in the stores unless you tell the staff that is where the information is, and that they must sign something to say they have read it. You have to make sure your staff understand the implications of the misuse of chemicals, as this could result in injury to themselves, another member of staff or a customer.

The types of document or source you would look for to assess COSHH risks include:

○ Safety Data Sheets (see page 134): supplied by law with all hazardous substances

○ informal discussions with staff: they can tell you if chemicals make them cough or give them itchy skin, for example

○ purchasing records: types of chemicals bought by the department

○ accident records: show how often certain chemicals have caused an accident; it would be good to replace any that have done so with something less dangerous

○ health surveillance records: monitoring use of cleaning chemicals known to irritate skin or lungs when used regularly by porters or cleaners (e.g. oven cleaner, floor stripper, grease remover).

You need to check whether your training records show that all staff have received appropriate training in the use of chemicals. Remember, if the instructions are only in English and you have non-English-speaking staff, they may not understand them properly; this could cause injury or damage to people and surfaces.

Evidence

Collect the training records for staff for health, hygiene, safety and security procedures. Collect the COSHH product sheets for all chemicals used in your department, and signpost to staff where they can be found by sending a memo or email, or writing a notice on a noticeboard. Remind any staff under your responsibility of internal health, hygiene, safety and security procedures.
1.1, 1.2, 2.1, 2.3, 2.4, 2.9, 2.10, 2.11, 2.12, 2.14, 2.23, 2.24, 2.25.

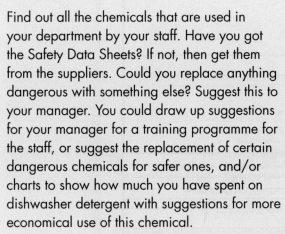

Evidence

Find out all the chemicals that are used in your department by your staff. Have you got the Safety Data Sheets? If not, then get them from the suppliers. Could you replace anything dangerous with something else? Suggest this to your manager. You could draw up suggestions for your manager for a training programme for the staff, or suggest the replacement of certain dangerous chemicals for safer ones, and/or charts to show how much you have spent on dishwasher detergent with suggestions for more economical use of this chemical.

Much of the information and records concerning risk assessment and COSHH will be stored on computer, and you may well generate evidence for key skills and the Level 3 NVQ Unit HS4 through your normal work duties.
1.1, 1.2, 1.5, 1.7, 1.8, 1.9, 2.6, 2.7, 2.11, 2.12, 2.14, 2.15, 2.16, 2.19, 2.20, 2.22.

Good practice

Replace dangerous chemicals with less dangerous ones for cleaning purposes. Nowadays some manufacturers are producing chemicals that are less harmful, both to people and the environment.

Procter&Gamble

Household Care Products – Europe

SAFETY DATA SHEET (2001/58/EC)

Reference: 0103 - Issue 1
PAnumber: PA00017560
Issue date: 3-Jul-08
Valid until superseded

1. **Identification of the Substance/Preparation**	**Bounce - Spring** (tumble drier sheets)
Company Name:	Procter & Gamble UK
Address:	Brooklands, Weybridge, Surrey, KT13 0XP, UK
Telephone #:	Tel: 01932 89 6000 Fax: 01932 89 6200
Emergency phone #:	0800 169 7679 (UK); 1800 409 535 (IRL)
Email Address:	rose.yd@pg.com

2. **Hazards identification**	This product is not classified as dangerous according to EU Directive 1999/45/EC.	
	Eye contact:	Transient superficial irritation.
	Skin contact:	Prolonged exposure may cause skin irritation.
	Ingestion:	Possible mild gastro-intestinal irritation with nausea and vomiting.
	Inhalation:	Inhaling aerosolized product may cause mild irritation of the respiratory system.

3. **Composition/information on ingredients**

Lotion loaded on wipes, containing:

Common Name	CAS	EINECS/ELINCS	Classification	Conc
Perfume	confidential	confidential	Xi, N; R43, R51/53	1-5%

4. **First-aid measures**	Eye contact:	Rinse thoroughly with plenty of water for several minutes. If symptoms persist, seek medical advice.
	Skin contact:	Rinse affected area with water. If needed apply cold compress to relieve irritation. If symptoms persist, discontinue use of product and seek medical advice.
	Ingestion:	Drink a glass of water to dilute lotion. Do not induce vomiting. Act immediately in order to prevent further irritation of mouth, throat and stomach mucosa. If symptoms persist, if persistent vomiting occurs or if blood tinged vomitus is present, seek medical advice.
	Inhalation:	Go into open air and ventilate suspected area. If irritation is experienced, mouth and throat may be rinsed with water. Aerosolized lotion adhering to the nasal cavity may be rinsed/diluted with saline/plain water. If irritation or asthma-like symptoms persist, seek medical advice.

5. **Fire fighting measures**	Not explosive. Not auto-flammable. Not flammable. The wipe lotion itself will not burn. If anything, packaging may be involved in a fire. Use CO2, dry chemical powders or alcohol resistant foam. If water is used, contain run-off.
6. **Accidental release measures**	Avoid spillage into sewers or surface water. For large spills: pump into plastic containers and rework/dispose as per local legislation. For small spills: use non- combustible absorbant and shovel into container for disposal.
7. **Handling and storage**	Store in a cool and dry area.
8. **Exposure controls / Personal protection**	Not a hazard in normal use. No personal protective equipment required.

9. **Physical and chemical properties**	Lotion:	
	Appearance:	liquid
	Odour:	perfumed
	pH (neat):	n/a
	Flammable:	NO
	Explosive:	NO
	Oxidizing:	NO
	Relative density (g/cm3):	n/a
	Water solubility:	High

10. **Stability and reactivity**	Stable under normal conditions.	
11. **Toxicological information**	Not acutely toxic; may cause vomiting. If very large quantities are ingested, symptoms of alcohol-like intoxication may be observed; treat symptomatically. Do not induce vomiting. If irritant effects are seen, these will be mild to moderate, depending on exposure. If in contact	
	Estimated acute oral toxicity:	LD50 (rats) > 5g/kg
	Eye irritation:	Slightly irritating to eyes
	Skin irritation:	Slightly irritating to skin
	Chronic toxicity:	Repeated exposure to low levels (e.g. on fabrics) will not cause adverse effects
	Contact sensitization:	Does not provoke a sensitization reaction

12. **Ecological information**	The product is intended for wide dispersive use and is compatible with the down-the-drain disposal route.
	The product is not considered harmful to aquatic organisms nor to cause long-term adverse effects in the environment.
	The surfactants contained in this preparation comply with the biodegradability criteria as laid down in Regulation EC/648/2004 on detergents.
13. **Disposal considerations**	Consumer products ending up down the drain after use. Observe safe handling precautions and local legislation.
14. **Transport information**	Not subject to ADR/IATA/IMDG codes.
15. **Regulatory information**	This product is not classified as dangerous according to EU Directive 1999/45/EC and national laws.
	All substances in the preparation are registered in the EU.
16. **Other information**	This product does not require any special training before use. Usage and handling instructions are mentioned on package and on this Material Safety Data Sheet.

Figure 4.6 Example safety data sheet.

Reporting of Injuries, Diseases and Dangerous Occurrences Regulations 1995 (RIDDOR)

Under the RIDDOR regulations, all employers, self-employed people and people in control of premises have a legal duty to report work-related deaths and major injuries. As a supervisor, it may be part of your responsibility to ensure this requirement is carried out consistently.

Major injuries in hospitality commonly include:
- fracture, other than to fingers, thumbs and toes (e.g. falling on a wet floor and breaking an arm)
- amputation (e.g. getting an arm trapped in a large-scale food processor, especially if the guard is not in place)
- dislocation of the shoulder, hip, knee or spine (e.g. through falling or attempting to carry heavy loads)
- loss of sight, temporary or permanent (e.g. by hot oil splashing into the eye)
- chemical injury to the eye or any penetrating injury to the eye; chemical splashes
- injury resulting from an electric shock or electrical burn leading to unconsciousness, or requiring resuscitation or admittance to hospital for more than 24 hours (e.g. caused by faulty wiring on a scrubber/polisher)
- injury leading to hypothermia (e.g. locked in a freezer), heat-induced illness (e.g. hot kitchens)
- unconsciousness caused by asphyxia or exposure to harmful substance or biological agent (e.g. a cleaner mixing cleaning chemicals with bleach causing a build-up of chlorine gas, which is highly toxic)
- acute illness requiring medical treatment, or loss of consciousness arising from absorption of any substance by inhalation, ingestion or through the skin (e.g. carbon monoxide poisoning from faulty gas equipment in a guest room).

Over-three-day injuries

An over-3-day injury is one that is not major, but results in the injured person being away from work or unable to do the full range of their normal duties for more than three days. The injury could be due to an accident, or to an act of physical violence. The injury must be reported to the Incident Contact Centre (ICC) within ten days.

Work-related diseases

If your employee gives you a note from the doctor indicating that they suffer from a reportable work-related disease, then you must report it to the enforcing authority.

Reportable diseases likely to be encountered in hospitality include:
- certain poisonings (e.g. mushrooms)
- some skin diseases (e.g. occupational dermatitis)
- infections (e.g. legionellosis and tetanus)
- other conditions such as certain musculoskeletal disorders (e.g. serious injury to someone's back through slipping on a wet floor, arm strain suffered by a waiter).

Dangerous occurrences or near-miss accidents likely in the hospitality industry

If something happens that does not result in a reportable injury, but that clearly could have done so, then it may be a dangerous occurrence, which must be reported immediately. These include:

- collapse, overturning or failure of load-bearing parts of lifts and lifting equipment
- explosion, collapse or bursting of any closed vessel or associated pipework (e.g. a steamer exploding)
- electrical short circuit or overload causing fire or explosion
- any unintentional explosion, injury caused by an explosion
- explosion or fire causing suspension of normal work for over 24 hours (e.g. kitchen extract ducting, if not cleaned regularly, poses a serious fire risk to a building).

Recording for RIDDOR

A record must be kept of any reportable injury, disease or dangerous occurrence. Each report should contain:

- the date and method of reporting
- the date, time and place of the event
- personal details of those involved
- a brief description of the nature of the event or disease.

Records can be kept by:

- keeping copies of report forms in a file
- recording the details on a computer
- using your accident book entry
- maintaining a written log.

Accident reporting: who reports to whom?

All accidents and near-misses, no matter how minor, must be recorded in the accident book. The person who suffers the injury can record the accident, but so can someone else on their behalf. The EHO will look at the accident book on their visit to the business. If there are few accidents, he or she will check that the premises and working methods really are that safe, or whether accidents are happening that are just not being written down.

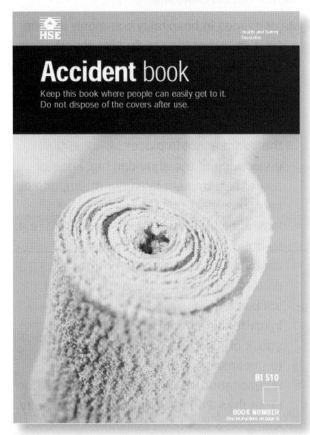

Figure 4.7 The Accident Book

All reportable accidents that happen at work are eventually reported to the Incident Control Centre at Caerphilly. In a small business it is usually the manager who deals with RIDDOR; in a large business it would be the appointed person. In a medium-sized organisation it could be the supervisor who has to fill in the forms and then pass them to the manager for authorisation.

Death, major injury and over-three-day injuries to employees of contractors working on your premises are reportable by their employer; for example, if an electrician is electrocuted on your premises and is off work for five days. If a self-employed contractor is working on your premises and has an accident, then it is the responsibility of the person in control of the premises at the time to report the accident.

The following examples of accidents would not be reportable as they did not 'arise out of or in connection with work':

○ a customer knocks their coffee over and is slightly burned
○ a customer has a heart attack while waiting in the lounge, and is taken to hospital.

First aid: Health and Safety (First-Aid) Regulations 1981

There are two types of first-aider in the workplace.

○ An official first-aider, who has passed a valid four-day (24-hour), HSE-approved training course for carrying out first aid at work.

○ An appointed person – someone who, in the case of an emergency, will find the trained first-aider and/or call an ambulance if required. They can only administer first aid to the level of the training they have received. It is usually this person who replenishes the first aid box and ensures that emergency equipment is kept in good working order.

Many small employers only need to make the minimum of first aid provisions, but the HACCP assessment of your workplace hazards may show that a trained first-aider is required. In a large hospitality business, there is always at least one first-aider on duty on the premises at any time. In each department, there may also be an appointed person. The number of first-aiders will depend on the risk level, for example, a member of the kitchen staff is often a first-aider (this could also be a porter or a member of the security staff), and a first aid box is often kept in the kitchen or bar/restaurant area because of the high risk of accidents happening in these areas.

Fire Regulatory Reform (Fire Safety) Order 2005

The Fire Regulatory Reform (Fire Safety) Order 2005 is a recent piece of legislation, which came into force in 2006, replacing the need to apply for a fire certificate. The changes in legislation covering fire mean that the 'responsible' person must carry out a fire safety risk assessment, which they must ensure is implemented and managed. The responsible person in a workplace is the employer. If the employer does not control the workplace, then it is the person who has control, or the owner.

As a supervisor, you will not be expected to carry out a fire risk assessment, but you may need to deliver staff training on what to do in the event of a fire, and you will have a role in the event of an evacuation. The responsible person can employ a professional company to do the risk assessment.

Fire risk assessment

This follows the principles of HACCP, whereby the responsible person must ensure a suitable and sufficient assessment of the risks is undertaken by a competent person. They must then identify the steps needed to eliminate or lessen the risk of fire. Also, the fire risk assessment must be reviewed regularly by the responsible person so as to keep it up to date.

Using HACCP, there are five steps to a fire risk assessment.

Step 1: Identify the hazards within your premises

The fire triangle shown here is a common way of expressing the cause of fire.

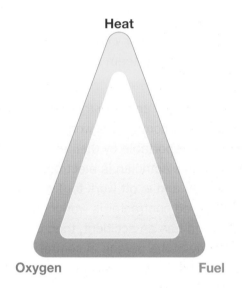

Figure 4.8 The fire triangle.

If all three conditions are present, then a fire is very likely to start. A risk assessment is about removing as many of these risks as possible; if at least one of these conditions is removed, then there will be no fire.

Fire hazards in the hospitality industry tend to be:

- naked flames in kitchens, hot surfaces, hot oil
- large amounts of paper and cardboard packaging, which is flammable
- large electrical equipment running on a high voltage
- the mixture of water and electricity (e.g. a floor-scrubbing machine)
- inflammable chemicals where they cannot be exchanged for safer ones (e.g. oven cleaner)

- smoking areas
- build-up of grease in ducting around food areas
- textiles and linen storage (flammable).

Find out!

Can you think of any other things that could cause a fire, which may exist in your area of work? It is good to be aware of them so that they can be safely controlled.

Find out!

When should fire drills happen in your workplace? Where are the fire exits? Does everyone in your department know where the exits are, and where to assemble outside the building? Do you have a fire warden, and does everyone know who this person is? Send a memo or email to staff reminding them of this essential fire safety information and keep it as evidence. All fire drills must be recorded, and if it is part of your role at your workplace to fill in the fire drill log book, keep copies of this for evidence.

Step 2: Who is at risk?

All people on the premises are at risk from fire, but particularly:

- those working in the kitchens
- people working alone (e.g. in the stores)
- guests in a hotel or restaurant with children
- elderly and disabled guests.

Step 3: Evaluate and reduce the risks; protect where necessary

- Ensure good housekeeping – keep the premises tidy. Store waste correctly and do not let waste packaging build up in kitchens or block escape routes.
- Make sure there is best practice when handling hot oil, and train the staff to use the equipment properly.
- Substitute the very dangerous for the less dangerous (e.g. use commercial frying oil for deep fat fryers rather than domestic cooking oil, as it is has a higher smoking point and does not catch fire so easily).
- Use safety signs where the risk cannot be eliminated (e.g. above dangerous equipment, when cleaning public areas, above unexpected steps).
- Install fire alarms and smoke detectors.
- Train staff in the use of emergency procedures and fire-fighting equipment (e.g. fire extinguishers, fire blanket). This should be done at induction, at regular intervals, and when there is some kind of change affecting the risk of fire.
- Practise evacuation procedures regularly and record these (usually every six months).
- Make sure all fire doors are kept closed and not wedged open with a fire extinguisher or blocked.
- Test fire alarms and smoke detectors (usually weekly).

Step 4: Record, plan and train

○ If there are more than five people at work, you must record the hazard findings and what you have done to remove or reduce them.

○ There should be a clear plan of fire prevention. This has to be coordinated with other users of the same building.

○ The staff – full time, part-time and temporary – must know about fire prevention and emergency procedures. These should also be communicated to contactors, guests and customers.

Step 5: Review

Do this:

○ especially when the risks change significantly

○ when dangerous substances are stored or used for the first time

○ when you have had a fire or a near miss.

Fire safety signs

The normal fire safety signs that you see around hospitality businesses indicate exit routes and what to do in the event of a fire. The fire officer in the building is responsible for the upkeep of these signs. As a supervisor, you must make sure they are always visible and not obstructed by anything.

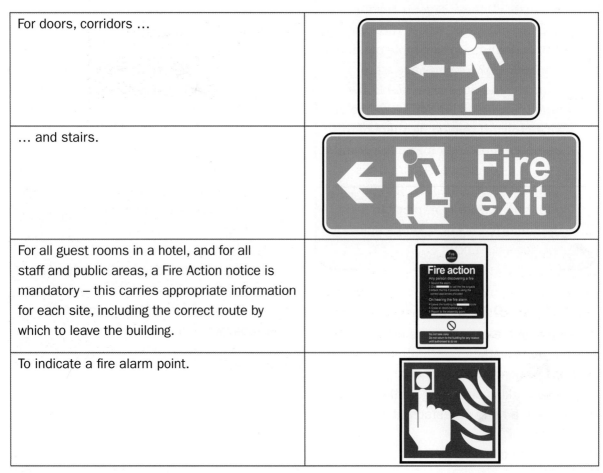

For doors, corridors ...	
... and stairs.	
For all guest rooms in a hotel, and for all staff and public areas, a Fire Action notice is mandatory – this carries appropriate information for each site, including the correct route by which to leave the building.	
To indicate a fire alarm point.	

Figure 4.9 Fire safety signs.

Fire extinguishers

Best practice indicates that someone in the department will normally be trained in the use of fire extinguishers. This may be you as supervisor, but it may not. If there is a fire officer, it will be their responsibility. In the event of fire, anyone can use an extinguisher, but no one should ever put themselves or others at risk by doing so.

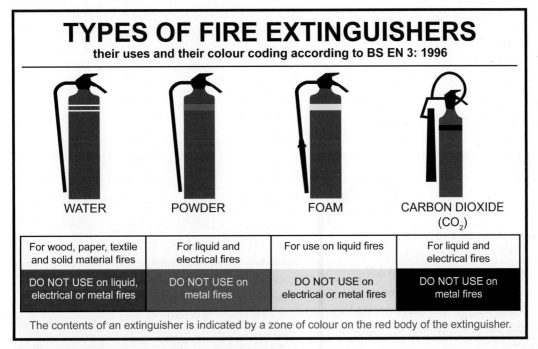

TYPES OF FIRE EXTINGUISHERS
their uses and their colour coding according to BS EN 3: 1996

WATER	POWDER	FOAM	CARBON DIOXIDE (CO$_2$)
For wood, paper, textile and solid material fires	For liquid and electrical fires	For use on liquid fires	For liquid and electrical fires
DO NOT USE on liquid, electrical or metal fires	DO NOT USE on metal fires	DO NOT USE on electrical or metal fires	DO NOT USE on metal fires

The contents of an extinguisher is indicated by a zone of colour on the red body of the extinguisher.

Figure 4.10 Different uses of fire extinguishers.

Emergency procedures

As a supervisor, you must fully understand the emergency procedures for your organisation, and ensure your staff also understand them and can implement them if necessary. In an actual emergency, your staff will look to you for leadership, so you must be prepared to act calmly and correctly and give direction to your team if necessary.

Find out!

Where are the emergency procedures for your department kept? What are they, and what is your role? Are they followed correctly in a drill? Do they need modifying and updating? (Often this is the job of the supervisor.)

Emergency procedures are related to the risk assessments. If there is a high risk of harm, the emergency procedure will usually involve evacuation of the premises, but at times a full evacuation is not necessary and would only encourage panic. Many businesses have different sounds for the alarm to 'alert' and the alarm to 'evacuate'. If the risk is a bomb, then searching is usually carried out by those familiar with the area, and this is often the supervisor. The emergency procedures indicate what to do in the case of an emergency and how to get out of the building quickly and safely in the case of evacuation.

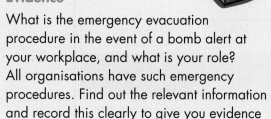

Evidence

What is the emergency evacuation procedure in the event of a bomb alert at your workplace, and what is your role? All organisations have such emergency procedures. Find out the relevant information and record this clearly to give you evidence for this unit.
1.1, 2.4, 2.23, 2.24, 2.25.

Bomb alerts

The following case study shows different procedures for dealing with bomb scares. They illustrate how people at different levels of authority acted in an emergency.

Case study

In the late 1980s there were a lot of bomb scares in Glasgow. A bomb was found one morning tucked at the back of a shelf of paint in a department store. The member of staff followed the procedure by alerting the supervisor, who set off the fire alarm so that the building was evacuated immediately. They also informed a senior member of staff, who alerted the police to the fact that it was a suspected bomb. The bomb disposal squad arrived from Edinburgh and defused the bomb with minutes to spare.

The next week, the supervisor of the restaurant in a different store found an abandoned package in the restaurant. It was slim and could have been a book or a magazine inside a brown paper bag. She did not touch the package, but called the security staff, who decided that because of its size it seemed unlikely that the package was a bomb. Some of the customers around asked what was going on, and to calm them they were told that there was a low-risk suspect package, but they were free to leave the premises if they felt uncomfortable; some customers left. A low-risk bomb alert was sounded (a series of bleeps) and staff followed the organisation's procedures by searching their own department and being ready for further action. The bomb squad was alerted to the package and arrived by helicopter from Edinburgh in 20 minutes. They entered the restaurant with sniffer dogs and as they did not react to the package, the bomb squad opened the package to reveal a small pile of birthday cards. The supervisor was very embarrassed, but the bomb squad praised her for acting sensibly, especially as the previous week she had received a phone call about a bomb in the restaurant.

BANFF & BUCHAN COLLEGE LIBRARY

Fire

The Fire Action notice illustrated on page 140 states that in an emergency you should:

- leave the building by the quickest route
- close all doors and windows
- make your way to the assembly point
- not return to the building until authorised to do so.

When the fire alarm sounds, it does not necessarily mean a full evacuation. You should never put your life at risk, but you may act as fire warden, making sure customers and staff leave the building before you do. People should not run out of a building or use the lifts in case of fire, as both are dangerous. Running causes panic and people are more likely to fall, becoming a hazard themselves.

Customers need to be directed to the assembly point, but equally they can leave the scene of the fire if they so wish, unless they are registered guests at a hotel, in which case they should wait to be registered as out of the building. Customers in a restaurant that is evacuated will not be expected to settle bills, and this adds to the losses of the restaurant.

All staff should know their roles in case of a fire, and practise them in the regular fire drills that the business must hold.

- After evacuation, the staff and, where necessary, the guests must report to the assembly point and be accounted for.
- Lists of names are taken out of the building on evacuation and used to account for those in it at any one time (see 'Security' on page 145).

- Reception can provide copies of visitors' names from their copies of the visitors' book, which all people entering the building must sign.
- In a hotel, not all visitors sign in – for example, in the restaurant and bar – so visitors there are always in danger in an evacuation as they are difficult to account for.
- No one can re-enter the building until the all-clear is sounded or communicated to them, so that they do not risk their or another person's life or become a security risk (for example, stealing may occur in an empty building).

Case study

A fire was discovered in the bottom of a lift shaft in a large store. The fire alarm was set off, but evacuation was not set in motion (evacuation is communicated to the staff by a series of bleeps, rather like during a bomb scare). On hearing the alarm, many customers left the building, but the fire brigade simply cleared the relevant area of people and dealt with the fire. People on the top floor may not even have smelled the smoke! An evacuation in these circumstances would simply have caused panic, as well as being expensive for the store through lost sales and even theft.

In the present climate of terrorist attacks, your organisation may well have special plans, which will be communicated like other emergency plans to the staff. It is up to each member of staff to be responsible in following the planned procedures to preserve as many lives as possible.

Crisis and contingency planning

Apart from bombs and fire, there are other, less obvious risks including:

○ natural disasters such as flooding, snowstorms, earthquakes, drought

○ loss of power supplies

○ an epidemic causing many staff to be absent at once, for example, flu

○ computer failure affecting booking systems, air-conditioning systems, financial records, etc.

○ organised crime, for example, large-scale theft from your premises.

How can you plan for the unexpected?

Contingency plans will be drawn up by experts in the matter or by senior members of staff. Your job will be to know your role and to train your staff in carrying out their roles. It is impossible to plan for every disaster that could happen. Risk assessments should be carried out for the most likely emergencies, and the results of the assessments used to train staff on how to act in different situations.

When you think of the possibility of something happening – a 'what if' situation – then a contingency plan is used. A contingency plan has two parts.

○ A plan of action to reduce the risk of things going wrong (e.g. installing back-up computer systems, keeping contact with employment agencies to provide staff at short notice, installing cut-off switches for gas and electricity – many pieces of equipment now have automatic cut-off systems as a safety measure).

○ Instructions on what to do in the case of an emergency.

The chain of command is important in a crisis. Staff should know well in advance who will be organising things in case a crisis occurs, so that people are not put at risk through confusion.

Food safety

A good general knowledge of food hygiene is desirable for people working in the hospitality industry, where food, drink and accommodation is our core business (see Unit 30 for more on food hygiene law).

Food Safety Act 1990

The Food Safety Act 1990 creates the 'umbrella' offence of selling or supplying food which does not meet food safety requirements, and allocates enforcement powers. The enforcement authorities are aided in their work by a number of Codes of Practice issued under the Food Safety Act (Section 40), which provide guidance on recommended enforcement practice.

Food Safety (General Food Hygiene) Regulations 1995

These regulations are made under the Food Safety Act and set out basic hygiene rules. They place a duty on the proprietor of a food business to:

○ make sure food is supplied or sold in a hygienic way

o identify hazards to the safety of food: physical, chemical or biological

o know which steps in their operation are critical for food safety; Critical Control Points (see HACPP page 125)

o ensure food safety controls are in place, maintained and reviewed (usually by the supervisor).

They set out the following regulations:

o basic requirements for food premises (including fixed, movable and temporary)

o equipment

o supply of raw materials

o quality of water in food

o personal hygiene for food handlers

o practices to prevent food contamination

o training and supervision requirements for food handlers.

Food Safety (Temperature Control) Regulations 1995

For food businesses, chiefly retail, catering, fruit and vegetables, the Temperature Control Regulations require foods that are likely to support the growth of pathogenic microorganisms or the formation of toxins to be held at or below 8°C (product) temperature or at or above 63°C.

Food Premises (Registration) Regulations 1990 and 1991

These regulations require that proprietors of food businesses must be registered as such with their local authority. This is to enable the local authority to enforce the law effectively.

Food Labelling Regulations 1984

These regulations relate to the labelling, presentation and advertising of foodstuffs for sale to the ultimate consumer, and include provisions on declaration of additives.

A HACCP risk assessment would take into account all of the above and, as with health and safety, procedures would be laid down by management as how to avoid the risk of food poisoning or food spoilage. Food poisoning is very serious as it can lead to severe illness or even death; hygienic food practices must be closely monitored by the supervisor to avoid any contamination.

Security

Security is an important issue in the hospitality industry, as it is a busy 'people' business. There are large numbers of people working in the same building, with many people passing through as customers each day, plus contractors, maintenance people and suppliers. Theft of personal property, business property and cash can be a real risk. Again, as with all these issues, the managers have to carry out a risk assessment and then put the necessary action and systems into place.

Some actions are very simple to carry out, like 'close the back door after deliveries'. However, all the staff have to know the procedure or this could lead to a situation as follows, which happened in a London hotel.

Case study

In a central London hotel kitchen deliveries came to the back door of the kitchen at the end of a small corridor where the chef's office was located. One day, some freshly-prepared bread disappeared from a trolley just inside the kitchen door. None of the staff knew where it had gone but it caused a problem, as the bread was just about to be sent up to the restaurant for lunch service. The next day, the chef decided to keep his office door open and he realised that the staff were leaving the back door open after deliveries because the kitchen was hot. He looked up in time to see someone enter the building. When he challenged the person to show his identity (by a delivery note or ID card), the person ran out of the door. The chef then realised how the bread, and possibly other things, had gone missing.

The solution was to retrain staff to close the door by drawing their attention to the fact that theft was occurring. Since this then meant that there was less ventilation, management agreed to the chef's request for a fan to be installed on the kitchen wall to help prevent the kitchen overheating.

Security is about safety, and about protecting staff and customers from becoming victims of crime. Security issues include:
- room safes for guests' convenience
- CCTV for security and protection
- automated kiosks for self-servicecheck-in/check-out
- computerised time and attendance recording for staff
- key cards for rooms, which change code with each new guest

- automatic charging of hotel mini-bars
- safe storage of staff members' personal belongings during working hours (e.g. lockers)
- closing doors properly.

Reception of guests or staff

Reception has a vital role to play in security. The supervisor of this area, along with the security staff, is very responsible for who comes in and out of the building. Everyone who comes in and out usually has to sign their name and time of arrival or departure. The arrival and departure lists are helpful in the case of registering people after an evacuation.

When a guest arrives at a hotel for sleeping accommodation, there is a legal requirement to register the arrival in writing. Guests have a system of registration to go through, which includes recording their credit card details. name and address, and nationality.
If the guest is an 'alien' (not of British nationality), then other details must be recorded, for example:
- passport number
- the place their passport was issued
- their next destination.

Staff names are recorded on arrival and departure at work by:
- signing in to the premises centrally, or
- signing in and out at arrival or departure from their department, or
- checking in on an automated system, which then generates a list of all people on site at one time.

Security is enforced by hotel rules, which sometimes state that guests are not allowed visitors in their rooms (but this is difficult to monitor). If visitors are allowed in rooms, they should never be sent up to a room without the guest's permission. Room numbers should not be revealed to anyone who asks.

Lost property

Usually when articles are found by an employee during their employment, they are awarded to the employer rather than to the employee who found them. Many organisations have a three-month rule whereby after this period they destroy or give away lost property handed in at the business.

Another major piece of legislation which affects the hospitality industry, this time under security issues, is the Data Protection Act and related Acts.

Data Protection Act 1998

○ The Data Protection Act 1998 gives people the right to know what information is held about them, and sets rules to make sure this information is handled properly. Organisations that hold personal information about staff and clients must use it fairly, keep it secure, make sure the information is accurate and keep it up to date.
○ The Privacy and Electronic Communications Regulations 2003 set out rules for people who wish to send out electronic direct marketing, for example, emails and text messages. This can affect mailing clients with information about your business.
○ The Freedom of Information Act 2000 and the Environmental Information Regulations

2004 give people the right to obtain other information held by public bodies unless there are good reasons to keep it confidential.

Data protection is very important when it comes to front office procedures, where personal information is handled all the time. Payment points are also sensitive areas, especially when people pay by credit or debit card. If you are supervising staff in one of these areas, you will need to be aware of the requirements for data protection.

To prevent card theft, a new system was introduced in February 2006 called 'Chip and PIN'. This means customers do not have to sign when making card payments, as the Chip and PIN machine will authorise the card only when the secret four-digit number is entered. In the hospitality industry, this has cut down fraud enormously because the personal identification number (PIN) has to be known whereas a signature could be copied (if the card had been stolen, for example). The sign illustrated below, which is often seen on windows of restaurants and other businesses, shows that the organisation operates the Chip and PIN payment system. This system has made supervising payments a much easier job.

Figure 4.11 The Chip and PIN symbol

Your responsibilities as supervisor

Monitoring

To monitor means to 'watch closely for purposes of control'.

You need to 'control' health and safety to comply with legislation and, more importantly, to prevent people being hurt in accidents.

Good monitoring also results in recording what is observed or uncovered by checking the different areas of the business, so that risks can be identified and action taken to eliminate or reduce them. This is a legal requirement for organisations with five or more employees. Checking usually means a physical check – going and having a look at the condition of the premises, the employees' facilities, or the front office database information, for example. The supervisor is usually the person responsible for keeping records of the monitoring carried out.

Evidence

Gather risk assessment documentation (memos, emails, letters, notes of phone calls) as evidence of dealing with and/or reporting hazards or equipment faults to a line manager or a supplier (e.g. a torn tile). If you have had to fill in an accident book, take a copy of this. Computer records of such information will usually be maintained, so this can also generate evidence for key skills at level 2 of Communication and ICT. 1.5, 1.6, 1.7, 2.7, 2.8, 2.13, 2.14, 2.15, 2.16, 2.18, 2.21.

Throughout this unit, many things have been mentioned which you will be responsible for checking. Here is a summary of things you will probably have to monitor and/or do.

○ Implementing the organisation's health and safety policy – the supervisor's role is to deal with risks and accidents promptly, following procedures and legal requirements for safeguarding customers and staff.

○ Accident reporting, including near-misses.

○ Observing the working practices of your team to ensure they are safe, hygienic and secure at all times, especially when working under pressure.

○ Recording refrigerator and freezer temperatures and service counter temperatures, and notifying management of anything unusual or dangerous (e.g. low hot plate temperatures, or an unusual pattern of automatic defrost on a freezer which may indicate a problem with temperature).

○ Checking the safety status of equipment (e.g. looking for bare wires, unsafe or dirty condition of floors, inadequate lighting especially on escape routes and in working areas).

○ Reporting signs of infestation in store rooms and service areas.

○ Checking the risks in your area are identified under the HACCP assessment, reporting any new risks.

○ Delivering training and keeping training records relevant to health and safety – make sure colleagues have relevant information on health, hygiene, safety and security issues within your area of responsibility; and make sure colleagues are aware of the importance of following health, hygiene safety and security procedures.

- Monitoring room status with regard to upkeep and repair.
- Passing on information relating to how procedures are working and how they can be improved with regard to identified health, hygiene, safety and security risks.
- Involving staff in health and safety issues – being a role model and motivating staff to comply and to actively suggest improvements when they can.
- Monitoring your area of responsibility for risks to health, hygiene, safety and security.

Alcohol and illegal drugs at work

As well as the more formal monitoring already described, your role as a supervisor will also include keeping a more informal eye on your staff in terms of their personal well-being. A particular issue in the hospitality industry is the abuse of drink and drugs. You need to be aware of this and be able to deal with it sensitively, but correctly, if you find it.

The Caterer and Hotelkeeper (6 December 2007), one of the industry trade press magazines, carried out a survey within the industry about the abuse of alcohol and illegal drugs. They found that 70 per cent of their sample of 300 employees said that employees found abusing alcohol or illegal drugs are dismissed. Two years earlier the industry was already concerned about drugs and alcohol abuse, as is shown in the following quote. 'This raises a variety of legal issues for employers, and points that need to be considered by all include whether drug abuse is an illness or misconduct; what exactly is a dismissible offence; and how can staff be tested and screened for drink and drugs?' (*The Caterer and Hotelkeeper*, 27 April 2005).

Other findings include:
- 40 per cent had witnessed others taking drugs at work (97 per cent cannabis, 65 per cent cocaine, 32 per cent ecstasy)
- 13 per cent had personally taken drugs at work (80 per cent cannabis, 57 per cent cocaine, 3 per cent ecstasy)
- more than seven in ten had witnessed other employees misusing drugs or alcohol (or both) at work or immediately prior to work.

A previous study, carried out in 2003, also revealed that the two most common reasons given by people who took drugs at their place of work were 'to stay awake during shift' (48 per cent) and 'to help cope with stress' (also 48 per cent). Some people estimate that 25 per cent of accidents in the hospitality industry are alcohol- or drug-related; however, this has not been proven yet.

'Publicans, managers of licensed premises and bar staff are the occupations most likely to be affected by alcohol-related deaths.' (*The Caterer and Hotelkeeper*, 23 August 2007)

The HSE has published a document entitled *Drug Misuse at Work – A Guide For Employers*. This document lists the signs of drug misuse that you might look for, including:
- sudden mood changes
- unusual irritability or aggression
- a tendency to become confused
- abnormal fluctuations in concentration and energy
- impaired job performance
- poor time-keeping
- increased short-term sickness absence
- a deterioration in relationships with colleagues, customers or management
- dishonesty and theft (arising from the need to maintain an expensive habit).

Good practice

The signs listed on the previous page *may* be caused by other factors, such as stress, and should only be regarded as indications that an employee may be misusing drugs or alcohol.

Since employers have a duty to assess the risks to the health and safety of their employees, they cannot knowingly allow an employee under the influence of drug misuse to continue working, because his or her behaviour places the employee or others at risk. Employers who do not abide by this part of the HASAW could be prosecuted. Employees are also required to take reasonable care of themselves and others who could be affected by what they do at work.

In a *Caterer* online poll, in November 2007, of nearly 300 hospitality professionals:
- 89 per cent felt alcohol and drug misuse was a problem in the industry.
- 39% of those believed it was 'widespread'.
- 85% felt that alcohol and drug misuse was having a negative impact on the image of the industry.

More than seven in ten of the respondents said they had witnessed other employees misusing drugs or alcohol (or both) at work or immediately before work. Just 20 per cent of the hospitality professionals said their employer undertook training with managers on how to manage alcohol and drug misuse; and 70 per cent confirmed that employees who were found to be abusing drink or drugs were dismissed.

This position was criticised by Alcohol Concern. A spokesman said: 'We view alcohol policies as fundamental to tackling alcohol-related problems at work. Misuse should be viewed as a health issue, rather than an automatic cause fo censure or dismissal.' British Hospitality Association Chief Executive Bob Cotton said: 'It's the responsibility of every good employer to look for signs of drug and alcohol abuse and to take steps to counter it. We can't just ignore it.' A spokesman for charity DrugScope said: 'Having a clear drug and alcohol policy in place, which includes the option to refer someone to counselling where appropriate, should be standard practice across British industry.'

These concerns are equally important for small- and medium-sized businesses. Absenteeism affects the workplace badly and can also contribute to the breakdown of working relationships in a team. Team members will only put up with someone not turning up on a Monday morning for a certain period of time before they start to complain. Alcohol consumption is known to affect work performance because it affects judgement and physical coordination. This is very dangerous when working with machinery, for example, for a chef using a meat slicer or cutting with sharp knives. It is also bad for customer relations, as the staff member may become irritable in response to a customer complaint, and can lead to mistakes; for example, when doing the final bill for a hotel guest, staff may miss items or add items to a bill, causing a difficult situation and maybe a loss of income for the business.

This is an important issue under health and safety – someone under the effects of alcohol or drugs is no longer in real control of their actions; therefore they are more likely to have or to cause an accident. Although people must take responsibility for their actions, long-term drug and alcohol abuse is now so widespread that employers are being urged to treat the issue as an illness rather than as a dismissible offence. The outcome of drinks or drugs misconduct should be clearly stated in the written rules within the employee contract or handbook, and brought to the attention of staff during the induction process. If you suspect that a member of staff has some problem in this area, then as their supervisor working closely with the team, it may be up to you to approach the member of staff informally to establish what help they need.

On the other hand, if you think someone may act in such a manner as to endanger their job by misconduct, they should be warned informally. For example, this could be done when you hear that a group of the staff are going out after their shift for a drink, and you know that one of them has to be in at 6.30 a.m. the next morning for the breakfast shift as the normal chef has a day off. It may be a good thing to remind them of the starting time, so that they behave responsibly when they are out and do not turn up late or unfit for work the next morning. These actions demonstrate good leadership and concern for team members.

Find out!

It will help you to find all the documents that you use, or will use, as a supervisor at work and compare them with the list on the following page. As you do this, note and remember where they are located. You may find you have different documents, but remember, each organisation applies the health and safety laws to its own business, and there will always be differences according to the type of business (e.g. a night club will be more affected by the noise regulations than a 50-seat café).

Evidence

Correctly-completed examples of your workplace forms for health, security, hygiene and safety in your workplace will give you evidence for this unit.
1.1, 1.2, 1.3, 1.4, 1.5, 1.6, 1.7, 1.8, 2.1, 2.2, 2.4, 2.5, 2.6, 2.7, 2.8, 2.11, 2.12, 2.14, 2.15, 2.16, 2.21.

Good practice

Differentiate between the social drinker who makes a mistake and the long-term alcoholic. People with serious problems of alcohol dependence would be in an even more difficult position if they were dismissed.

Below is a list of the main records to which you will have access as a supervisor in the hospitality industry. These documents should always be up to date and available for inspection by the appropriate people. Your monitoring may not include all these documents.

o Health and safety policy, including food hygiene policy where applicable.
o Staff training records.
o Forms for recording temperatures of fridges, freezers, food cooking and holding temperatures.
o Health and safety checklists for all departments (e.g. rooms, offices, kitchens, public areas, equipment, cleaning records). These are for the cleanliness and state of repair of fittings and fixtures, staff and public facilities, etc.
o Maintenance checklists for repairs, forms for reporting repairs (see example on the following page).
o A place for staff suggestions to be recorded.
o Electrical testing recording forms.
o A fire risk assessment, including a form for recording fire drills, safety equipment checks, alarm testing.
o Health surveillance records.
o HACCP risk assessments and outcomes.
o RIDDOR documents and records along with the accident book.
o COSHH documents (e.g. safety data sheets, storage procedures).
o Display screen risk assessment records (especially for office and front office staff).
o Safety committee meeting minutes.
o First-aid facilities.

The simple repair notification form on the previous page is an example of a form created so that the floor supervisor can physically check the status of the building and report repairs needed. This seating and bedroom type of check is probably done once a month, or even once every three months. This form is then passed on to the manager with suggestions for maintenance and replacement of items. In a hotel, the check might be carried out every time a room is vacated, as significant damage will be added to the client's bill before they check out, or charged to their bank account after check-out.

Repair Note		
Date	Department	Area
Short description of Malfunction or Hazard:		
Suggested Action:		
Signatures		
Staff reporting:		(To be filled in by Manager) Action taken
Supervisor:		
Manager:		

A housekeeping supervisor's checklist for rooms

1 = Present, of acceptable standard 2 = Missing 3 = Broken/Damaged 4 = Needs attention

SEATING AREAS

	Sofas/Chairs (should not be restricting access)	Fire Door	Phone Sockets	Phones	Walls	Ceilings	Windows	Light Switches	Lights	Emergency Lights	Plug Sockets	Glass Panel Call Points (fire)	Carpet	Smoke Detector	Radiator	Fire Escape Route (directions displayed)	Tables
Ground Floor*	4 access	1	1	1	1	1	1	1	3								
1st Floor*	1				1	1		1	1								
2nd Floor*	1				1	1		1	1								

BEDROOMS

Room No.*	Main Door	Wardrobe	Washbasin Unit (Doors & Unit only)	Walls	Ceilings	Carpet	Light switches	Lights	Plug Sockets	Hand Basin	Taps	Towel Rail	Mirror/ Toiletry Cupboard	Bed	Headboard	Bed Boxes	Desk & Drawers
C01																	
C02																	
C03																	

Figure 4.12 Example repair notification form.

Communicating and training

The information you have to give your staff is regulated by different legislation. We have seen how the employer and employee have different responsibilities. But as supervisor, what do you have to communicate?

Evidence

What kind of training have you delivered to your staff regarding health and safety, security or hygiene? How did you record it? What did you do with the record? Did you then monitor the staff to see the improvements after training? If you found someone not doing well, what did you do? Did you suggest further training or some sort of support? How did you communicate your information?
1.2, 1.3, 1.4, 2.5, 2.9, 2.10.

Evidence

What is your role in communicating risk assessment findings to your team members? It is important to communicate the risk assessment outcomes to the staff in order to prevent accidents and to improve working methods. How can you show that this communication has been effective?
1.2, 1.5, 1.7, 2.9, 2.10, 2.11, 2.12, 2.15, 2.16, 2.18, 2.19, 2.20, 2.22.

What you must communicate to your staff

The main information about your organisation's health and safety policies will be given to employees as part of the induction process. Within the department, you as supervisor will also need to do some or all of the following, as shown in Table 4.1.

Action	Reason	Method
Draw their attention to where the statutory poster or leaflet is displayed	Comply with the law	Show them
Inform staff what to do in this department if they, a colleague or a customer is taken ill or has an accident at work	Comply with RIDDOR	Show them the accident book, where it is kept and how to fill it in; also where to hand in the completed pages
Distribute or organise the giving of suitable personal protective equipment (PPE) where necessary (e.g. rubber gloves, plastic aprons, goggles for oven cleaning)	Comply with PPE regulations	Physical or delegated; monitor the use of PPE by observation; correct those working unsafely according to the organisation's procedures
Provide first-aid equipment, trained employees and facilities relative to the organisation's size and assessed risks	Comply with the law	Show them where the first-aid box is, especially if they work in the kitchen or food and beverage service areas
Display specified safety signs to warn of remaining risks	Comply with regulations	Tour of department indicating safety signs when first employed; reminder in team meetings
Display your statement on employees' liability insurance	Comply with law	Show them or tell them about the statement
Draw attention to local hazards other than those indicated by a safety sign	Comply with law and to prevent them having an accident	Show them
Encourage suggestions and good working practices among your team	Comply with law	During team briefings, and always after an accident
Refer to staff handbook regarding the organisation's policies, etc.	Comply with law	Make sure they understand the English – it is important the team understands, not just that you tell them
Draw their attention to any changes or new risks.	Comply with law	Department memo on a board, team meetings, individual warning if necessary
Draw their attention to evacuation and emergency procedures.	Comply with law	Handbook, posters, signs, verbal instruction and revision in team meetings; monitor drills and feedback to staff either through memo or team briefing

Table 4.1 What you must communicate to staff.

External authorities

We have seen that there are a number of external authorities that have powers to inspect and to require records to be submitted by hospitality organisations. As a supervisor, you will often be dealing directly with these authorities by providing them with information or showing them round premises. Many of the documents required will be your responsibility to keep up to date.

The following table provides a summary of external authorities who may need information regarding health, hygiene, safety and security of the working environment.

Authority	Documentation/information they are likely to require
Environmental Health Officer (EHO) working for the local authority	Temperature charts, accident book, date monitoring for fridges and freezers, health & safety policy, food hygiene policy, training records, induction records risk assessment
Health and Safety Executive (HSE) inspector	A health and safety inspector may visit your organisation to examine the arrangements in place for assessing and controlling risks from work-related pressures or other health and safety at work issues. Inspectors will be looking for evidence that your organisation has undertaken or plans to complete a suitable and sufficient risk assessment (www.hse.gov.uk)
Police (regarding security issues, e.g. theft, personal attack, acts of violence)	CCTV footage, duty rotas, personal information of staff and customers, e.g. addresses, witness interview
Insurance company of the business and of customers, in the case of a claim	Record of incident initiating the claim, accident book, Health and Safety Information (records and policy), Food Hygiene Information (records and policy)
Fire officers and the fire brigade	Fire documentation, risk assessment, records of fire fighting equipment servicing, escape routes and plans, records of fire drills, Fire Policy, evacuation and emergency plans
Medical staff and emergency services.	Accident book, duty rota, entrance instructions / building plans, witness interview

Table 4.2 External authorities and what information they require.

Test yourself!

1 What are your main responsibilities as a supervisor (team leader) towards your staff regarding COSHH?

2 What is HACCP and why is this system important?

3 Where should waste be left, and what should it never block?

4 How do you know where to assemble in the case of a fire?

5 If you see a member of staff working and they are very drowsy, what should you do? What could this indicate, and what can you do to prevent injury to the person or others because of their actions?

6 What procedures should you follow in your workplace in order to store information regarding health and safety at work?

7 What information regarding health and safety are you required to make available to external authorities? Why?

8 What kinds of checks can be made on small electrical equipment to ensure it is safe to use?

9 What sort of information is gathered by the receptionist about foreign guests?

Further information

The Caterer and Hotelkeeper magazine

CIEH (2003) *Supervising Health and Safety at Work*, Chartered Institute of Environmental Health, Chadwick House.

Health and Safety at Work Notice (ISBN 978 0 717624 93 5)

Useful weblinks:

Parliament – www.parliament.uk

The Health and Safety Executive: information and publications relating to the hospitality industry – www.hse.gov.uk

The Chartered Institute of Environmental Health (CIEH) – www.cieh.org

The Royal Society for Public Health (RSPH) – www.rsph.org.uk

The Institute of Occupational Safety and Health (IOSH) – www.iosh.co.uk

Business Link: advice provided by the Small Business Service UK – www.businesslink.gov.uk

Reference for local authority professionals with links to health and safety websites – www.info4localgov.com

HS5

Improve the customer relationship

This chapter covers the following units:

○ Level 3 Diploma Hospitality Supervision and Leadership (NVQ) Unit
   HSL5: Lead a team to improve customer service
○ Technical Certificate Unit 2: Supervision of operations in the
   hospitality industry – 1.1, 1.2, 1.3, 1.4, 1.5, 1.6.
This unit is Unit 26 from the Institute of Customer Service standards.

**Working through this chapter could also provide
evidence for the following key skills:**

○ C2.1a, C2.2, C2.3, N2.1.

In this chapter you will learn about:

○ customer service fundamentals
○ motivation of the team
○ who the customers are
○ defining customer service and its delivery
○ working with excellence models
○ dealing with customer service problems
○ going the extra mile
○ using the whole team to improve customer service
○ legislation to consider when providing customer service.

Likely sources of evidence

1.1 treat team members with respect at all times
Witness testimony. Observation. PD.

1.2 agree with team members their role in delivering effective customer service
Induction training, briefing sessions, appraisals, emails, memos, etc.

1.3 involve team members in planning and organising their customer service work
Briefings, dept meetings, memos, emails, handover books.

1.4 allocate work which takes full account of team member's customer service skills and the objectives of the organisation
Team briefings, rotas, function sheets, liaising with other depts to second staff, emails, memos, records of telephone conversations. PD to determine how they match the organisational objectives for staffing.

1.5 motivate team members to work together to raise their customer service performance
Team briefings, minutes of meetings, training, feedback sessions. PD.

2.1 give team members support and direction when they need help
Witness testimonies, PD, emails, help notes.

2.2 encourage team members to work together to improve customer service
PD pointing to e.g. use of customer feedback to identify areas for improvement, response to complaints, targets set to reduce number of complaints or address a particular area of weakness.

2.3 check that team members understand what they have to do to improve their work with customers and why that is important
Briefings, appraisals, follow up from a customer complaint. Witness testimony. Letters of compliments. PD. Observation of team briefing or training session.

2.4 check with team members what support they feel they may need throughout this process
Reviews, team meetings, appraisals, witness testimony.

3.1 provide sensitive feedback to team members about their customer service performance
Debriefs, feedback from compliments, letters or oral, PD to ascertain that they understand the need for sensitive feedback

3.2 encourage team members to discuss their customer service performance
Team meetings, debriefs, observation. PD/narrative.

3.3 discuss sensitively with team members action they need to take to continue to improve their customer service performance
One-to-one discussions, appraisals, witness testimony, PD.

Introduction

This unit is about looking at both your organisation and your staffing resources, and bringing these together in a constructive way to improve overall customer service. You need to give support and guidance to your team to encourage them to improve their customer service delivery. It is about having a passion for customer service, and sharing this enthusiasm with your colleagues and staff team. It is about leading by example.

In the world of business, there is ever-increasing competition on costs, products and the delivery of service. Customers generally select a product for many reasons, such as the cost of the product or for ethical or moral reasons, for example, their preference for organic or vegetarian food. The main point is that customers do have a choice as to whether they visit your establishment. Often, the key to that choice is driven by the service level they receive – this can be the deciding factor when someone is making up their mind which establishment to choose.

Customer choice is heavily influenced by the level of customer service.

Customer service fundamentals

Mission statements, visions and values

Organisations spend a lot of time and energy on the development of good customer service. Many strive for excellence in service, and will use all sorts of management tools, as discussed below (page 174). Larger organisations will have a mission statement that sets out the purpose of the business (see page 64). Often, the senior management of a business creates a vision to set out how they wish the organisation to develop. Values describe the understanding and expectation of the organisation in terms of behaviour underpinning internal and external relationships. These values are usually written down and linked to the personal objectives agreed for each team member. The values set out the ethos or culture of the business, and are based on factors such as trust, support and truth.

A mission statement is about treating people with respect and dignity. It is not just words, but should be a creed injected from the top to the whole organisation. To expect employees to exceed the expectations of the customers, the management should strive to exceed the expectations of the employees.

There is usually an open commitment to communication, recognising achievement and empowering people; at the heart of this will be a focus on the importance of the individual to the whole business. Like the different-sized cogs in a big machine, the managing director of an organisation relies on his or her staff to make the business work; if one person does not fulfil their role, the whole business will suffer.

The same principles also apply to the work of small businesses. They may not need to be written down or communicated formally, because of the size of the business, but what is important is that everyone understands what they are doing and that their personal contribution is valuable. Staff should receive praise, encouragement, training and communication to help motivate and empower them. This is where you, as a supervisor, play a key role. Developing the right people skills is vital to success in your role.

Leading your team

As a supervisor, how do you lead your team in order to improve customer service?

There is a saying that you should lead by example. In practice, that means you should exhibit all the good features of customer service and 'live those values', so that you treat not only your external customers with value and respect, but also everyone else you encounter – that means all of your internal 'customers'.

Staff like to be valued – they want to be clear about what is expected from them and to have clear communication channels. This should start with the induction process at the beginning of their employment, a clear job description, and the provision of training to the organisation's standards of performance. The ongoing process should include regular communication via one-to-one meetings or staff briefings, and regular appraisals or reviews where all relevant parties are involved in the review process (see page 70).

People value feedback when they have done a good job; they will also need feedback when they need to improve their performance.

Roles in delivery of customer service

Everyone has a role in the delivery of customer service, and it is important that everyone can see how the whole process fits together. Beyond the actual point of service, there are many other support roles without which the service person could not deliver: the food staff are reliant on the food preparation staff, who are reliant on the suppliers of equipment, energy and commodities. If any of these links breaks, it is likely to have an impact on service. There are also some vital staff behind the scenes, for example, those who wash the plates or the laundry.

It is important that this is understood by your staff through clear setting of their objectives, and a clear understanding of the other roles. There should be no room for an 'us-and-them' culture to emerge. An ongoing negative attitude between staff is counter-productive and will affect customer service. Some businesses have a policy of encouraging people to carry out short periods of work in other departments, or hold team exercises to encourage team spirit, understanding and mutual respect. As a supervisor, you need to think about the ways in which you can foster respect within your team.

Planning and organising work

It is important to plan and organise staff to enable the delivery of customer service. Rotas will play a role in the delivery of service, since the business level will dictate the level of staff required, for example, for a shift preparing for a special function, or when making up rooms for a busy conference. It is the supervisor's role to identify the resources necessary to deliver the service level required. Calculating staff levels from business information and translating that into the staff rota is an important skill, but is not the only thing the supervisor needs to do. You must also make sure the staff are briefed adequately about the day's workload. This communication needs to be two-way, with the supervisor making sure staff have opportunities to ask questions and seek clarification, making notes if necessary.

Motivation of the team

Customer service is not just about smiling – it is a whole philosophy of how to care for your customer. It begins with the quality of the product and service, and continues throughout the relationship we build with our customers. From the first tentative phone call from a prospective customer, to the final letter from them saying how much they have enjoyed themselves, we can have a direct influence on their experience through our attitude, attention to detail, and much more.

Serve customers as they expect to be served

Keep existing customers happy

Exceed customers' expectations

Figure 5.1 Exceeding customers' expectations is at the core of customer service.

It is essential in **hospitality** that we constantly look for ways to improve the relationship we have with our customers. This is at the very heart of the business, and the definition of hospitality.

> **Definition**
> **Hospitality:** the act, practice or quality of offering a generous welcome to guests or strangers.

Your role is to ensure the quality standard is maintained across the whole customer experience. Each department, whatever the type of establishment, is dependent on excellent customer relationships to function effectively. As a supervisor, you will generally be the primary link between the customer, the management and the staff. All will be depending on you to deal with everyday issues in a competent and professional manner as they arise. What this means in reality is that you should show a passion for service delivery that will be transmitted by actions and deeds to those you are working alongside, to ensure the customer's experience is positive and meets their needs. In this unit we are looking at how you can build on and improve customer service by your own attitude and that of your staff. Different customers will need different methods of communication, and you will need to recognise the most appropriate method of communication for your various customers. We will look at some of the benefits of alternative forms of communication as we progress through the unit.

As a supervisor, you should always aim to exceed a customer's expectations. If the customer tells you they have been to your establishment before, look at historic records within the organisation to see what their preferred services were. Can you discover what they thought of the room service and the restaurant from their customer survey report? Repeat bookings are crucial business opportunities. If a new organisation books your venue for a function, do some research on it – how long has it been running, what does it do, and what do its customers say about it? You will be able to use the information to help your team meet the organisation's requirements and exceed expectations.

Actions

○ Set an example for your staff, with positive, open body language that will welcome the customer. Slouching, scowling and sulking are all negative forms of body language that your customer – whether a member of staff or of the public – will interpret as your lack of enthusiasm for the organisation. You will send out a signal that they are not welcome. A good posture and a smile are examples of open body language that portray sincerity, candour and reliability. These set an example to the staff for whom you are responsible. Even when things go wrong, you need to remain positive and professional.

Positive body language.

○ Set realistic and achievable targets for the staff. For example, if in the restaurant, set realistic and timely targets for taking orders once the customer has been seated.

- Use team meetings to ensure staff are fully aware of the standards you expect from them at all times, and encourage them to suggest ways in which the service could be improved.
- Make use of customer surveys to discover what customers think you're doing well, and what needs to be improved. After all, you may think you are all doing a wonderful job, but if the customer feels differently then all your hard work will not deliver the customer service excellence that you are striving towards.

Working together

- Train staff to identify positive and negative body language (see pages 17–18) and empower them to consciously recognise the difference. *Waitrose Magazine* (February 2008) reported that Waitrose had been named the best high street retailer for customer service, as shoppers said they were increasingly willing to pay a little extra for better service. You can have all the technology in the world, but survey after survey shows that it is the people delivering the service who make the real difference. Why? Because people can be more flexible than machines and demonstrate an implicit understanding of the particular needs of individual customers. Positive personal contact really does matter.
- Monitor the staff to ensure they are following through their training. You have to be confident that the standard will be maintained at all times. Staff should be corrected if they allow personal issues to affect the level of service delivery.

- Having collected customers' comments, analyse them thoroughly to help you set targets for improvements. One survey found that UK customers spend, on average, 2 hours 16 minutes a week dealing with customer service staff – as a nation, that equates to 5.8 billion hours a year. In a poor economic climate, with customers having to be persuaded to spend their money, the importance of excellent customer service becomes more and more vital.

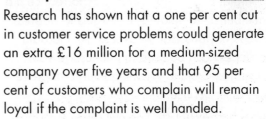

Good practice

Research has shown that a one per cent cut in customer service problems could generate an extra £16 million for a medium-sized company over five years and that 95 per cent of customers who complain will remain loyal if the complaint is well handled.

Who the customers are

A customer is anyone to whom you deliver a service.

External and internal customers

The external customer has no direct association with your organisation. In most cases they will be paying for the services your organisation provides. They may be guests, companies using conference facilities, or event organisers. Other external organisations, such as suppliers or outside contractors, are also customers for your services in terms of good communication, prompt action, etc., even if they are not paying for them. They will all have different motivations for coming to your organisation. Value for money, loyalty to a brand, past reputation or a new experience can all have an influence on the local reputation of your organisation.

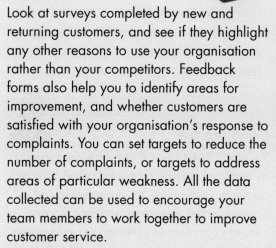

Evidence

Look at surveys completed by new and returning customers, and see if they highlight any other reasons to use your organisation rather than your competitors. Feedback forms also help you to identify areas for improvement, and whether customers are satisfied with your organisation's response to complaints. You can set targets to reduce the number of complaints, or targets to address areas of particular weakness. All the data collected can be used to encourage your team members to work together to improve customer service.
HSL 1.2, 1.3, 1.4, 1.5, 3.1, 3.2, 3.3, 4.3, 4.4, 4.5, 4.6, 4.7, 4.8.

Internal customers are those people who work for your organisation, and may be colleagues, managers, or anyone who is part of the team. Internal customers are very important – the way you treat them can have a direct effect on the type and quality of service that you and your team can provide. Respect has to be earned and mutual for it to be real. Some examples of external and internal customers are given in the table.

External customers	Internal customers
General public coming to dine	Staff in the restaurant
Customers arranging a function	Function organiser
An organisation arranging a party	Kitchen staff

Table 5.1 Examples of external and internal customers of a restaurant.

 Find out!

List the external and internal customers with whom you and your team need to build a good relationship.

Defining customer service and its delivery

The average satisfied customer will tell five other people about their positive experience. The average dissatisfied customer, on the other hand, will tell 15 people. It is therefore vital to get it right as often as possible, if the reputation of your organisation is to grow. It is also estimated that it costs ten times more to attract a new customer than to retain an existing one.

Generally, customers have high expectations of the level of care they should be receiving.

○ Customers now expect more than good products at good prices. As the Internet and other forms of information are more and more accessible, people can very easily make comparisons with other, similar services. So you must be aware of the competition to help ensure your standard of service delivery is outstanding.

○ Many businesses apparently forget to take customer service into account when planning training and development programmes. This can lead to the customer rating the overall service lower than the organisation might expect. Investment in the training and personal development of staff will always bring benefits to the organisation.

○ Customers do appreciate a personal touch. Remembering the names of previous customers can really put you ahead of the competition. This is not being over-familiar with your customers; it just means treating them as individuals who are valued by your organisation.

○ If your staff are poorly equipped in their interpersonal skills and lack product knowledge, then the customer will become frustrated. They might forgive initially, but if the issue continues on further visits, they will be less likely to return. This can be addressed by training and monitoring your staff.

○ Customers are entitled to feel they are doing your organisation a favour by choosing you over the rest. After all, without their patronage your organisation will not survive. Always remember they are your customers, and you are providing the service.

○ Value for money is really important. If someone has worked hard for their money, they do not want to give it away without feeling the experience was worth it (see Case study, page 170).

○ In the hospitality industry, it is inevitable that the hours worked will be reflected by the needs of the customer. Flexibility to accommodate different needs and requirements is all part of the job. Staff need to be motivated to offer service at the same standard. It can be very rewarding to be part of someone's special occasion and witness the pleasure your excellent service gives that customer.

○ Customers expect an immediate response. They do not want to be served at a time that suits you. If you are not available, then the task of dealing with immediate issues should be delegated. If there is a problem, the member of staff dealing with the customer should have some empowerment to handle the situation. If things have gone wrong, the customer wants matters to be resolved, without fuss and as quickly as possible. If the person dealing with the problem initially cannot make the necessary decision as to how to handle the situation, they should know who is available to offer that support.

○ Customers often ask for information. For example, they may wish to access their room earlier than originally agreed. The person dealing with this customer should know the policy of the organisation, be able to check on availability and confirm whether the customer's request can be granted.

○ Customers have a right to expect good service, if they are to return to your business rather than looking elsewhere.

Find out!

Where does your organisation perform well, and where can improvements be made? An organisation should be constantly looking to improve performance. As supervisor, you can play a key role in this through your involvement in staff appraisals, reviews and team briefings. Check with your team members that they understand both what they have to do to improve their work with customers, and why that is important. Check through meetings, reviews and appraisals what support they feel they may need during this process. Letters of compliment on a job well done, especially when addressed to the individual member(s) of staff, are enormously motivating. The more your team feel involved in your organisation's drive for excellence in customer service, the better they will perform.

Progression of customers

With a sustained high standard of service, it can be possible to develop a customer's loyalty to your organisation. They may start as potential customers, but you can move them up the hierarchy of the customer relationship to be an advertiser or advocate. You should be aiming, through the quality of your service, to move customers from the point of being a potential customer to a situation where they become advocates or ambassadors of the business.

Customer	Definition	How to develop their loyalty
Advertiser Advocate Ambassador ↑	An actively loyal customer who can tell others about you	It is important to keep information current about them – acknowledge that they are important to you, perhaps with a birthday card, notice of any special offers, brochures, etc.; offer rewards for loyalty
Regular ↑	A loyal customer who has used your service or product more than once	Identify how you can give them preferential treatment – record information in order to be able to meet their needs, and be as flexible as possible to exceed expectations
Mover ↑	Moving from another supplier to you	Be proactive with any feedback they give you – use a complaint in a positive way to raise the service level, try to identify future needs and collate key information
Explorer ↑	Interested in becoming a customer	Listen carefully to what they want so you can exceed their expectations – focus on what you can provide, use their name and give them a contact name
Potential customer ↑	Could be a potential customer	Know what you can offer – respond positively and be interested, give contact details

Table 5.2 Developing a customer's loyalty to your organisation.

Cooperating with other teams

Your team will often need to work closely with other teams in the organisation in order to move the customer 'up the hill of satisfaction'. After all, you will be judged on their latest experience with your business. The standard has to be consistent. The supervisor plays a key role here in setting targets and motivating the team to succeed. It is not sufficient to be efficient, you must aim to be effective in ensuring not just that things are done right, but that the *right* things are done right. What that means is that customers are given individual attention, are made to feel valued, and have their individual needs and expectations met. Some customers may not know what they expect – but they will know if the service has been inadequate. Part of the supervisor's role is to be able to anticipate needs. For example, if a family arrives, the receptionist should be trained to have readily available any information regarding family dining, children's clubs and play areas. This information will involve liaising with the kitchen, the childcare team, and also having a knowledge of local amenities.

All the teams need to link together. If there has been a change to the menu, the kitchen needs to inform the reception and dining room staff as soon as possible. If housekeeping has detected a problem with the facilities in one of the rooms, this should be given to reception as soon as possible, with an estimation of how long the room will be out of use. No one team can function in any aspect of the hospitality industry without the full support of all the others. You will need to show 'hard' skills of team building, such as knowledge of the organisation, the general customer service strategy and the systems that are in place, as well as the 'softer' skills of team building, such as leadership, recognition of the culture of the organisation, and confidence in your own skills (see pages 32 and 64).

Families with young children have special requirements.

Case study

A business had built a huge reputation as a place to dine. People came from miles away to eat because of the quality of the food. The chefs were given full training and support by the senior management. Unfortunately, cuts were made in the number of dining staff, and people were taken on who were unable to cope with the standard expected. As a result, complaints started to increase, people stopped coming because they did not feel the service in the dining area matched the service from the kitchen, and the business started to lose its reputation as a centre of excellence. The restaurant could no longer charge the higher prices that were necessary to maintain the kitchen staff, and it came to a point when people would have to be laid off. The supervisors came together and recognised that the problem was in the front of house, put together an intensive training programme, and looked at individual staff and how they could be motivated to improve the service. Issues were resolved, the front-of-house staff felt valued again, the overall service delivery improved, customers returned, and no jobs were lost. It took good communication and motivational skills by the senior staff to make the difference, leading by example. Customers now really felt they were getting value for money.

Working with excellence models

It is vital that the attitude of everyone connected to the business is positive towards the organisation, in order for them to be able to promote it to the customer. A supervisor can foster this role by the following means.

- Having very good communication with other team supervisors. A good way of developing the lines of communication is through well-planned meetings that are minuted. Meetings allow those involved to see what action points have been agreed, and the timescales. They allow different departments to become aware of some of the problems or commitments that other groups have, and therefore will help develop a feeling of mutual support.
- Showing you have confidence in the business through the way you discuss the organisation with staff and in front of customers. Here you can use your knowledge of how your organisation has grown and responded to customer comments over time to reflect the development of a thriving business. Negativity from key members of staff will be picked up by your team as well as your customers, and will affect how far you can motivate them to strive for further improvement.
- Not allowing personal feelings to affect the way you work with team members. Individuals will quickly sense any favouritism or bias. Workplaces where everyone gets on with each other

are rare, but as a team leader you have to keep your own prejudices and preconceptions away from the workplace. Valuing a diversity of staff, using their strengths to develop within the team, and understanding different types of behaviour all go towards strengthening the service delivery your team will be able to provide (see page 69).

○ Generally portraying a positive role model. Your team will be watching everything you do. If you are regularly late for your shift, why should you expect them to be on time? If you are always finding an excuse for not doing something you have agreed to do, why should you look to your team to be more diligent? The team leader or supervisor who is willing to do extra work will have a team who want to go that extra mile themselves.

○ Making sure messages are passed on to the relevant person promptly. There is nothing more frustrating than not being able to trust someone to pass on information that they have agreed to pass on. The whole strength of a business depends on an information highway that is built on trusting people to communicate and inform.

The table summarises some of the main attributes you will need to demonstrate.

Attitude	Action
Resilience	Do not take criticism personally
Care for all customers	Value diversity
Positive attitude	Much more effective than a negative mental state
Belief in oneself	Show outwardly your belief in your skills
Willingness to learn	We can all learn more
Desire to succeed	Want the organisation to grow
Outgoing and friendly	Be approachable
Valuing colleagues	Respect those you work with
Caring and empathetic	Understand people will have personal problems at times
Flexible and genuine	When giving feedback, give praise when due; try to meet the individual needs of customers by looking at issues from different perspectives

Table 5.3 Through demonstrating these attributes, you can encourage more positive atttitudes from your staff.

Figure 5.2 A hospitality team meeting.

Behaviour

There is never an excuse to be anything other than professional, courteous and patient, but this is not always easy to achieve in practice. The team may be tired and customers can be very demanding. Again, it is the role of the supervisor to use motivational skills to keep the team together.

○ Give immediate positive verbal feedback if a member of the team has had to deal with a difficult customer. You could also use this at the next team meeting as a real example of how a situation should be dealt with in line with the guidelines of the organisation.

○ Allow the team to voice their individual concerns at team meetings and through the appraisal system. In your team, you will have all types of people. Some may feel their views are not regarded as valid; others may think they are the only ones who are right. You must listen to everyone, analyse the different points of view, and then develop a strategy that will move the team forward.

○ Listen to comments from the team and the customer, and use them to highlight what works well. This is another form of customer survey that you should use, along with written surveys, to give yourself an idea of your customers' general opinions on the service they are receiving.

○ Be prepared to intervene if a member of the team is under pressure. Some people really struggle to deal with a conflict situation, whether that conflict is with a member of the internal organisation or an external customer. People should not feel harassed or bullied at work, and you need to be aware of the body language the staff member is showing as an indication that they are in an uncomfortable position. Once the situation has been resolved, you can give advice on handling similar situations in the future.

○ Use appropriate humour to lighten a tense moment. Humour is a really good form of defusing a situation that threatens to lead to aggression or conflict, as it can allow both parties to step back from the tension.

Competence – skills and knowledge

Competence can be divided into two parts: skills and knowledge.

Skills in:	Knowledge of:
communication	products
listening	the business
positive body language	key personnel
interpersonal relationships	the organisation's reputation
developing relationships	the industry
being outgoing and friendly	the administration system
use of technology	the job role
competence in role	

Table 5.4 Examples of skills and knowledge.

Generally, we can all recognise strengths and weaknesses more easily in our colleagues than in ourselves. As supervisor, you need to be very honest about areas you could develop and those that are your particular strengths.

Some people are very good at handling personal problems in a way that will allow the situation to be resolved. Others are much better at dealing with problems to do with a breakdown in a system. When you start to identify these strengths and areas that need improvement, it is possible to plan ways to use the attributes you have.

Find out!

Make a list of your own skills, knowledge and attitude. Can you recognise areas that could be improved? Setting demanding but achievable (and SMART; Unit 1, page 29) targets for yourself is an important part of your role. Supervising others does not mean neglecting your own skill development. Lead by example.

Identifying areas for improvement

The management of your organisation will be constantly looking at the business as a whole, to identify how well it is performing against targets and against the competition.

To assist with this, they may carry out a SWOT analysis. This is a way of identifying:

○ **S**trengths
○ **W**eaknesses
○ **O**pportunities
○ **T**hreats.

The table shows a typical SWOT analysis for a small hotel.

Strengths	Weaknesses
Good team spirit Excellent reputation	Premises need updating Poor local transport Two experienced waiters due to retire
Opportunities	**Threats**
Training for staff Loans available for development	New establishment just opened

Table 5.5 A SWOT analysis.

As the supervisor, you will be in a key position to work with the management to change threats to opportunities, and focus on building the reputation to capitalise on your sound customer base. You need to identify which parts of the SWOT analysis relate to your department.

○ If customers are making negative remarks about the conduct of any of the team, then you should be reviewing the levels of service being delivered.
○ Your SWOT analysis may well identify that there is a good team spirit that is not always shown to customers, and through highlighting areas that need improvement you can then develop this strength and use it to motivate the whole team into raising the level of customer service delivery.
○ If overall comments from the customers are good, and you already have a good reputation, build on this and ensure all the teams have the same high standard.
○ Motivate the team to develop new skills.

Set up a meeting with your manager to look at possible options to develop those strengths you have identified. Remember that customer service depends on the commitment of everyone in the business. Positive feedback is easy to give to someone. But any negative feedback you give to team members should be communicated sensitively and in a positive spirit, so you can work out some good action points. Everyone has off days. Try to treat issues in proportion to their importance: a one-off, silly mistake needs a different approach from repeated carelessness and failure to carry out basic responsibilities. You should give feedback in a way that encourages the team member to discuss it with you, not to become defensive and uncommunicative.

- Business objectives (the long-term plan) have an impact on…
- functional objectives (how to achieve the plan), and on…
- team objectives (who is doing what), to enable the achievement of…
- individual objectives (customer and personal satisfaction).

Possible options for improving staff performance might be:

- put experienced staff on duty with less experienced members of the team, so they can take on the role of mentor to new staff – this will make the experienced staff feel valued and give confidence to the new team member

Figure 5.3 Monitoring in the kitchen

- if introducing new procedures or equipment, allow time for training to ensure competence
- look at the methods of communication used when contacting customers.

Models used to improve customer service and businesses in general

Many theories on how to improve the customer service element of a business use models of excellence, such as:

- EFQM Excellence Model
- Six Sigma
- Investors in People (IiP)
- the 'naïve to natural' customer relationship model.

The essence of each is to aim for total quality management, so that improvements and support flow from the top down.

EFQM Excellence Model

The EQFM Excellence Model was introduced in 1992 as a framework for assessing organisations for the European Quality Award, now called the EFQM Excellence Award. It can be used as a tool for self-assessment to improve performance, a benchmark with other similar organisations, a guide to identifying areas for improvement, a structure for the organisation's management system, and as a basis for a common vocabulary and way of thinking across the organisation. This is not a checklist that has to be followed – it allows different organisations to achieve the criteria in ways that suit their business. It is based on the premise that:

> 'Excellent results with respect to performance, customers, people and society are achieved through leadership driving policy and strategy, that is delivered through people, partnerships, resources and processes.'
>
> *Source: www.efqm.org*

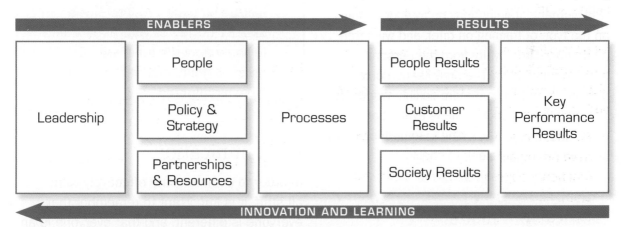

Figure 5.4 EFQM Excellence Model © 1999-2003 EFQM

Including people at all levels in the business encourages a sense of belonging, and this in itself motivates individual members to achieve improvements within the organisation.

Six Sigma

Six Sigma is a business management strategy, originally developed by Motorola, that is used today in many sectors of industry. It seeks to identify and remove the blockages in processes. It uses different quality management methods toso that there are people within the organisation who are experts in these methods (termed 'black belts'). They, in turn, are driven by the 'master black belts' (senior management). The black belts will assist champions who are dedicated to implementing the management's strategies for development (green belts). The green belts will show the employees how to implement the improvement strategy. This particular formula for improvement is driven down from the top. It helps the bottom line, and also encourages teamwork across all levels of the business.

Investors in People

Investors in People (IiP) recognises where there is investment in the people working within an organisation. This recognition is often in the form of training and personal development opportunities. It uses the strengths of people already in the organisation to move the whole organisation forward to achieve care of the customer and development of the services available. Individual members of the organisation will receive personal benefit through knowledge, and certificates of achievement. Training may be free, depending on the type of training on offer, and will often result in greater loyalty from the personnel to the organisation. The organisation also benefits from having a more flexible workforce. The main contribution of IiP is evaluation of the effectiveness of training – something many businesses do not seek to check.

The 'naïve to natural' customer relationship model

Another customer service strategy is the 'naïve to natural' model. Here the organisation works in all areas to take a customer who is new to the business through such a positive experience that they will pass through different stages to become a 'natural' customer, one who would choose your organisation first, rather than looking elsewhere. This approach relies on total management systems that foster a positive customer service experience through the systems in place, the marketing strategy, and a channelled approach to customer service at the highest possible level at all times. If properly implemented and followed, it can give the organisation a very loyal customer base.

Setting SMART targets for improvement

Once you have decided on the areas for improvement in your department, and agreed with management on the approach that will be used, you need to set SMART targets for customer service (see page 29).

Find out!

Look at the ideas for improvement that you identified in the Find out! feature on page 170. Produce a SMART target for your department to show how the team will make improvements in areas that you have highlighted.

Communication

In order to communicate effectively with all staff, it is important to remember that everyone is different, and that everyone is an individual. To do this, you need to be able to adapt your method of communication to them (see page 21).

If you are effective in your method of communication you will motivate your staff to want to be part of something larger than just their individual goals. They will be proud of the achievements of everyone and will fight for the team; this will be part of the building of trust within the team.

Dealing with customer service problems

Recognising different types of customer service problems

Meeting customers' expectations

All customers have different needs and expectations, but these are not always obvious.

> **Case study**
>
> McDonald's has often come under attack for the quality of the product it delivers. The company's approach to deal with this is to develop an interesting campaign that entices the customer in and guarantees the same quality every time a product is bought. It has also developed its own training scheme to ensure the product and customer service are consistent. It has recently received good publicity over its cleanliness and hygiene. The overall result is a product the customer can trust to be exactly what is advertised, every time they buy it – with no surprises!

Empowering staff to deal with complaints

- Identify the problem. What really went wrong?
- Listen to what the customer is saying – show attentive listening techniques.
- Repeat the problem back (this clarifies the problem).
- Ensure you know your organisation's policy for dealing with problems.
- Remain calm and polite.
- Do not get drawn into a shouting match.
- Know where you have back-up if needed.
- Give the customer a predicted time of response.
- Keep them involved throughout.
- Ensure they are happy with the outcome.
- It can be useful for future reference to have a standard form that you can complete during the conversation.

Customer complaint form

Customer name:
Company (if relevant):
Address:
Contact numbers:
Customer reference number:

What is the complaint about?

When did it happen?

Where did it happen?

Staff involved:

Action taken so far:

Any follow-up action (with timescale):

No further action required:
(document ready for filing)

Signature:

Date:

Figure 5.5 Example of a customer complaint form.

The previous page shows an example customer complaint form.

Turning the complainant into an ambassador

If a customer feels that the problem has been satisfactorily resolved, this will give them a positive impression of your organisation, and they then become a repeat customer.

> **Find out!**
>
> Find your customer complaints book. Record which are the most common complaints over the past three months and how they were resolved. What were the outcomes? Did these outcomes suit the customer or the organisation, or both? Have the complaints been fully resolved? Did this cost the organisation? What impact would this have on the organisation?

The complaint-handling policy needs to be clearly communicated to your team. Team meetings are a very good way of doing this. They are also an opportunity to encourage the whole team to look at the options, as they are the people dealing directly with the customer. You need to be sure each team member knows their role and can handle different situations as they arise – use team meetings as an opportunity to look at the policies and procedures in place, involving the team in the general customer service attitude of the organisation, and – as always – leading by example. At times there may be conflict within the team, but this is a natural part of team development. As supervisor, deal with this by giving clear leadership, firm targets and guidelines.

If some team members cannot raise their standard of performance, you will have to consider whether they are in the right role. You need to monitor any changes and the effect they are having on both internal and external customers. Conflict within the team is not always obvious, but needs to be managed before it affects performance. The feedback process, both formal and informal, is a very important role for the supervisor. It can clear up any misunderstandings, help develop trust, and break down barriers. The advantage in involving the whole team in improving customer service delivery is that they will be as diverse as the customers. Staff will have different backgrounds, skills, abilities, beliefs and feelings, and this will provide a holistic view of any areas that could be improved.

Going the extra mile

Going the extra mile means providing exceptional customer service from day to day, in order to deliver a service to the customer which is beyond their expectations. Some examples might include the following.

○ Knowing not only about your own organisation, but also about others in your area. If you have details of other restaurants that you can recommend, the customer will appreciate that you are being frank. The organisation you recommend will then return the compliment if there is mutual understanding and respect.

- Providing information on local areas of interest, such as museums, places to visit and shopping areas. Customers are grateful for advice about local amenities. Some establishments now put together an information book, with comments from other guests. This is another excellent way of getting feedback from the customers.

Go the 'extra mile' to help customers.

- Knowing about dietary requirements, doctors, hospitals and chemists. As a growing number of people have some form of allergy or specialised diet, having details about specialist food shops is really helpful, and knowing where the emergency facilities are can give the sufferers of particular illnesses reassurance.
- Making travel services available. It is really helpful if travel information is clearly set out. Public transport can be confusing to people who are unfamiliar with the area.

All the above can be provided if you know the customer needs them. This is achieved by asking the correct questions, in the correct way, to obtain quick and accurate answers. As a supervisor, you need to train your staff to carry out this kind of questioning.

Type of question	Leading words
Open	Who, what, where, when, how, why? 'How can I help you?' will lead to a detailed answer, whereas 'Can I help you?' could lead to a *No*
Closed	These questions lead to a quick response that could not be acted on. 'Would you like another drink?' could lead to a *No*
Probing	Once you have led with an open question, follow it up with a probing question that will gain more information. 'How can I help you?' (open) 'I am looking for a new coat' (response) 'What particular brand do you require?' (probing)

Table 5.6 Asking the right questions in the right way leads to quiet and accurate answers.

A customer feels valued as an individual if their needs are fully met. The outlay costs to the business for this level of service may not be excessive but the return of a happy customer will be reflected in the bottom line showing a profitable benefit.

Evidence

Hold a team meeting and identify ways in which the customer service role could be improved. Team meetings are about two-way communication. This is a good chance to empower staff to improve customer service within the limits of their authority, encouraging them to make the best use of their abilities. If you approach customer service problems as a challenge, and with a 'can-do' attitude, this approach will be transmitted to your team. Agree at least one action point, taking account of people's particular skills, as well as their job roles, so that team members feel respected and involved. Recap on these roles and meet again after a reasonable period of time to review progress.

1.2, 1.3, 1.5, 1.7, 1.8, 1.11, 2.4, 2.5, 2.6, 2.7.

Acme Hotel

Front-of-house team   13th January 2009

Venue: Restaurant

Present: HB, AD, TD, JW, SJ
Apologies: BT, SC

Minutes/Action Points

1. **Welcome and introductions, review notes from last meeting:** Hilary welcomed all and invited quick introductions around the table.   **All to note**

    Previous minutes were reviewed and updated: the new booking summary form has been implemented and is working well. This is allowing us to have full details of new arrivals and be fully prepared and organised.

2. **Review standards:** Hilary again stressed the urgency in maintaining the standards as set out through the initial induction and staff development programme. Reporting any issues promptly enables earlier communication between the team and the management team and highlights any areas that may need further staff development.   **All to do!**

3. **Menu:** We are hoping to develop a new menu in the next month. Chef is currently looking at some exciting new dishes and will welcome suggestions, particularly if they are coming from comments you have heard from the customers. We will organise a training session when the new menu is finalised to ensure you are all understand the make-up and content of each dish, and we will bring in Tony to talk about wines that would be suitable to offer as an accompaniment with each.   **All**

4. **Health and safety reminder.** Make sure you are checking your access routes through the room when carrying hot meals. A recent incident has occurred with a customer being splashed by a soup being taken to an adjoining table. We have ensured that there is space to get around but some customers do leave belongings in the way.

5. **Heating:** The heating problems are supposed to be fixed but if there any issues please report them to Sue, who is taking action if needed.   **All to note**

6. AOB

7. Date of next meeting

Figure 5.6 Example meeting minutes.

Using the whole team to improve customer service

If you select an appropriate method of communication, you and your team are more likely to meet the needs of the customer. The team will benefit from guidance from you on the different ways of communicating (see page 21).

Using feedback from the customer can be a very effective tool in showing the level of service being offered, and if there are areas that you need to improve.

- **Questionnaires** can be used to identify the day-to-day positive experiences and problems that may be noted by your customers, as they are often quantitative.
- **Surveys** can give a bigger picture over a longer period of time, as they are generally a qualitative form of gathering feedback.
- **Informal feedback** gives the ability to change requirements and services quickly if necessary. This could be in response to something to do with legislation, such as a health and safety issue.

Evidence

Look at the different ways in which you and the team communicate with your customers. Show how they differ in their effectiveness. 1.12, 2.8.

Evidence

Find out if your organisation has feedback forms, and collect some of the responses to these. Is there someone within your department who is given the responsibility for dealing with the feedback? If the customer is looking for a service you do not offer, this gives you a real customer service opportunity – make a list of these opportunities. 1.2, 2.4.

Customer survey

The Acme Hotel

Please complete the following survey as we welcome your comments and aim to develop our customer service standards to meet the needs of our customers. It will only take you a few moments.

Area	Very good	Good	Poor	Additional comments
Greeting on arrival	○	○	○	
Cleanliness of the rooms	○	○	○	
Service in the restaurant	○	○	○	
Service in the bar	○	○	○	

Figure 5.7 Example customer survey.

Having held a meeting to look at customer service comments and results, it is important that the whole team is involved in making the improvements you have agreed on. Use the individual strengths of each team member to improve the overall service delivery. If one of the team is particularly good at meeting and greeting customers on arrival, are you using them in that role? Some of the team may be much happier doing routine tasks, while others prefer to have new things to do. You should be able to identify the best person for the task and use them to develop customer service.

You might identify underperformance in the team. It is important that this is dealt with promptly. If not, the whole team will start to be affected, as your team will only be as strong as its weakest member. It is very demotivating for a team to see one member's poor performance not dealt being with. You will need to give the person an opportunity to talk about why they are not completing their job to the standard expected. They may identify a personal problem that they are having outside work, but they should not allow this to affect their commitment to the rest of the team.

Legislation to consider when providing customer service

The whole range of legislation that applies to the hospitality industry – on health and safety at work, food safety, trade descriptions, licensing, weights and measures, equal opportunities, race relations, disability discrimination, harassment in the workplace, data protection, and employment regulations – may apply when you are considering all the various aspects of customer service.

Law and policy

For detailed information on all the major legislation applying to the hospitality industry, see Legislation, page 199.

Case study

Jenny arrived for work 30 minutes late on certain days. After four weeks, the rest of the team started to notice this and grumble to their supervisor, Gill. She took care to record the incidents of lateness for the next few days. She then asked Jenny to have a coffee, away from the glare of the team. After a few minutes' general chat, she raised the evidence she had that Jenny was always late on certain days of the week. Jenny became very upset, apologised, and explained that she was having problems with the carer she had engaged to stay with her son, who had spina bifida and could not be left alone. Gill suggested that Jenny should change her hours to fit in with the carer, and Jenny agreed to work later to compensate for arriving later. The solution was given to the team, and Jenny was eventually able to explain to them what had been happening.

Test yourself!

1 Identify the following customers: (a) external; (b) internal.

2 What do you perceive as value for money?

3 Why are first impressions so important to your organisation?

4 How can you turn an explorer into an advertiser?

5 How can you ensure the communication in your organisation has been effective?

6 Give three examples of an open question.

7 How could you develop your three open questions into probing questions?

8 How could you use a team meeting to motivate your staff?

9 What type of training would be appropriate if the complaints system had been altered?

10 How would you give individual feedback to address a team member who is underperforming?

Further information

Six Sigma: www.isixsigma.com

EFQM Excellence Model: www.efqm.org

Investors in People: www.investorsinpeople.co.uk

Simple calculations and costings

Working through this chapter could also provide evidence for the following key skills:

o N2.1, N2.2.

In this chapter you will learn about:

o stakeholders and financial matters
o calculating profit
o controlling food costs; costing a dish
o calculating gross profit and food cost as a percentage of sales income
o target-setting: calculating selling price and mark up.

Introduction

This unit aims to help you to undertake the basic calculations you will carry out at work. It gives an overview of the importance of costing and profit in the hospitality industry.

As well as offering a service to others, getting job satisfaction from a day's work and getting a buzz out of being busy – the trademark of hospitality – business is about making money. Most hospitality businesses make their money by selling a lot of low-value items. Usually the most expensive items sold are rooms, especially when they are sold at a **premium rate**. As supervisor, you may be involved at different stages in calculating how to make your business profitable. For example, if the business is planning to put a new dish on the menu, you may be involved in working out how much it costs to make, and at what price it will be sold. Getting these calculations wrong could have a disastrous effect on your business, and could mean that sooner or later you end up without a job. So it is important that you feel very confident with carrying out the basic calculations that are used in the hospitality industry.

Part of the supervisor's job, along with the manager, is to analyse the daily, weekly, monthly and yearly sales from the department. Then you need to plan and budget how to increase sales and reduce costs so that the business stays successful.

Stakeholders

People who are interested in a business have something 'at stake', and are therefore called 'stakeholders'. Each stakeholder will be interested in the business for a different reason (see the table on the next page). Not only are people who own the business stakeholders; you, too, are a stakeholder.

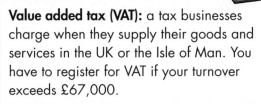

Definition

Value added tax (VAT): a tax businesses charge when they supply their goods and services in the UK or the Isle of Man. You have to register for VAT if your turnover exceeds £67,000.

Your job as a supervisor is to make sure the financial decisions and plans of the senior managers are carried out in your department.

Definition

Premium rate: a high price, usually for something like a room in a four- or five-star hotel.

Stakeholders	What they are interested in	Why they are interested
Owners/ shareholders/ managers	Has the business made a profit? Can the business pay its way? Are the sales figures increasing?	To see how much profit can be paid by the business to the owners/ shareholders To assess if the business will continue in the foreseeable future To see if the business is growing
HM Revenue and Customs	Has the business made a profit? What were the sales figures and what **VAT** was charged on these sales?	To calculate the tax due on the profit To ensure the VAT charged on the products is paid to HM Revenue and Customs
Bank manager/ lender	Has the business made a profit? What is the bank balance or overdraft? What is the value of the business?	To check if the business can afford to make loan repayments To decide how much the bank can lend to the business
Employees/trade unions you (the supervisor)	Has the business made a profit? Can the business continue to pay its way?	To assess if the business will continue to provide jobs in the foreseeable future To see if the business can afford to give pay rises and offer promotions To understand how their contribution will contribute to the profitability of the business
Customers	Is the business reliable and will it continue to trade?	To see if the business has the financial stability to carry out work for its customers
Suppliers (people to whom the business owes money)	Is the business trading profitably? Are the bills being paid on time?	To assess if the business is able to pay its bills on the due date
Competitors	What are the sales figures?	To see if their business is expanding or declining – how hard they compete with your business To consider whether your business is worth taking over

Financial matters

In a food business, as in any other business, **costs** have to be kept to a minimum while **sales** have to be at a maximum in order for the business to maximise profit. A business needs to be profitable in order to have money to pay its staff and its bills, and to use for the development of the business.

> ## Definitions
>
> **Sales (income) or revenue:** money that is received in payment for services (e.g. food, a room).
> **Costs:** money that must be spent in order to create and sell the goods and services offered by a business.

A simplified cycle of business could be as follows:

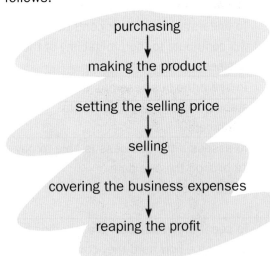

purchasing
↓
making the product
↓
setting the selling price
↓
selling
↓
covering the business expenses
↓
reaping the profit

Any successful business must plan to be financially successful. Part of this planning process lies in the **purchasing plan** of the business.

> ## Definition
>
> **Purchasing plan:** plan formulated by management to control the purchasing cycle, e.g. how to select suppliers, defining quality standards, who authorises payment, who can make an order.

The hospitality industry involves three main sales activities:

o food

o drinks

o accommodation.

Where food and beverages are concerned, the goods have to be purchased, held in stock and then sold. Once the cycle has been completed, the process starts all over again. The more times the cycle happens, the more profit you are making.

Food and beverages are a **buy–store–sell** cycle.

Accommodation is different. If you have a 20-room hotel, then you should aim to sell 20 rooms every night. If the price of every room is £50, then the hotel could potentially earn revenue of 20 × £50 = £1,000. However, if only six rooms are let, their revenue is only £300 and the remaining revenue of £700 is lost.

Accommodation is a **sell–sell–sell** cycle.

Hotels adopt a different method for costing and selling rooms than they do for costing and selling food and beverages.

Calculating profit

Calculating profit correctly is important for the survival of the business.

Costs relating to catering businesses are usually divided into:

- **food cost**: the cost of purchasing the food and beverages that are sold in a catering business
- **direct labour cost**: salaries paid to full-time and part-time permanent staff where the cost can be placed directly against income from food and drink (e.g. chefs, waiters and bar staff)
- **indirect labour cost**: salaries paid to staff such as managers, office staff and maintenance staff, who work for all departments – a proportion of indirect labour costs should be charged to all departments
- **overhead costs**: other costs that have to be paid by the business, regardless of whether it makes any sales or not (e.g. rent, council tax, water rates, services such as gas, electricity and telephone, maintenance and repairs, advertising and sundry expenses).

Gross profit: sales income less the cost of food and drink – usually expressed as a percentage of sale income.

$$\text{gross profit (\%)} = \frac{\text{gross profit}}{\text{sales income}} \times 100$$

Net profit: the profit remaining after food costs and all other costs have been deducted – also usually expressed as a percentage of sales.

$$\text{net profit (\%)} = \frac{\text{net profit}}{\text{sales}} \times 100$$

Break even: the point at which the amount of sales income is equal to the cost of making the sales.

Sales mix: the ratio of the sales of each product/department to the total sales – usually expressed as a percentage of total sales.

$$\text{sales mix (\%)} = \frac{\text{departmental sales}}{\text{total sales}} \times 100$$

Average spend: the total sales divided by the total number of customers during a given period.

$$\text{average spend} = \frac{\text{total sales}}{\text{number of customers}}$$

$$\text{average spend} = \frac{\text{weekly sales}}{\text{no. people served (covers)}} \quad \frac{4685}{365} = 12.835 = \text{£}12.84 \text{ each}$$

(rounded up: see page 192)

Turnover: income from all areas of a business (e.g. a whole hotel rather than just the housekeeping department).

Capital: money put into the business by its owner.

Liabilities: money the business owes to its suppliers and other creditors.

Percentage room occupancy: the proportion of the total number of rooms that were occupied during a given period – usually expressed as a percentage of the total number of rooms.

$$\text{percentage room occupancy} = \frac{\text{total number of rooms occupied during the period}}{\text{total rooms}} \times 100$$

Controlling food costs

In order to make a profit, a business can control two things:

○ **cost of sales**: by buying cheaper goods, having fewer staff and reducing wages
○ **sales income**: by increasing the prices or selling more food.

The correct balance of costs and income has to be achieved in order to make a profit. Most managers set targets for the profit margins they want to achieve.

Case study

At the end of a week, a restaurant earns £10,000 from selling food and drink.

Is that all profit? No – they may have had to spend £4,000 on buying in the ingredients to make the recipes, as well as on the drink.

Therefore the gross profit is:

sales   – cost of sales   =   gross profit
£10,000   –   £4000   =   **£6,000**

How do you work out the sales income for a week?

You work out the sales income for a week by adding up all the money taken at the till in the restaurant (including card payments) for the whole week. Most automatic payment points such as electronic tills calculate the total sales automatically each day. The manager or supervisor simply logs the information in their recording system in order to know how much money they have taken in during the week.

To calculate the gross profit, you need to know all the food and drink costs involved (e.g. the cost of all the ingredients used to make the meals).

Dish costing

Dish costing can be very tedious, but there are many advantages to doing it:

○ You will know exactly how much the dish costs you, so you can easily work out the selling price.
○ You will produce consistently high-quality goods, because once costed the recipes can be repeated at the same cost.
○ Your selling price will give you the same gross profit every time, unless the food costs increase.

How do you calculate the cost of an ingredient? Look at the recipe below. We are going to cost this recipe.

Chicken chasseur – serves 4

Ingredient	Quantity
Butter	50g
Parsley	10g
Chicken	1.25kg
Shallots	50g
Button mushrooms	100g
White wine	30ml
Chicken demi-glace	250ml
Tomatoes	200g
Tarragon	10g

Notice in particular the unit of measurement for each item (e.g. grams, millilitres).

Now look at the prices for each ingredient:

Ingredient	Cost per unit
Butter	£1.22 per 250g
Parsley	£0.90 per 25g
Chicken	£2.79 per kg
Shallots	£2.49 per kg
Button mushrooms	£5.27 per kg
White wine	£2.22 per 750ml
Chicken demi-glace	£2.00 per litre
Tomatoes	£0.12 each
Tarragon	£0.68 per 25g

Butter costs £1.22 per 250g and the recipe requires 50g. Here's how to work out the cost for the recipe:
- first work out the cost for 1g
- then multiply the answer by the number of grams required in the recipe.
- If butter costs £1.22 per 250g, what is the price of 50g butter?

$$\text{price for recipe quantity} = \frac{\text{purchase price}}{\text{purchase units}} \times \text{recipe units}$$

$$= \frac{1.22}{250} \times 50 = 0.244 = 24p$$

Tarragon cost 68p for 25g but the recipe requires 10g:

$$\frac{0.68}{25} \times 10 = 0.272 = 27p$$

Note: if a cost comes out with more than two decimal places after the point, it should be **rounded down** or **rounded up**, e.g.:
- 1.864 becomes £1.86 (extra digit is below 5, so rounded down)
- 1.865 becomes £1.87 (extra digit is 5 or above, so rounded up).

Sometimes the calculation is very obvious and you don't need to find the cost of one unit before calculating the cost for the recipe. For example, if the chicken costs £2.79 per kg and you need 1.25 kg, then you can simply multiply £2.79 by 1.5:

£2.79 × 1.5 = £3.49

The table on the next page shows how each of the ingredients for this recipe were costed.

Chicken chasseur					
Ingredient	Quantity	Unit	Cost per unit	Calculation	Cost (£)
Butter	50	g	250g = £1.22	1.22 ÷ 250 × 50	0.24
Parsley	10	g	25g = £0.90	0.90 ÷ 25 × 10	0.36
Chicken	1.25	kg	1kg = £2.79	2.79 × 1.25	3.49
Shallots	50	g	1kg = £2.49	2.49 ÷ 1000 × 50	0.12
Button mushrooms	100	g	1kg = £5.27	5.27 ÷ 1000 × 100	0.53
White wine	30	ml	750ml = £2.22	2.22 ÷ 750 × 30	0.09
Chicken demi-glace	250	ml	1 litre = £2.00	2 ÷ 1000 × 250	0.50
Tomatoes	200	g	Each = £0.12	approx. 3 × 12	0.36
Tarragon	10	g	25g = £0.68	0.68 ÷ 25 × 10	0.27
Total cost					5.96
Number of portions: 4					
One portion cost (£5.96 ÷ 4)					1.49
Selling price					4.97

Calculating the gross profit

See Definitions on page 190.

Gross profit = sales – cost of sales (in this case, the food cost).

The gross profit for the chicken chasseur per portion is:

(selling price) £4.97 – (food cost) £1.49 = (gross profit) £ 3.48

Say you sell 500 portions of chicken chasseur at £6.00 per portion.

Sales will be 500 × £6.00 = £3,000

Food cost will be 500 × £1.49 = £745

sales income – food cost = gross profit
£3,000   –   £745   =   £2,255

Usually the GP is expressed as a percentage of the total sales. This calculation helps to plan the profit, and control the costs, i.e. I need to get at least 70 per cent gross profit from my sales so I control the food cost and I price the dish carefully to enable this to happen. In this example the GP is 75 per cent of sales, i.e. for every pound that is received from sales, 75p is Gross Profit.

The gross profit is 75 per cent of sales.

Percentage: the proportion or rate per hundred. For example, 30 per cent (%) means 30 parts out of 100 parts.

gross profit ÷ sales income × 100 = gross profit as a percentage of income

   2,255   ÷   3,000   × 100 = 75%

Calculating food cost as a percentage of sales income

Food costs can also be expressed as a percentage of sales income.

Food cost ÷ sales income × 100 = food cost as a percentage of sales income

  £745   ÷   £3,000   × 100 = 25%

The food cost is 25% of sales income.

A simple way to calculate the percentage food cost or the percentage gross profit is to calculate one of them and take it away from 100: this gives you the other figure.

percentage food cost (25) + percentage gross profit (75) = 100

Target setting

Companies normally set targets for their gross profit so that they know they will have enough money to pay their bills and their staff. Many food businesses aim to achieve 70 per cent gross profit on food sales. This means that gross profit is 70% and food costs are 30 per cent of sales income. This is a hard figure to achieve, especially when food prices are on the increase, but setting and keeping gross profit targets is essential if the business is to survive.

Calculating the selling price

Once the cost of food has been kept under control, the next thing to do to improve profits is to get the selling price right. Once you know the food cost, you can calculate the selling price that will give you the required gross margin. This is known as 'cost plus' pricing.

To calculate the selling price, you need to know:
○ the food cost (in £)
○ the target food cost (as % of sales).

The formula you need is:

(food cost ÷ food cost as % target) × 100 = selling price

  (1.49   ÷   30)   × 100 = £4.97

If food is being sold for consumption on the premises, you will need to include VAT in the price charged. To calculate the selling price of the dish, you need to know how much it costs in food terms. Then you have to include VAT and meet the required gross profit of 70 per cent (see previous page).

$$\text{selling price} = \frac{\text{food cost}}{\text{percentage food cost}}$$

$$= \frac{1.49}{30} \times 100 = £4.97$$

To calculate £4.97 plus VAT @ 15 per cent

4.97 × 0.15 = 0.7455
0.7455 + 4.97 = 5.7155
selling price = £5.72

So in order to keep the food cost at 30 per cent of the sales income, the selling price (including VAT) of each portion of chicken chasseur should be £5.72; any increase in the selling price will increase the gross profit.

Calculating mark-up

The mark-up is the gross profit expressed as a percentage of the food cost.

$$\text{mark-up} = \frac{\text{gross profit}}{\text{food cost}} \times 100$$

$$= \frac{£3.48}{£1.49} \times 100 = 234\%$$

Another example:

If the food cost of a cake is 40p and the selling price is £1, then the gross profit is 60p and the mark-up is 150 per cent.

$$\text{mark-up} = \frac{£60}{£40} \times 100 = 150\%$$

The final table

Chicken chasseur – makes 4 portions					
Ingredient	Quantity	Unit	Cost per unit	Calculation	Cost (£)
Butter	50	g	250g = £1.22	1.22 ÷ 250 × 50	0.24
Parsley	10	g	25g = 90p	0.90 ÷ 25 × 10	0.36
Chicken	1.25	kg	1kg = £2.79	2.79 × 1.25	3.49
Shallots	50	g	1kg = £2.49	2.49 ÷ 1000 × 50	0.12
Button mushrooms	100	g	1kg = £5.27	5.27 ÷ 1000 × 100	0.53
White wine	30	ml	750ml = £2.22	2.22 ÷ 750 × 30	0.09
Chicken demi-glace	250	ml	1 litre = £2.00	2 ÷ 1000 × 250	0.50
Tomatoes	200	g	Each = £0.12	3 × 12 200 g is about 3 tomatoes	0.36
Tarragon	10	g	25g = 68p	0.68 ÷ 25 × 10	0.27
Total cost for 4 portions					£5.96
Cost for 1 portion					£1.49
Selling price (excl. VAT)					£4.97
Selling price (incl. VAT)					£5.72
Mark-up					234%
Food cost					30%
Gross profit					70%

Exercise 1: Calculating gross profit, percentage gross profit and mark-up

FC	SP (no VAT)	GP	% GP	Mark-up
80p	£1.00	20p	20%	25%
35p	£1.40		75%	300%
90p	£3.50			
£1.50	£2.40			
£3.50	£9.75			

Exercise 2: Setting the selling price

	FC	% GP	% FC	SP	SP incl. VAT
1	40p	60%			
2	25p	30%			
3	£1.06	50%			
4	94p	45%			
5	85p	49%			
6	32p	33%			
7	56p	20%			
8	75p	70%			
9	£2.00	30%			
10	55p	35%			

Exercise 1: Solutions

FC	SP	GP (SP − FC = GP)	% GP (GP ÷ SP × 100)	Mark-up (GP ÷ FC × 100)
80p	£1.00	20p	20%	25%
35p	£1.40	£1.05	75%	300%
90p	£3.50	£2.60	74%	289%
£1.50	£2.40	90p	38%	60%
£3.50	£9.75	£6.25	64%	178.5%

Exercise 2: Solutions

	FC	%GP	%FC	SP (FC ÷ %FC × 100)	SP incl. VAT (at 15%)
1	40p	60%	40%	£1.00	£1.15
2	25p	30%	70%	36p	41p
3	£1.06	50%	50%	£2.12	£2.43
4	94p	45%	55%	£1.71	£1.97
5	85p	49%	51%	£1.66	£1.92
6	32p	33%	67%	48p	55p
7	56p	20%	80%	70p	81p
8	75p	70%	30%	£2.50	£2.88
9	£2.00	30%	70%	£2.85	£3.29
10	55p	35%	65%	85p	98p

Appendix: Legislation

Club Premises Certificate

Relevant units

HSL 11

Summary

A Club Premises Certificate authorises a members' club to carry out licensable activities. The licensable activities it can carry out are:

○ sale or supply of alcohol to members or guests

○ provision of regulated entertainment

○ provision of hot food/drink at any time between 11 p.m. and 5 a.m.

There is no requirement for a qualifying club to have a Designated Premises Supervisor named on the certificate or personal licence holder present to authorise the supply of alcohol.

Control of Noise at Work Regulations 2005 (Noise Regulations)

Relevant units

HSL 4

Summary

Working in a night club behind a bar can damage your hearing. In April 2008 the existing Noise at Work Regulations 1989, protecting workers in the music and entertainment sectors from exposure to excessive noise were replaced by the Control of Noise at Work Regulations 2005 (Noise Regulations). For other industry sectors these Regulations have been in force since April 2006. These regulations recognised that music is unusual as it is noise deliberately created for enjoyment and therefore practical guidelines are necessary to help workers, employers and freelancers in the music and entertainment sectors protect their hearing and safeguard their careers. Music and entertainment sectors are defined in the Noise Regulations as all workplaces where a) live music is played or b) recorded music is played in a restaurant, bar, public house, discotheque or nightclub, or alongside live music or a live dramatic or dance performance.

The Sound Advice website and Sound Advice HSG 260 publication, were launched in July 2008. They provide practical advice on controlling noise at work in the music and entertainment sectors, and identify good practice to help avoid the harmful effects of prolonged exposure to noise. The aim of Sound Advice is to control or reduce exposure to noise at work without stopping people from enjoying music, whether you are an employer, freelancer or employee.

Control of Substances Hazardous to Health Regulations) (COSHH), as amended 2002

Relevant units

HSL 4, HSL 6, HSL 7

Summary

COSHH identifies dangerous chemicals, such as cleaning agents. The regulations require that chemicals must be labelled accurately and must be used only after suitable training has been given. The correct protective clothing, e.g. gloves and goggles, must always be used. The COSHH Regulations form part of the Health and Safety at Work Act and consist of rules controlling substances that are considered hazardous to health. The COSHH Regulations state that:

○ chemicals that may be dangerous to people must be clearly identified
○ those chemicals must be stored, issued and used safely
○ training must be given in the use of these chemicals
○ suitable protective clothing must be provided when using the chemicals.

When using any type of chemical you should:

○ always follow the manufacturer's instructions carefully
○ never mix one chemical with another
○ never move any chemical from its original container into a different one that is incorrectly labelled or has no label at all
○ never use food containers to store a cleaning chemical
○ always store chemicals in the correct place.

To comply with COSHH you need to follow these eight steps:

1 Assess the risks to health from hazardous substances used in or created by your workplace activities.
2 Decide what precautions are needed to protect your employees from hazardous substances.
3 Prevent, or if prevention is not possible, adequately control exposure.
4 Ensure that control measures are used and maintained.
5 Monitor the exposure of employees to hazardous substances.
6 Carry out appropriate health surveillance.
7 Prepare plans and procedures to deal with accidents, incidents and emergencies.
8 Ensure employees are properly informed, trained and supervised.

Copyright, Designs and Patents Act 1988

Relevant units

HSL 6

Summary

The Copyright, Designs and Patents Act 1988 is the main law that covers intellectual property rights in the United Kingdom and the work to which the rights apply. The law gives rights to the creators of literary, dramatic, musical, artistic works, sound recordings, broadcasts, films and typographical arrangement of published editions, in order to control the ways in which their material may be used. The rights cover:

○ broadcast and public performance
○ copying
○ adapting
○ issuing
○ renting and lending copies to the public.

In many cases, the creator will also have the right to be identified as the author and to object to distortions of his or her work. International conventions give copyright protection in most countries, subject to national laws.

Data Protection Act 1998

Relevant units

HSL 4, HSL 6, HSL 8, HSL 17/18, HSL 21/22, HSL 25

Summary

The Data Protection Act 1998 defines a legal basis for handling information relating to people living in the UK. It is the main piece of legislation that deals with the protection of personal data such as names, addresses and other personal details like a person's date of birth. Although the Act does not mention privacy, in practice it provides a way in which individuals can enforce the control of information about themselves. Most of the Act does not apply to domestic use, for example, keeping a personal address book. However, anyone holding personal data for other purposes is legally obliged to comply with this Act, subject to some exemptions. It applies to all data, whether this is stored on computer (electronically) or in a paper-based traditional filing system.

The Act defines eight data protection principles:

- Data may only be used for the specific purposes for which it was collected.
- Data must not be disclosed to other parties without the consent of the individual whom it concerns, unless there is legislation or another overriding legitimate reason to share the information (for example, the prevention or detection of crime). It is an offence for other parties to obtain this personal data without authorisation.
- Individuals have a right of access to the information held about them, subject to certain exceptions (for example, information held for the prevention or detection of crime).
- Personal information may be kept for no longer than is necessary (e.g. if a child has left a school, information should not be kept on them).
- Personal information may not be transmitted outside the European Economic Area unless the individual whom it concerns has consented, or adequate protection is in place, for example, by the use of a prescribed form of contract to govern the transmission of the data.
- Subject to some exceptions for organisations that only do very simple processing, and for domestic use, all bodies or organisations that process personal information must register with the Information Commissioner's Office.
- Organisations holding personal information are required to have adequate security measures in place. These include technical measures (e.g. firewalls) and organisational measures (e.g. staff training).
- Subjects have the right to have factually incorrect information corrected (note: this does not extend to matters of opinion).

Disability Discrimination Act 1995

Relevant units

HSL 2, HSL 6, HSL 21/22, HSL 24

Summary

The Disability Discrimination Act 1995 (updated 2005) makes it unlawful to discriminate against people in respect of their disabilities in relation to employment, the provision of goods and services, education and transport.

It is still permissible for employers to require reasonable medical criteria for employment, and to expect adequate performance from all employees once any reasonable adjustments have been made.

In addition to imposing obligations on employers, the Act places duties on service providers and requires 'reasonable adjustments' to be made when providing access to goods, facilities, services and premises.

The duties on service providers have been introduced in three stages.

○ Since 2 December 1996 it has been unlawful for service providers to treat disabled people less favourably for a reason related to their disability.
○ Since 1 October 1999 service providers have had to make 'reasonable adjustments' for disabled people, such as providing extra help or making changes to the way they provide their services.
○ Since 1 October 2004 service providers may have to make other 'reasonable adjustments' in relation to the physical features of their premises to overcome physical barriers to access.

The Act requires public bodies to promote equality of opportunity for all disabled people. The website for the Department for Work and Pensions offers further information, including details on the changes made by the Disability Discrimination Act 2005 (see www.dwp.gov.uk/employers/dda).

Electricity at Work Act 1989

Relevant units

HSL 4

Summary

Electricity at Work Regulations 1989 (EAWR) places a legal responsibility on employers and employees to ensure that electrical systems used at work under their control are safe.

To achieve compliance with the legal requirements of the Electricity at Work Regulations 1989, proof is required that an electrical system is safe. This involves, amongst other things, proper inspection and testing of a system by competent people and the creation and maintenance of records. Different regulations are applied to small portable appliances and to large pieces of stationary equipment.

Portable equipment is defined as equipment that has a lead (cable) and plug and which is normally moved around or can easily be moved from place to place, e.g. floor cleaners, kettles, heaters, fans, televisions, table lights. Equipment in hotel bedrooms, such as hairdryers or kettles, with a permanently wired lead, also comes into this category, as does equipment that could be moved, e.g. photocopiers, fax machines, and desktop computers. There may also be kitchen equipment such as mixers or food processors and laundry equipment.

203

Environmental Protection Act 1990

Relevant units

HSL 3

Summary

The EPA 1990 imposes duties on certain landowners and occupiers to keep specified land clear of litter and refuse, and also upon local authorities and the secretary of state to keep clean public highways.

The duty of care regulations explain part of the EPA (1990), which imposes a legal duty on businesses to take all reasonable steps to keep waste safe whilst it is in their possession. It also requires businesses to make sure they only pass waste on to an authorised person in order to dispose of it correctly.

If there is a litter problem related to particular kinds of commercial premises, such as takeaway restaurants, cinemas, sports centres, service stations and others, then the local authority has powers to issue Street Litter Control Notices (SLCN).

Where a litter problem can be clearly traced to certain types of business, such as 'food on the go' establishments, mobile vendors or market stalls, a local authority can issue a street litter control notice. This can be used to compel the occupier, or the owner of business or retail premises, to clear up litter and implement measures to prevent the land from becoming defaced again. Local authorities are allowed to issue a fixed penalty notice to any person who has not complied with a street litter control notice.

Remember:
- Provide enough litter bins, preferably covered ones.
- Ensure bins are of a sufficient size for the quantity of litter produced.
- Empty and clean bins on a regular basis.
- Set aside adequate storage space for trade waste, either inside the building or in an enclosed area outside.
- Trade refuse containers must be of adequate capacity and in good condition.
- Takeaway food shops should have litter bins outside their premises (by agreement with the council) and display notices encouraging customers to use them.
- Carry out regular clean ups, including the rear of premises, car parks and delivery and storage areas.
- Keep within the law by having a trade refuse collection agreement with either the council, the council's contractor or a private contractor authorised to carry waste.

Fire Precautions (Workplace) Regulations 1997, amended 1999

Relevant units

HSL 7, HSL 21/22

Summary

The Workplace Fire Precautions Legislation brings together existing health & safety and fire legislation to form a set of dedicated Fire Regulations. The aim is to have in place a risk-appropriate standard of fire safety for persons in the workplace.

These regulations were amended on 1 December 1999 in order to confirm the concept of the employer having unconditional responsibility for the safety of employees. As a result, most workplaces are now subject to the legal requirements of these regulations. The regulations apply to all workplaces where persons are employed to work. This means that those workplaces that are subject to the requirements of a fire certificate (or application) have additional legal obligations in respect of the Workplace Regulations. An existing fire certificate may form the basis of the fire risk assessment, but it is not a substitute for a fire risk assessment.

Employers are required to:
- carry out a fire risk assessment
- monitor and review the risk assessment and revise as appropriate
- inform staff or their representatives of the risks
- plan for an emergency
- provide staff information and training
- nominate persons to assist.

Employers are required to provide and maintain (to the extent that it is appropriate as determined by the fire risk assessment):
- means for detecting and giving warning in case of fire

emergency lighting
- means of escape
- fire safety signs
- fire-fighting equipment.

Fire Precautions Act 1971

Relevant units

HSL 7, HSL 21/22

Summary

The Act furthers the provisions for the protection of persons from fire risks. If any premises are put to use and are designated, a certificate is required from the fire authority. Classes of use cover: the provisions of sleeping accommodation; use as an institution; use for the purposes of entertainment, recreation, instruction, teaching, training or research; use involving access to the premises by members of the public; and use as a place of work.

Applications for a fire certificate must be made on the prescribed form and the fire authority must be satisfied that there are adequate means of escape in case of fire, means of fire-fighting and means of giving persons in the premises warning in case of fire. Every fire certificate issued shall specify particular use or uses of the premises, its means of escape, details of the means of fire-fighting, and of fire warning and, in the case of factories, particulars of any explosive or highly flammable materials which may be stored or used on the premises. The certificate may impose such restrictions as the fire authority considers appropriate and may cover the instruction or training of people about what to do in case of fire, or it may limit the number of individuals who may be in the premises at any one time.

Fire Regulatory Reform (Fire Safety) Order 2005

Relevant units

HSL 4

Summary

The Order, made under the Regulatory Reform Act 2001, replaces many of the references to fire safety in other legislation such as the Fire Precautions Act, Licensing Act and Housing Acts with a simple, single Order. It requires any person who exercises some level of control in premises to take reasonable steps to reduce the risk from fire and ensure occupants can escape safely if a fire does occur.

In many premises, fire safety is often a matter of common sense but you will have to ensure that sufficient time is put aside to work through the necessary steps. In more complicated premises, or those with a high life risk, more expert help may be required.

The Order applies to virtually all premises and covers nearly every type of building, structure and open space. These include:

- offices and shops
- premises that provide care
- community halls
- the common areas of houses in multiple occupation including common fire warning systems, etc.
- pubs, clubs and restaurants
- schools and libraries
- tents and marquees
- hotels and hostels
- factories and warehouses.

Food Hygiene (England) Regulations 2006

Relevant units

HSL 6, HSL 7, HSL 3

Summary

On 1 January 2006 the Food Hygiene (England) Regulations 2006 introduced a requirement on all food businesses to put in place procedures which are based on the principles of Hazard Analysis and Critical Control Points (HACCP). There is a legal requirement on all food businesses to provide appropriate documents and records showing how the HACCP principles are being applied.

Food Labelling Regulations 1984, amended 1996

Relevant units

HSL 4

Summary

The main provisions of the regulations are to require all food which is ready for delivery to the ultimate consumer or to a catering establishment, subject to certain exceptions, to be marked or labelled with:

- the name of the food
- a list of ingredients
- the appropriate durability indication (i.e. how long it might last)
- any special storage conditions or conditions of use

- the name and address of the manufacturer, packer or seller

... and in certain cases:
- particulars of the place of origin of the food
- instructions for use.

Food Premises (Registration) Regulations 1990 and 1991, amended 1993

Relevant units

HSL 4

Summary

Food poisoning can be disastrous for a new business – word gets around. When starting a new catering business it is very important to get things right at the start because it will make it much easier for you to run your business well in the future. You must register your premises with the environmental health service at your local authority at least 28 days before opening – registration is free

Registration applies to most types of food business, including catering businesses run from home and mobile or temporary premises, such as stalls and vans. If you use two or more premises, you will need to register all of them.

If food premises are used by several catering businesses (for example, a village hall or conference centre), the person who allows the premises to be used for this purpose is responsible for registering them.

Registration is simple. You can download a registration application form from some local authority websites, which can be completed and emailed, faxed or posted to the food team in the environmental health department. Other local authorities offer online registration, where an electronic form can be completed and submitted online. Contact your local authority to find out how you can register.

Food Safety (General Food Hygiene) Regulations 1995 Amended, 2006

Relevant units

HSL 6, HSL 7

Summary

These regulations cover general requirements for the design, construction and operation of food premises. The premises must be designed to allow food to be prepared safely with minimal risk of cross-contamination. The design must allow for adequate cleaning and/or disinfection. The kitchen should be at least one-third of the size of the dining area and planned so that work flows progressively from delivery of goods to service of the food. 'Dirty' work, such as washing/preparing raw food and washing up, should be carried out away from preparation of 'ready to eat' foods. Separation can be achieved by allocating separate areas or work surfaces. This will depend on the size of the proposed operation.

Food Safety (Temperature Control) Regulations 1995

Relevant units

HSL 4, HSL 6, HSL 7

Summary

Food which is susceptible to the bacteria, toxins and viruses that can cause food poisoning needs to be stored at the correct temperature. The Food Safety (Temperature Control) Regulations 1995 require potentially dangerous foods to be held at or below 8°C at or above 63°C. Certain exceptions to this are allowed for practical considerations relating to, for example, processing or handling food, as long as food safety is not put at risk. The regulations do not list specific foods which need to be held under temperature control conditions and it is up to the food businesses to decide for themselves which foods should be held under temperature control.

Food Safety Act 1990

Relevant units

HSL 4, HSL 6, HSL 7, HSL 10

Summary

The Food Safety Act 1990 regulates the statutory obligation to treat food intended for human consumption in a controlled and managed way. The key requirements of the Act are that food must comply with food safety requirements, must be 'of the nature, substance and quality demanded', and must be correctly described (labelled).

Food Standards Act 1999

Relevant units

HSL 7

Summary

The main purpose of the Act is to establish the Food Standards Agency, provide it with functions and powers, and to transfer to it certain functions in relation to food safety and standards under other Acts.

It sets out the Agency's main objective of protecting public health in relation to food and the functions that it will assume in pursuit of that aim. The Act also gives the Agency the powers necessary to enable it to act in the consumer's interest at any stage in the food production and supply chain. The Act provides for the Agency's main organisational and accountability arrangements. In addition to this, it provides powers to establish a scheme for the notification of the results of tests for food-borne diseases.

Gas Safety (Installation and Use) (Amendment) Regulations 1990

Relevant units

HSL 4

Summary

The Gas Safety regulations ensure that:
○ the employer of any person carrying out gas work shall ensure that no person shall carry out any work in relation to a gas fitting unless he is competent to do so

○ no employer shall allow any of his employees to carry out any work in relation to a gas fitting, and no self-employed person shall carry out any such work, unless the employer or self-employed person is a member of the gas Safe Register.

Hazard Analysis and Critical Control Points (HACCP)

Relevant units

HSL 1, HSL 3, HSL 4

Summary

HACCP is a systematic preventive approach to food safety and pharmaceutical safety that addresses physical, chemical, and biological hazards as a means of prevention rather than finished product inspection. HACCP is used in the food industry to identify potential food safety hazards, so that key actions, known as Critical Control Points (CCPs), can be taken to reduce or eliminate the risk of the hazards being realised.

The system is used at all stages of food production and preparation processes including packaging, distribution, etc. HACCP has been recognised internationally as a logical tool for adapting traditional inspection methods to a modern, science-based, food safety system. Based on risk assessment, HACCP plans allow both industry and government to allocate their resources efficiently in establishing and auditing safe food production practices. HACCP has been increasingly applied to industries other than food, such as cosmetics and pharmaceuticals. This method, which in effect aims to root out unsafe practices, is different from traditional 'produce and test' quality assurance methods which are less successful and not appropriate for highly perishable foods.

Health and Safety (Display Screen Equipment or DSE) Regulations 1992

Relevant units

HSL 4

Summary

The Health and Safety (DSE) Regulations 1992 came into effect from January 1993 (some small changes were made in 2002). The Regulations require employers to minimise the risks in VDU (Visual Display Units) work by ensuring that workplaces and jobs are well designed.

The Regulations apply where staff habitually use VDUs as a significant part of their normal work e.g. management and administrative staff. Other people, who use VDUs only occasionally, are not covered by the requirements in the Regulations.

Health and Safety (First-Aid) Regulations 1981

Relevant units

HSL 4

Summary

The Health and Safety (First-Aid) Regulations 1981 place a duty on employers to provide adequate first-aid equipment, facilities and personnel to their employees. In the Act, first aid is included under 'welfare facilities' to be made available to 'persons at work'. In its guidance, the Health and Safety Executive (HSE) strongly recommends that employers should also include non-employees in their assessment of first-aid needs and should make provision for them.

Health and Safety (Safety Signs and Signals) Regulations 1996

Relevant units

HSL 4

Summary

These regulations bring into force the EC Safety Signs Directive (92/58/EEC) on the provision and use of safety signs at work. The purpose of the Directive is to encourage the standardisation of safety signs throughout the member states of the European Union so that safety signs, wherever they are seen, have the same meaning.

Some examples of these signs are shown below:

General danger

Ear protection must be worn

Industrial vehicles

Eye protection must be worn

The regulations cover different ways of communicating health and safety information. They can include the use of illuminated signs, hand and acoustic signals (e.g. fire alarms), spoken communication and the marking of pipework containing dangerous substances. These are in addition to traditional signboards such as prohibition and warning signs. Fire safety signs (i.e. signs for fire exits and fire-fighting equipment) are also covered.

The regulations require employers to provide specific safety signs whenever there is a risk that has not been avoided or controlled by other means, such as by engineering controls and safe systems of work. Where a safety sign would not help to reduce that risk, or where the risk is not significant, there is no need to provide a sign.

Health and Safety at Work Act 1974 (HASAW)

Relevant units

HSL 3, HSL 4, HSL 7, HSL 10, HSL 17/18, HSL 21/22

Summary

The Health and Safety at Work Act 1974, also referred to as HASAW or HSWA, is the primary piece of legislation covering occupational health and safety in the UK. The Health and Safety Executive is responsible for enforcing the Act and a number of other Acts and Statutory Instruments relevant to the working environment.

Health and Safety Information for Employees Regulations 1989

Relevant units

HSL 7, HSL 21/22

Summary

These regulations require employers to display a poster telling employees what they need to know about health and safety.

The Hotel Proprietors' Act 1956

Relevant units

HSL 3

Summary

This Act refers to the security of guests' property when staying in a hotel. The proprietor of any hotel has a duty to take reasonable care of the property of his guests brought to the hotel, whether resident or not. If it is lost or damaged through the negligence of the hotel, the proprietor may be liable. The proprietor can avoid his liability only if he can prove that the loss or damage was caused by the guest's own negligence, or by an act of God (flood, earthquake etc.), or by an act of the Queen's enemies (during times of war).

Immigration (Hotel records) Order 1972

Relevant units

HSL 4

Summary

Under the Immigration (Hotel Records) Order 1972, all hotels, boarding houses, etc. must keep a record of the full name and nationality of their guests over 16 years of age. Aliens must also record the number and place of issue of their passport, their nationality and their next destination. Records of this information must be kept for at least 12 months and be available for inspection by any police officer.

Licensing and the Licensing Act 2003

Relevant units

HSL 10, HSL 11

Summary

To control the sale of alcohol, anyone wishing to sell alcohol must have certain licences. There are different sorts of licences that allow the sale of alcohol. In order to carry out your role effectively, you must familiarise yourself with licensing hours, trades descriptions and age restrictions when selling and serving alcohol.

Premises licence

All premises where alcohol is sold need a Premises licence. This allows alcoholic drinks to be sold and served only at stated times and on the named premises.

Personal licence

In addition, a Personal licence is required. This states the named person who is legally authorised to sell alcohol on the premises. Only the licence holder and staff approved by the licence holder can sell alcohol on the premises.

Licensing hours

The licensing laws have changed over the last few years and now there are no set permitted hours. Trading could be up to 24 hours per day, but in reality most bars do not operate 24 hours a day. The Premises licence states the hours during which alcohol can be sold and drunk on the named premises. As a waiter you need to know the correct times when you can sell and serve alcohol at your orkplace.

When applying for a licence, the times of opening throughout the year must be stated. Applications are made to the local authority and are subject to the approval of police, local residents and the environmental health department. The local authority will grant a licence and state the approved hours in which alcohol can be sold and consumed on the premises.

Under-age drinking

Only customers aged 18 years or over can be served alcoholic drinks. If you are not sure about a customer's age, then you should request and check some form of personal identification. It is an offence to knowingly serve anyone under the age of 18 years with alcohol.

When you must not sell alcohol

You must not sell alcohol:

- to customers under 18 years of age
- out of legal opening hours
- to a customer who is drunk, violent, quarrelsome or disorderly
- to an associate of a drunk person, if the purchase is intended to be consumed by the drunk person
- to customers who are under the influence of drugs
- to a policeman on duty.
- to a known prostitute
- to those previously barred.

The Licensing Act 2003 introduced new types of licence and changed the way alcohol licensing is controlled. The new licensing Act was intended to increase the prevention of crime and disorder, public safety, the prevention of public nuisance, and the protection of children from harm. One major change was the new personal licence. Before alcohol can be supplied, the person selling or supplying the alcohol must have a personal licence or be authorised to supply the alcohol by someone who holds a personal licence.

Management of Health and Safety at Work Regulations in 1999

Relevant units

HSL 17/18

Summary

These regulations require employers to carry out risk assessments, make arrangements to implement necessary measures, appoint competent people and arrange for appropriate information and training.

Manual Handling Operations Regulations 1992, amended 2002

Relevant units

HSL 7, HSL 21/22

Summary

The Manual Handling Operations Regulations 1992, as amended in 2002, apply to a wide range of manual handling activities, including lifting, lowering, pushing, pulling or carrying. The load may be either inanimate (a 'dead weight') – such as a box or a trolley, or animate (alive) – a person or an animal. This guidance gives useful practical advice for employers, managers, safety representatives and individual employees on how to reduce the risk of injury from manual handling.

Offices, Shops and Railways Premises Act 1963

Relevant units

HSL 4

Summary

This Act was originally drawn to provide legislation to cover health, safety and welfare of employees (general provisions). These provisions were repealed and superseded, as far as they applied to "workplaces", by the Workplace (Health, Safety and Welfare) Regulations 1992 .

Sections 4 to 16 defined general broad requirements for safe and healthy workplace working conditions:

4 Cleanliness;

5 Overcrowding;

6 Temperature;

7 Ventilation;

8 Lighting;

9 Sanitary conveniences;

10 Washing facilities;

11 Supply of drinking water;

12 Accommodation for clothing;

13 Sitting facilities;

14 Seating for sedentary work;

15 Eating facilities; and

16 Construction and maintenance of floors, stairways and passageways.

Under this Act up until the 6th April 2009, employers had to register the factories, offices and shops in which their employees work with the relevant health and safety authority. Now employers no longer have to register. This is because new rules have removed the requirements to register under the Factories Act 1961 and the Offices, Shops and Railway Premises Act 1963.

PAT Testing (Portable Electrical Appliance Testing)

Relevant units

HSL 4

Summary

It is not necessary for the sort of portable equipment normally used in hotels to be inspected on an annual basis by a qualified electrician. Any sensible (competent) member of staff can do it if they have been given enough knowledge and training.

Checks can be carried out simply by looking at the equipment. This is the most important maintenance precaution. Around 95% of faults or damage can be found by visual inspection.

First, identify your equipment and where and how it is used. The things you are looking for on the equipment, the cable and plug, after disconnecting it, are signs of:

- damage, e.g. cuts, abrasion (apart from light scuffing) to the cable covering;
- damage to the plug, e.g. the casing is cracked or the pins are bent;
- non-standard joints including taped joints in the cable;
- the outer covering (sheath) of the cable not being gripped where it enters the plug or the equipment. Look to see if the coloured insulation of the internal wires is showing;
- equipment that has been used in conditions where it is not suitable, e.g. a wet or dusty workplace;
- damage to the outer cover of the equipment or obvious loose parts or screws;
- overheating (burn marks or staining).

In addition, formal inspection could include removal of the plug cover and checking that:

- a fuse is being used (i.e. it is a proper fuse not a piece of wire, a nail, etc);

- the cord grip is holding the outer part (sheath) of the cable tightly;
- the wires, including the earth where fitted, are attached to the correct terminals
- no bare wire is visible other than at the terminals;
- the terminal screws are tight;
- there is no sign of internal damage, overheating or entry of liquid, dust or dirt.

(This does not apply to moulded plugs where only the fuse can be checked).

PPE at Work Regulations 1992

Relevant units

HSL 4

Summary

The main requirement of the PPE at Work Regulations 1992 is that personal protective equipment is to be supplied and used at work wherever there are risks to health and safety that cannot be adequately controlled in other ways.

The Regulations also require that PPE:
- is properly assessed before use to ensure it is suitable;
- is maintained and stored properly;
- is provided with instructions on how to use it safely; and
- is used correctly by employees.

Prescribed Dangerous Machinery Order 1964

Relevant units

HSL 3

Summary

This order ensures that all work equipment is suitable for use. The law states that every employer shall:

- ensure that work equipment is so constructed or adapted as to be suitable for the purpose for which it is used or provided.
- have regard to the working conditions and to the risks to the health and safety of persons which exist in the premises or undertaking in which that work equipment is to be used and any additional risk posed by the use of that work equipment.
- when selecting work equipment, ensure that work equipment is used only for operations for which, and under conditions for which, it is suitable.

It also enforces the following:
- Equipment at work must be properly maintained and an up-to-date Maintenance Log must be kept
- Health and safety information should be made available to the workforce. Where appropriate, written instructions about the use of the work equipment should be easily available.
- Every employer shall ensure that everyone who uses or supervises the use of work equipment has received adequate training for purposes of health and safety, including training how to use specific

215

work equipment, e.g. meat slicers, steam cleaners, etc.

In kitchens 'dangerous machinery' usually includes:

- mincing machines
- chopping machines (rotary blade)
- mixing machines
- slicing machines
- potato chipping machines
- food processors.

Remember that the risk assessment will show who is at risk and what the level of risk is (see Unit HS4)

Provision and Use of Equipment Regulations 1992

Relevant units

HSL 3

Summary

These regulations concern the suitability of work equipment and are very similar to the Prescribed Dangerous Machinery Order of 1964.

The regulations stipulate that:

- every employer shall ensure that work equipment is so constructed or adapted as to be suitable for the purpose for which it is used or provided. They should have regard to the working conditions and to the risks to the health and safety of persons which exist in the premises or any additional risk posed by the use of that work equipment.

- regular maintenance is carried out
- where the use of work equipment is likely to involve a specific risk to health or safety, every employer shall ensure that:
  (a) the use of that work equipment is restricted to the people given the task of using it; and
  (b) repairs, modifications, maintenance or servicing of that work equipment is restricted to people who have been specifically designated to repair, modify or service it e.g. gas and electrical engineers have to have specific qualifications to allow them to carry out certain jobs. Gas engineers must be on the 'Gas Safe Register' otherwise they are working illegally.
- proper training and supervision is carried out with reference to work equipment.
- the information and instructions required by work equipment shall include information and, where appropriate, written instructions on:
  (a) the conditions in which and the methods by which the work equipment may be used;
  (b) foreseeable abnormal situations and the action to be taken if such a situation were to occur; and
  (c) any conclusions to be drawn from experience in using the work equipment (usually instruction manuals come with a section on 'What to do if the following goes wrong' i.e. a problem solving page.)

Public Health (Control of Diseases) Act 1984

Relevant units

HSL 4

Summary

This Act is not the same as the Reporting of Injuries, Diseases and Dangerous Occurrences Regulations 1995 (see page x). This Act affects employees and guests in the hospitality industry because of the contact there is with tourists and the high level of immigrant workers. In this Act, 'notifiable disease' means any of the following diseases:

- cholera
- plague
- relapsing fever
- smallpox
- typhus

Cases of notifiable disease and food poisoning must be reported when:

- a registered medical practitioner becomes aware, or suspects, that a patient whom he is attending within the district of a local authority is suffering from a notifiable disease or from food poisoning
- he must then send to the proper officer of the local authority for that district a certificate stating:
- the name, age and sex of the patient and the address of the premises where the patient is,
- the disease, or, as the case may be, particulars of the poisoning from which the patient is, or is suspected to be, suffering and the date, or approximate date, of its onset, and

- if the premises are a hospital, the day on which the patient was admitted, the address of the premises from which he came there and whether or not, in the opinion of the person giving the certificate, the disease or poisoning from which the patient is, or is suspected to be, suffering was contracted in the hospital.

A person who (among other things), knowing that he is suffering from a notifiable disease, exposes other persons to the risk of infection by his presence or conduct in any street, public place, place of entertainment or assembly, club, hotel, inn or shop, shall be liable on summary conviction to a fine.

Public Health (Infectious Diseases) Act 1988

Relevant units

HSL 4

Summary

The main provisions are:

- a requirement for any registered medical practitioner to notify the local authority if s/he becomes aware of any case of food poisoning or of certain diseases. Some diseases are identified as notifiable in the Act itself; others are identified in regulations made under the Act;
- powers for the local authority and its officers to take certain action in order to control outbreaks of disease, including:
- (a) environmental control measures (such as arranging for the disinfection/ destruction of material exposed to notifiable disease);

(b) powers to require certain actions of individuals. For example, a person responsible for the care of a child who has or has been exposed to a notifiable disease can be ordered by the local authority's proper officer not to allow the child to go to school;

(c) powers to apply to a Justice of the Peace for an order requiring a person thought to have a notifiable disease to be medically examined, or removed to hospital, or detained there in certain circumstances;

○ a duty on members of the public not to expose others to notifiable disease, for example by using public transport when they know themselves to have a notifiable disease.

This Act affects the hospitality industry because food poisoning has to be reported to the local authority and because there is a lot of contact with members of the public therefore staff are always at risk as are other customers.

Public Interest Disclosure Act 1998

Relevant units

HSL 7

Summary

The Public Interest Disclosure Act 1998 is designed to protect workers from detrimental treatment or victimisation from their employer if, in the public interest, they 'blow the whistle' or go public on wrongdoing at work.

Race Relations Act 1976, amended 2003

Relevant units

HSL 2

Summary

The Race Relations Act 1976 was established to prevent discrimination on the grounds of race. This includes discrimination on the grounds of race, colour, nationality, ethnic and national origin in the fields of employment, the provision of goods and services, education and public functions. The Act also established the Commission for Racial Equality with a view to reviewing the legislation. The Act incorporates the earlier Race Relations Act 1965 and Race Relations Act 1968, and was later amended by the Race Relations Amendment Act 2000. This notably included a statutory duty on public bodies to promote race equality, and to demonstrate that procedures to prevent race discrimination are effective.

In 2003, additional regulations also made illegal certain forms of discrimination due to religious belief.

Reporting of Injuries, Diseases and Dangerous Occurrences Regulations 1995 (RIDDOR)

Relevant units

HSL 4

Summary

These regulations concern the reporting of major or fatal injuries to any person in an accident connected with the business where you work. The report must usually be made to the Environmental Health Department of the local authority. RIDDOR regulates the statutory obligation to report deaths, injuries, diseases and 'dangerous occurrences' that take place at work or in connection with work. Even today, hundreds of people are killed at work each year in the UK.

The Regulations require responsible persons to report deaths at work, major injuries caused by accidents at work, injuries to persons at work that require hospital treatment, injuries arising from accidents in hospitals and dangerous occurrences. Additionally, the law requires registered gas fitters to report poor and dangerous gas installations.

Responsible persons are generally employers but may also include various managers and occupiers of premises. Although the regulations do not impose a specific obligation on employees, all workers have a general obligation under the Health and Safety at Work Act 1974 to take care of safety. The Health and Safety Executive recommends that workers report incidents to their employer and it encourages voluntary notification to the relevant regulating authority.

Safety Representatives and Safety Committee Regulations 1977

Relevant units

HSL 4

Summary

These Regulations enforce the legal requirement for employers to consult with their employees on matters of health and safety.

The law sets out how you must consult your employees in different situations and the different choices you have to make. There are two sets of general regulations about your duty to consult your workforce about health and safety:

o The Safety Representatives and Safety Committees Regulations 1977
o The Health and Safety (Consultation with Employees) Regulations 1996

These regulations will apply to most workplaces. The flow chart below shows the relationship between the two sets of regulations and how they affect you and your workforce.

It is quite common to have some parts of a business where employees are members of recognised trade unions and others where they are not. In this case, you may have to consult both:

o health and safety representatives appointed by recognised trade unions under the Safety Representatives and Safety Committees Regulations 1977.

o the remainder of your workforce, either directly where practical, or through elected health and safety representatives under the Health and Safety (Consultation with Employees) Regulations 1996.

These regulations are designed to enable you and your employees to work together:

o to develop, maintain and promote measures that ensure health and safety at work; and

o to check the effectiveness of such measures.

The presence of a union health and safety representative does not prevent managers from communicating directly with the workforce as a whole. Managers remain responsible for managing health and safety in the workplace and should consult the workforce as necessary.

Sale of Goods Act 1979, amended 2003

Relevant units

HSL 17/18

Summary

The Sale of Goods Act 1979 regulates contracts in which goods are sold and bought. Within six months, beginning at the time at which the goods were purchased or delivered, the buyer can require the seller to repair the goods, reduce the price, or rescind (giving back the property and requiring the return of any payment) the contract if the buyer can successfully claim that the goods were not in accordance with the contract at the time of delivery. The seller can defeat this claim if (a) it is established that the goods

did so conform at the time of delivery, or (b) the measure is incompatible with the nature of the goods or the nature of the lack of conformity (Source: www.berr.gov.uk).

Supply of Goods and Services Act 1982, amended 2002

Relevant units

HSL 17/18

Summary

The Supply of Goods and Services Act 1982 requires a supplier of a service acting in the course of business in England, Wales and Northern Ireland to carry out that service with reasonable care and skill and, unless agreed to the contrary, within a reasonable time and make no more than a reasonable charge.

If a supplier of a service breaches the conditions of a contract (for example, by failing to carry out the work ordered) the consumer then has a choice. It is possible either to affirm the contract (i.e. treat it as still in existence) and claim compensation from the trader for his failure to carry out what was agreed or rescind (cancel) the contract. If the supplier does not carry out the work with reasonable care and skill, the law treats the matter as a breach of contract and the consumer can seek redress. Often reasonable compensation in these circumstances will be repair or replacement.

A supplier of a service who has broken a contract may also be liable for any consequential loss which is suffered by the consumer. Ultimately, the courts would decide whether or not a breach of contract has occurred and the redress, in the form of damages (compensation), to which a consumer might be entitled. A claim can be pursued though the courts for up to six years, providing it can be shown that the problem was due to the work not being carried out properly or the goods or materials used not being of satisfactory quality.

The Tourism (Sleeping Accommodation Price Display) Order 1977

Relevant units

HSL 10

Summary

In this Order, 'hotel' means any establishment in Great Britain at which sleeping accommodation is provided by way of trade or business; but excluding any establishment which is a bona fide members' club. (the full definition can be found on the HM Revenue and Customs website).

At each hotel a legible notice shall be displayed in a prominent position in the reception area or at the entrance. The notice should state the current prices (including any service charges) payable per night. The notice must be easily read by prospective customers and contain the following information. The price of:

(a) a bedroom for occupation by one adult person,

(b) a bedroom for occupation by two adult persons, and

(c) a bed, other than as in (a) or (b) above, for occupation by an adult person and stating also whether it is situate in a dormitory or room to be shared with other guests.

Where Value Added Tax is payable, then either:

(a) the price shall include and be stated to include the amount of VAT, or

(b) the price shall be stated to exclude the VAT and that amount shall be stated in money terms as the amount of VAT payable in addition to the price.

(3) if the accommodation is only provided inclusive of meals, this shall be clearly stated and the meals provided shall be suitably identified.

(4) If the prices in respect of each of the above categories of sleeping accommodation are not standard throughout the hotel it is sufficient to state the lowest and highest current price for accommodation of each category.

Trade Descriptions Act 1968

Relevant units

HSL 10

Summary

The Trade Descriptions Act 1968 prevents manufacturers, retailers or service industry providers from misleading consumers about what they are spending their money on.

Advertising is a crucial part of successful commercial enterprises and, with fierce competition, the temptation can be strong to push the boundaries of truth when making claims for a product. This law empowers the courts to punish companies or individuals who make false claims about the products or services that they sell.

Applying a false trade description to goods is a strict liability offence; this means that a person is responsible for the damage and loss caused by their acts. Provided it is shown that the description was applied and was false, the accused has to prove certain defences in order to escape conviction.

Each product sold must be as described, of satisfactory quality, and fit for purpose. 'As described' refers to any advert or verbal description made by the trader. 'Satisfactory quality' covers minor and cosmetic defects as well as substantial problems. It also means that products must last a reasonable time. But it does not give you any rights if a fault was obvious or pointed out to you at point of sale. 'Fit for purpose' covers not only the obvious purpose of an item but any purpose you queried and were given assurances about by the trader.

The advertising industry has often managed to get round this obstacle by using a disclaimer in small print, and, to some extent, through creative associations of products with the things that people desire.

Workplace (Health, Safety and Welfare) Regulations 1992

Relevant units

HSL 7

Summary

The Workplace (Health, Safety and Welfare) Regulations 1992 stipulate general requirements on accommodation standards for nearly all workplaces.

Breach of the regulations by an employer, controller of work premises or occupier of a factory is a crime, punishable on summary conviction with a fine of up to £400. If convicted on indictment in the Crown Court, an offender can be sentenced to an unlimited fine. It can be either an individual or a corporation who is the offender and who can be punished. Enforcement is the responsibility of the Health and Safety Executive (HSE) or, in some cases, local authorities.

The HSE publishes a code of practice on implementing the Regulations. The regulations do not, however, create duties as to members of the public.

Weights and Measures Act 1985 and Weights and Measures (Intoxicating Liquor) Order, as amended 1988

Relevant units

HSL 3, HSL 10, HSL 11

Summary

The Weights and Measures Act governs the way alcohol and other goods measured and sold. The Weights and Measures (Intoxicating Liquor) Order controls the manner in which alcohol must be sold in restaurants, cafes, bars, etc. The purpose is to standardise the size of the measures used to serve wine, beer or spirits, and to ensure customers are aware of the sizes of those measures.

How should beer and cider be sold?

Draught beer and cider may be sold in any of the following quantities:

- $\frac{1}{3}$ pint, often found in specialist draught beer pubs
- $\frac{1}{2}$ pint
- in multiples of $\frac{1}{2}$ pint, e.g. one pint glasses, 2-pint and 4-pint jugs.

Glasses and jugs must be stamped. Some bars use automatic beer and cider dispensers instead of glasses. These too must be stamped to show accuracy. At the moment there is no provision allowing draught beer and cider to be sold in metric quantities such as 250ml or a litre. All bottles and cans are, however, pre-packed in metric quantities. If you sell pre-packed beer and cider, you must make the quantity known to the customer.

How should gin, rum, vodka and whisky be sold?

If sold by the glass, the above spirits should only be sold in quantities of 25ml, 35ml, or multiples of those amounts. You must choose either 25ml or 35ml measures. It is illegal to mix the sizes. Also, you must inform customers of the size of measure used. If customers buy their drinks from a bar, this information may be provided on a notice. Alternatively, the measure size may be indicated on the price list or menu. This will

be more appropriate if customers are served at tables, such as in a restaurant. Thimbles and measuring instruments (optics) must be stamped to show they are accurate.

Glossary

Allergens: a substance which causes an allergic reaction – the reaction may result after exposure through inhalation, digestion, injection or contact.

Anaphylactic shock: a hypersensitive allergic reaction to a substance which the body views as a toxin.

Appraisal: a periodic review (which can be monthly or quarterly, but is usually annually) which assesses the standard and efficiency of the work completed by an employee. This is also a time when the employee can discuss their future career development and raise any other issues they may have with their work. Some companies have different names for the same process, for example, 'performance review'.

Appraisee: the person who is being appraised by the appraiser.

Appraiser: the person who conducts the appraisal of the appraisee.

Average room revenue: room sales divided by the number of rooms.

Average spend per customer: the total customer sales divided by the number of customers.

Bacterium (pl. bacteria): micro-organism(s), some of which can cause disease.

Barista: an employee who serves coffee-based espresso drinks.

Benchmarking: a reference point/standard by which to measure something, e.g. comparing the cost or quality of a specific process to another that is considered to be the industry norm or best practice – provides a snapshot of performance at a particular moment in time.

Bin cards: cards (may be colour coded) assigned to large storage containers – they usually record: product, date filled, batch number, quantity in the container and the use-by date.

Budget: a financial document that is a summary of the expected income and expenditure over a given period; the total amount of money allocated for a specific purpose during a specified time.

Compliance: conforming to a specification, policy, standard or law that has been clearly defined; may also be known as legal compliance.

Contact dermatitis: a skin reaction resulting from exposure to allergens or irritants; also known as irritant dermatitis.

Contaminant: a poisonous or polluting substance.

Contingency plans: plans devised for a specific situation when things could go wrong; also known as back-up plans, worst-case scenarios, or plan Bs; they often include specific strategies and actions to deal with specific assumptions based on an identified problem; they should always include a monitoring process which triggers the planned actions.

Contract: a written or spoken agreement that is intended to be enforceable by law.

Contractors: a person or company that undertakes a contract to do a job or provide a service

Critical control point: this is a point, step or procedure to which controls can be applied thereby preventing, eliminating or reducing a food safety hazard. The most common CCP is cooking.

Cross-contamination: the transfer of microbial/chemical contamination from one food product to another, usually from low-risk food to high-risk food e.g. from cooked to raw meat.

Dermatitis: inflammation/infection of the skin.

Due diligence: a term used for a number of concepts involving either the performance of an investigation, business, person, or act which needs to provide a standard of care. It can either be a legal obligation or a voluntary one.

Department for Work and Pensions (DWP): this is the government department responsible for welfare. It works with people of working age, employers, disabled people, pensioners, families and children, providing services through a number of agencies.

Environmental Health Officer: usually employed by local government to advise on and enforce public health standards.

Equipment costs: including maintenance and replacements.

Etiquette: the customs or rules governing behaviour regarded as correct in social life.

FIFO: An acronym for First in First Out, FIFO is usually associated with stock-taking, to ensure all food is used within the correct rotational timeframe to maximise freshness.

Food/Beverage costs: the cost per dish/drink.

Food miles: refers to the distance food is transported from the time of its production until it reaches the consumer; it is sometimes used to help assess the environmental impact of food.

Gross profit: the profit achieved after food and beverage costs have been taken off.

Gueridon service: food partially prepared in the kitchen and finished at the table, or completely cooked at the table.

HASAW: Health and Safety at Work Act.

Hazard: a situation which poses a level of threat to life, health, property or environment.

Hazard Analysis Audit: an assessment of an organisation's systems and procedures of internal control to minimise the potential of a situation which could pose a threat.

Health surveillance monitoring: the systematic collection, analysis and interpretation of data that may have a significant impact on public health; this data is then used to make decisions about health policy and education.

Health and Safety Executive (HSE) Inspectors: HSE inspectors have the power to: enter premises; inspect and investigate; take measurements, samples and photographs; require an area or machine to be left undisturbed; seize, render harmless or destroy dangerous items; and obtain information and take statements.

Hospitality: the reception and entertainment of guests with liberality and goodwill. Hospitality frequently refers to the hospitality industry jobs for hotels, restaurants, casinos, catering, resorts, clubs and any other service position that deals with tourists. Hospitality is also known as the act of generously providing care and kindness to whoever is in need.

Leading indicators: usually measured more frequently than lagging indicators, they are the result of a measurement process that is driven by the organisation itself and it is entirely within their span of control, e.g. measuring process cycle times. Leading indicators are those that predict, with a degree of confidence, a future outcome. Employee satisfaction, although a lagging indicator for the morale of staff, is usually recognised as a leading indicator of customer satisfaction. Sometimes referred to as driving indicators.

Learning: the acquiring and understanding of information which may lead to improvement or change. Examples of organisational learning activities include benchmarking, internally- and externally-led assessments and/or audits, and best practice studies. Examples of individual learning include training and professional qualifications.

Legislation: the act or process of making laws.

Management system: the framework of processes and procedures used to ensure that the organisation can fulfil all tasks required to achieve its objectives.

Microbiological: the study of microscopic organisms, e.g. bacteria, fungi or viruses.

Mission: a statement that describes the purpose of an organisation. It describes why the business or function exists.

Mould: a fungus that grows on organic matter, including food.

Net profit: profit achieved after all costs have been taken off.

Non-profit-making: catering outlets where the catering is a service and will not be seeking to make money.

Organisational agility: the ability of an organisation to react positively to required changes in speed, focus, goals, actions, and timescales that affect its ability to deliver.

Partnerships: a working relationship between two or more parties creating added value for the customer. Partners can include suppliers, distributors, joint ventures, and alliances. Note that suppliers may not always be recognised as formal partners.

Pathogenic: an infective organism, either bacterial or viral, which may cause a disease or illness to its host.

People: all of the individuals employed by the organisation, including full-time, part-time, temporary and contract employees.

Perception: the opinion of an individual or group of people.

Performance: a measure of attainment achieved by an individual, team, organisation or process.

Pesticides: a substance used to destroy insects or other organisms harmful to cultivated plants or to animals.

Process: a sequence of activities which adds value by producing required outputs from a variety of inputs.

Process indicators: leading indicators relative to the performance of the process.

Profit-making: catering outlets whose objective is to make money.

RADAR: Results, Approach, Deployment, Assessment and Review.

Risk: a situation which would lead to negative consequences.

Risk assessment: a careful examination of what activities your business might be vulnerable to and which ones could cause harm to people; this is a vital part of providing a safe and secure environment for staff and customers.

Room revenue: the amount of income generated by a specific room.

Safety representatives: appointed safety reps have normally either worked for their present employer for the preceding two years or have had at least two years' experience in similar employment. Functions of safety representatives are: investigating potential hazards, dangerous occurrences and accidents; investigating employees' complaints; making representations to the employer on health and safety matters; carrying out workplace inspections; receiving information from inspectors; representing employees in consultations at the workplace with inspectors; and attending meetings of safety committees.

Safety Representatives and Committees Regulations 1977: the Safety Representatives and Safety Committees Regulations 1977 were made under section 15 of the Health and Safety at Work Act 1974. They have been subsequently amended by the Management of Health and Safety at Work Regulations 1999, and the Health and Safety (Consultation with Employees) Regulations 1996. The Regulations and associated Codes of Practice provide a legal framework for employers and trade unions to reach agreement on arrangements for safety representatives and safety committees to operate in their workplace.

Service Level Agreement: agreement negotiated between two parties where one is the customer and the other the service provider. It may be legally binding, formal or informal and is a record of understanding of the services, responsibilities and guarantees between the two parties.

Society: all those who are, or believe they are, affected by the organisation, other than its people, customers and partners.

Staff costs: usually expressed as a percentage of sales.

Stakeholders: all those who have an interest in an organisation, its activities and its achievements. These may include customers, partners, employees, shareholders, owners, the government and regulators.

Standard operating procedure: a set of written instructions detailing all the steps and activities of a procedure. These should be carried out without any deviation or modification to guarantee an expected outcome.

Supply chain: the integrated structure of activities that procure, produce and deliver products and services to customers. The chain can be said to start with the suppliers of your suppliers and ends with the customers of your customers.

Sustainable excellence: excellent results with respect to performance, customers, people and society are achieved through leadership driving policy and strategy that is delivered through people, partnerships and resources, and processes.

Toxin: a poison, especially one produced by micro-organisms.

Unique selling point (USP): the unique selling point of a product or service makes specific claims that only it can fulfil. The product/service must be such that the competition either cannot or does not offer it; i.e. it is unique to that product/service.

Values: the understandings and expectations that describe how the organisation's people behave and upon which all business relationships are based (e.g. trust, support and truth).

Vision: a statement that describes how the organisation wishes to be in the future.

Write off: to remove or disregard a worthless asset from an account.

Technical Certificate Mapping Grid

Textbook Unit \ Technical Certificate Unit	Unit 1: Principles of leading a team in the hospitality industry	Unit 2: Supervision of operations in the hospitality industry
HSL1 Provide leadership for your team	1.1, 1.2, 1.3, 1.4, 2.1, 2.2, 2.3, 2.4, 2.5, 2.6, 2.7, 2.8, 2.9, 2.10, 2.11	
HSL2 Develop productive working relationships with colleagues	1.1, 1.2, 1.3, 1.4, 2.1, 2.2, 2.3, 2.9, 2.10	
HSL3 Contribute to the control of resources	3.1, 3.2, 3.3, 3.4, 3.5	2.1, 2.2, 2.3, 2.4, 3.1, 3.2, 3.3, 3.4, 3.5
HSL4 Maintain the health, hygiene, safety and security of the working environment	3.1, 3.2, 3.3, 3.5, 3.6, 3.7, 3.8	
HSL5 Lead a team to improve customer service		1.1, 1.2, 1.3, 1.4, 1.5, 1.6

Index